THE WELSH

THE MEDIEVAL WORLD
Editor: David Bates

Already published

THE WELSH PRINCES

THE NATIVE RULERS OF WALES
1063–1283

ROGER TURVEY

Longman

An imprint of **Pearson Education**

London · New York · Toronto · Sydney · Tokyo · Singapore · Hong Kong · Cape Town
New Delhi · Madrid · Paris · Amsterdam · Munich · Milan · Stockholm

Pearson Education Limited

Head Office:
Edinburgh Gate
Harlow CM20 2JE
Tel: +44 (0)1279 623623
Fax: +44 (0)1279 431059

London Office:
128 Long Acre
London WC2E 9AN
Tel: +44 (0)20 7447 2000
Fax: +44 (0)20 7240 5771
Website: www.history-minds.com

First published in Great Britain in 2002

ISBN 0 582 30811 9

British Library Cataloguing in Publication Data
A CIP catalogue record for this book can be obtained from the British Library

Library of Congress Cataloguing in Publication Data
A CIP catalogue record for this book can be obtained from the Library of Congress

10 9 8 7 6 5 4 3 2 1

Set in 10.5/13pt Galliard by Graphicraft Limited, Hong Kong
Printed in Malaysia

The Publishers' policy is to use paper manufactured from sustainable forests.

CONTENTS

EDITOR'S PREFACE

The history of Wales before Edward I's conquest in the 1280s has been the subject of much research and stimulating interpretation in recent times. Yet until now, there has not been a book published devoted specifically to the country's ruling elite. As a historian who has already contributed a major study of one of the most important of the Welsh princes of this period, the Lord Rhys, Roger Turvey is supremely qualified to write such a book. The result, the first in the Medieval World series to be devoted specifically to the history of Wales, fills a crucial gap in the historiography of Western Europe and the British Isles in the Central Middle Ages, and in a vigorous and lively style presents a positive assessment of the Welsh princes.

From the outset of the book, Roger Turvey makes it clear that the history of the Welsh princes is a part of the history of European aristocracies. The princes participated fully in the vast cultural and social changes which are identified with the developments known collectively as the Twelfth Century Renaissance. Like their contemporaries elsewhere, they consciously evolved new courtly life-styles and consolidated their power in their principalities through violence, administrative reorganisation and political symbolism. They responded to and adopted the religious changes of the time, patronising the new religious orders which spread across western Europe, and become steadily more integrated into the life of western Christendom. Yet at the same time princely life drew on a powerful Welsh ethnic consciousness and on cultural traditions which were distinctively Welsh. At the same time it was influenced (some might say was imprisoned) by local economic and social conditions. At all levels the actions of the princes interacted not just with each other, but with the mighty military and cultural presence of the English kingdom, itself in the process of absorbing the changes which followed the conquest of 1066. Yet although these influences and the military might of the English kingdom and its aristocracy might at times threaten to overwhelm not just the small principalities of the Welsh rulers, but also the culture of the land, they did not do so. The resoluteness of the princes, epitomised by military skill and political astuteness, was central to this resilience.

There is a school of thought which sees the history of Wales in this period in terms of tragedy or failure, or both. That the princes of Wales did not, or more accurately could not, unite to form a single Welsh polity as many of their contemporaries elsewhere in western Europe were apparently doing is seen as a disaster. In rejecting such arguments as anachronistic and by concentrating on princely achievement, Roger Turvey successfully portrays this period as a vibrant and dynamic one in the history of Wales. The paradox – or so it now seems – is that the violence and dynastic conflict which characterise princely politics were central elements to an ethos and to attitudes which were intensely constructive. Central to the long-term achievement of the princes was a sense of honour and dignity which drove them forwards, a particularism imbued by self-interest and long-standing independence, and a sense of ethnic difference which ultimately derived from a belief in their descent from the earliest inhabitants of Britain. All who write on Welsh History in this period do have the inestimable benefit of the writings of Giraldus Cambrensis to draw on. Not the least of Roger Turvey's achievements is to bring his subject alive through many other types of evidence, including charters, chronicles, poetry and archaeology. The result is an important contribution to the history of Wales, of Britain and of western Europe.

DAVID BATES

PREFACE

⸙

In a recently published survey of medieval Welsh history A.D. Carr concluded that

> there are so few working in this field and so much basic work is still to be done that . . . much opportunity remains for individual historians to make significant and original contributions. With so much fresh ground still to be broken there has been little scope for the kind of debates which have developed in other fields.[1]

Clearly, the field is a fertile one and no more so than in the study of the Welsh ruling class – the princes. The subject matter is of great intrinsic value for those seeking fresh insights into the role and influence of a significantly powerful group of individuals and their families. Therefore, one of the primary aims of the book will be to provide a synthesis of the history of an important and influential ruling elite during a significant period in Welsh history by incorporating the results of the latest scholarship. It seeks to provide those readers with little or no knowledge of the history of pre-conquest Wales, much less its princes, with a relatively brief and generally broad-ranging introduction to the subject of the late medieval rulers of Wales which, it need hardly be stressed, is deserving of further and more detailed study. This is not to imply that the 'history' of the native princes is in any sense a neglected field of study, a Cinderella topic. Far from it – a glance at the select bibliography will bear testimony to that. Indeed, such has been the explosion of interest in the past thirty-five or so years in the history of medieval Wales that a number of princes and their dynasties have been fortunate enough to find their academic champion which has resulted in the publication of some classic studies, among them *Llywelyn ap Gruffudd, Tywysog Cymru* (1986), republished in a substantially revised English-language edition in 1998, *Yr Arglwydd Rhys* (1996) and *Gruffudd ap Cynan: A Collaborative Biography* (1996), and some fine theses such as that entitled 'The Native Welsh Dynasties of Rhwng Gwy a Hafren, 1066–1282' (1989). Careful reading of the bibliography will reveal the extent to which we owe these, and a host of other works, to a relatively small group of industrious and committed historians whose dedication to elucidating the history of pre-conquest Wales is deserving of our gratitude. Nevertheless, much remains to be done, and in spite of the labours of these historians, it is probably true to say that, hitherto, piecemeal studies only have been published on the princes. This study is modest in comparison to the many outstanding works listed in the bibliography but it has the virtue of being the first publication to focus specifically on the princes, providing for the first time a scholarly overview of their activities and their contribution to the history of Wales.

This book developed out of my interest in and work on the Lord Rhys and twelfth-century Deheubarth in respect of which Ifor Rowlands deserves special mention for his encouragement of my research. I am grateful to David Bates, the general editor of the series, and Andrew MacLennan, former editorial director of the academic department at Longmans, for giving me the opportunity to take my interest a stage further by studying the native ruling class as a whole. I only hope this book is worthy of their faith and support. I would also like to thank the friends and colleagues with whom I have discussed parts of this book, but my greatest debt is to my wife and fellow historian Carol for her sound advice and unfailing support.

Roger Turvey
November 2001

Note

1. A.D. Carr, *British History in Perspective: Medieval Wales* (London, 1995), 24.

Acknowledgements

We are grateful to the following for permission to reproduce copyright material:

Maps 3 and 10 redrawn from *An Introduction to the History of Wales*, published and reprinted by permission of University of Wales Press (Williams, A.H. 1948); Map 8 redrawn from *Llywelyn ap Gruffudd Prince of Wales*, published and reprinted by permission of University of Wales Press (Smith, J.B. 1998); Maps 9 and 12 redrawn from *Edward I and Wales*, published by University of Wales Press, reprinted by permission of the Welsh History and its Sources Project of the Open University in Wales (Herbert, T. and Jones, G.E. eds 1987).

In some instances we have been unable to trace the owners of copyright material and we would appreciate any information which would enable us to do so.

ABBREVIATIONS

Ann. Camb.	*Annales Cambriae*, ed. J. Williams ab Ithel (Rolls Series, 1860)
Autobiog.	H.E. Butler, *The Autobiography of Giraldus Cambrensis* (London, 1937)
BBCS	*Bulletin of the Board of Celtic Studies*
BT. Pen.	*Brut y Tywysogion or The Chronicle of the Princes. Peniarth Ms 20 Version*, translated with introduction and notes by Thomas Jones (Cardiff, 1952)
BT. RBH	*Brut y Tywysogion or The Chronicle of the Princes. Red Book of Hergest Version*, translated with introduction and notes by Thomas Jones (Cardiff, 1955)
B. Saes.	*Brenhinedd y Saeson or The Kings of the Saxons*, translated with introduction and notes by Thomas Jones (Cardiff, 1971)
Cal. Anc. Corr.	*Calendar of Ancient Correspondence concerning Wales*, ed. J.G. Edwards (Cardiff, 1935)
CW	'Cronica de Wallia and other documents from Exeter Cathedral Library MS 3514', ed. T. Jones, *BBCS*, 12 (1946–8)
DWB	*Dictionary of Welsh Biography* (London, 1959)
Journey & Description	Gerald of Wales, *The Journey through Wales and the Description of Wales*, trans. Lewis Thorpe (Harmondsworth, 1978)
Litt. Wallie	*Littere Wallie preserved in Liber A in the Public Record Office*, edited with introduction by J.G. Edwards (Cardiff, 1940)

Lloyd, *Hist. Wales*	J.E. Lloyd, *A History of Wales from Earliest Times to the Edwardian Conquest* (2 vols, 2nd edn, London, 1912)
Mediaeval Prince	D.S. Evans, ed. and trans., *A Mediaeval Prince of Wales. The Life of Gruffudd ap Cynan* (Llanerch, 1990)
Medieval Welsh Society	T. Jones Pierce, *Medieval Welsh Society*, ed. J.B. Smith (Cardiff, 1972)
PBA	*Proceedings of the British Academy*
TRHS	*Transactions of the Royal Historical Society*
WHR	*Welsh History Review*

GENEALOGICAL TABLES AND MAPS

Genealogical tables

Maps

Table 1 The dynasty of Gwynedd

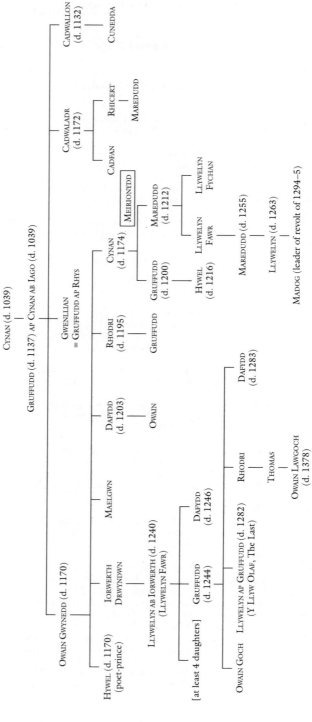

Table 2 The dynasty of Deheubarth

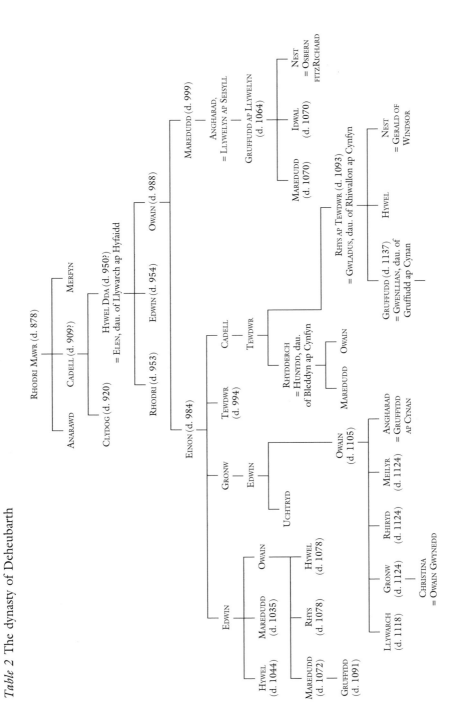

Table 2 The dynasty of Deheubarth (*cont'd*)

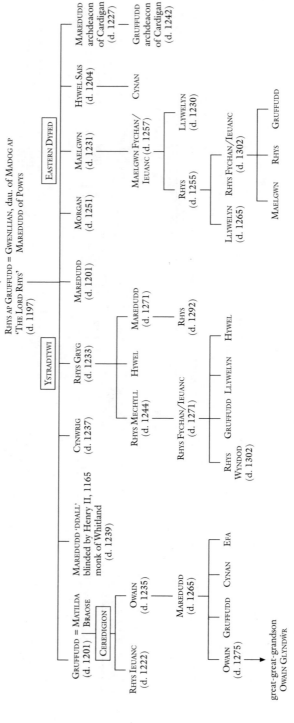

Table 3 The dynasty of Powys

BLEDDYN AP CYNFYN (d. 1075)

RHIRID (d. 1081) — MADOG (d. 1081) — ITHEL (d. 1124) — IORWERTH (d. 1111) — CADWGAN (d. 1111) — MAREDUDD (d. 1132)

MADOG

OWAIN (d. 1116) — EINION (d. 1123) — MORGAN (d. 1128) — MAREDUDD (d. 1124)

GRUFFUDD (d. 1128)

MADOG (d. 1160)

IORWERTH GOCH — MADOG

OWAIN CYFEILIOG (d. 1197) — MEURIG — LLYWELYN (d. 1160) — ELISE

SOUTHERN POWYS WENWYNWYN

GRUFFUDD MAELOR (d. 1191)

NORTHERN POWYS FADOG

OWAIN FYCHAN (d. 1187)

MECHAIN

OWAIN BROGYNTYN

PENLLYN, EDEIRNION

CADWALLON

GWENWYNWYN (d. 1216) = MARGARET CORBET

GRUFFUDD (d. 1286) = HAWISE LESTRANGE

OWAIN DE LA POLE (d. 1293) (five other sons)

GRUFFUDD DE LA POLE (d. 1309)

HAWISE = JOHN CHARLTON →

CHARLTONS, barons of Powys

MADOG (d. 1236)

GRUFFUDD (d. 1238)

HYWEL (d. 1268)

GRUFFUDD MAELOR (d. 1269) = EMMA AUDLEY

MAREDUDD (d. 1256)

MADOG FYCHAN (d. 1269)

MADOG (d. 1277)

LLYWELYN — OWAIN — GRUFFUDD FYCHAN →

OWAIN GLYNDŴR

LLYWELYN — OWAIN FYCHAN (d. 1245) — OWAIN

LLYWELYN FYCHAN (d. pre-1277) — MAREDUDD — GRUFFUDD — MAREDUDD

BLEDDYN — OWAIN — GRUFFUDD — ELISE — DAFYDD

IORWERTH — GRUFFUDD

The major regional division of Powys according to the partition effected after the death (1160) of Madog ap Maredudd. These divisions proved to be permanent. Further sub-divisions, temporary or permanent, were effected in each generation, notably in northern Powys (Powys Fadog) in 1236 and 1269 (revised 1277) and recurrently in Penllyn and Edeirnion

Table 4 The lesser dynasties

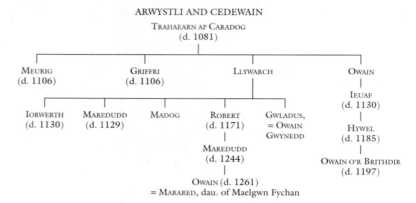

ARWYSTLI AND CEDEWAIN

TRAHAEARN AP CARADOG
(d. 1081)

MEURIG	GRIFFRI	LLYWARCH	OWAIN
(d. 1106)	(d. 1106)		

IEUAF
(d. 1130)

IORWERTH	MAREDUDD	MADOG	ROBERT	GWLADUS,
(d. 1130)	(d. 1129)		(d. 1171)	= OWAIN
				GWYNEDD

HYWEL
(d. 1185)

MAREDUDD
(d. 1244)

OWAIN O'R BRITHDIR
(d. 1197)

OWAIN (d. 1261)
= MARARED, dau. of Maelgwn Fychan

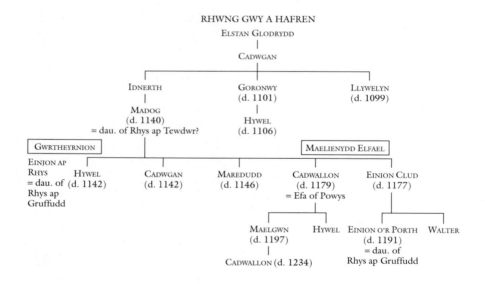

RHWNG GWY A HAFREN

ELSTAN GLODRYDD

CADWGAN

IDNERTH	GORONWY	LLYWELYN
	(d. 1101)	(d. 1099)

MADOG
(d. 1140)
= dau. of Rhys ap Tewdwr?

HYWEL
(d. 1106)

GWRTHEYRNION

MAELIENYDD ELFAEL

EINJON AP
RHYS   HYWEL   CADWGAN   MAREDUDD   CADWALLON   EINION CLUD
= dau. of   (d. 1142)   (d. 1142)   (d. 1146)   (d. 1179)   (d. 1177)
Rhys ap   = Efa of Powys
Gruffudd

MAELGWN	HYWEL	EINION O'R PORTH	WALTER
(d. 1197)		(d. 1191)	
		= dau. of	

CADWALLON (d. 1234)   Rhys ap Gruffudd

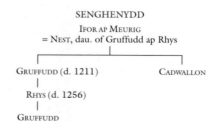

SENGHENYDD

IFOR AP MEURIG
= NEST, dau. of Gruffudd ap Rhys

GRUFFUDD (d. 1211)	CADWALLON

RHYS (d. 1256)

GRUFFUDD

Table 4 The lesser dynasties (*cont'd*)

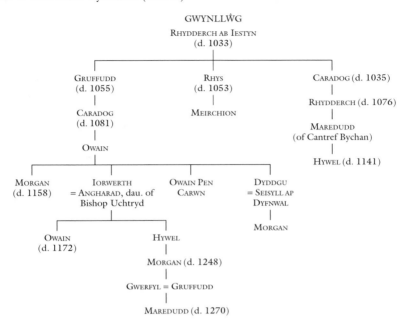

GWYNLLŴG

RHYDDERCH AB IESTYN
(d. 1033)

GRUFFUDD
(d. 1055)

CARADOG
(d. 1081)

OWAIN

MORGAN
(d. 1158)

IORWERTH
= ANGHARAD, dau. of
Bishop Uchtryd

OWAIN
(d. 1172)

HYWEL

MORGAN (d. 1248)

GWERFYL = GRUFFUDD

MAREDUDD (d. 1270)

RHYS
(d. 1053)

MEIRCHION

OWAIN PEN
CARWN

DYDDGU
= SEISYLL AP
DYFNWAL

MORGAN

CARADOG (d. 1035)

RHYDDERCH (d. 1076)

MAREDUDD
(of Cantref Bychan)

HYWEL (d. 1141)

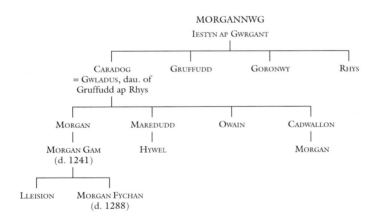

MORGANNWG

IESTYN AP GWRGANT

CARADOG
= GWLADUS, dau. of
Gruffudd ap Rhys

MORGAN

MORGAN GAM
(d. 1241)

LLEISION

MORGAN FYCHAN
(d. 1288)

GRUFFUDD

GORONWY

RHYS

MAREDUDD

HYWEL

OWAIN

CADWALLON

MORGAN

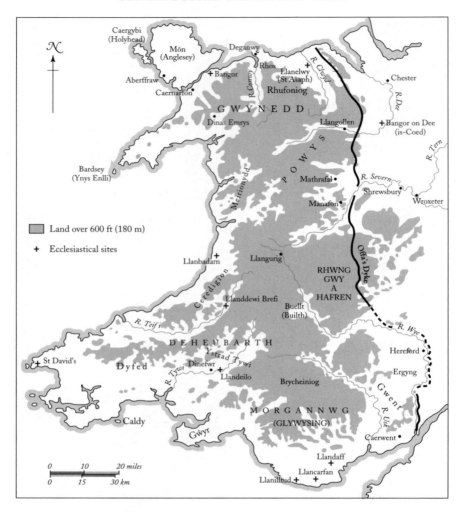

Map 1 Medieval Wales

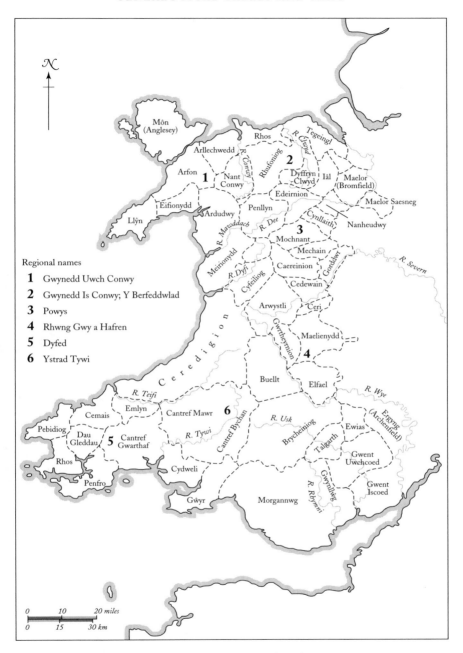

Regional names

1 Gwynedd Uwch Conwy
2 Gwynedd Is Conwy; Y Berfeddwlad
3 Powys
4 Rhwng Gwy a Hafren
5 Dyfed
6 Ystrad Tywi

Map 2 Regional and local divisions of medieval Wales

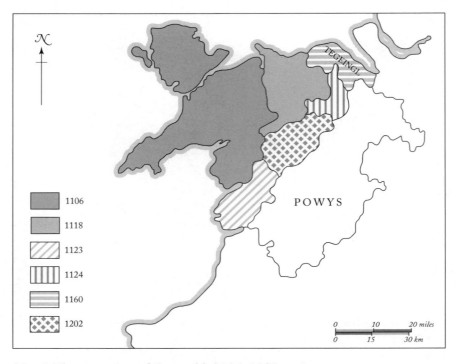

Map 3 The expansion of Gwynedd, 1106–1202

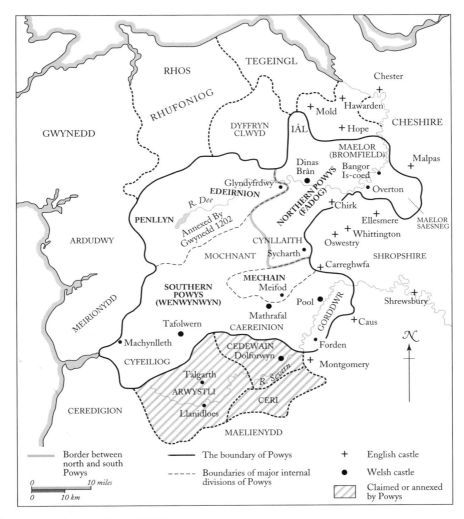

Map 4 Powys, 1160–1282

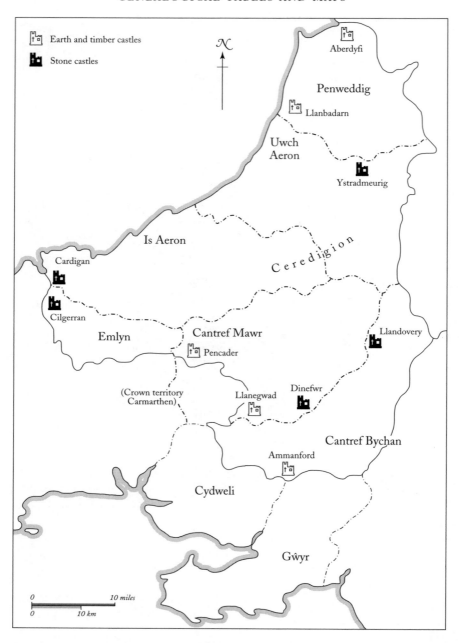

Map 5 Deheubarth under the Lord Rhys, 1166–97

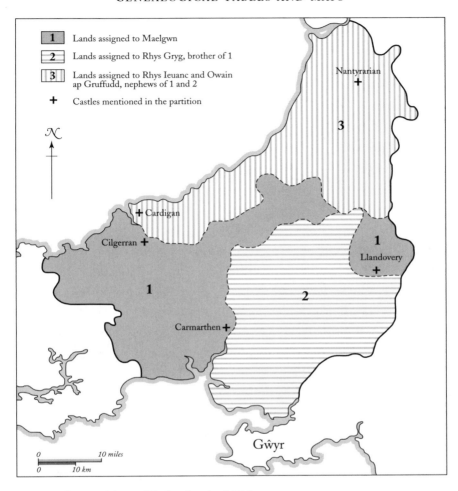

Map 6 The partition of Deheubarth, 1216

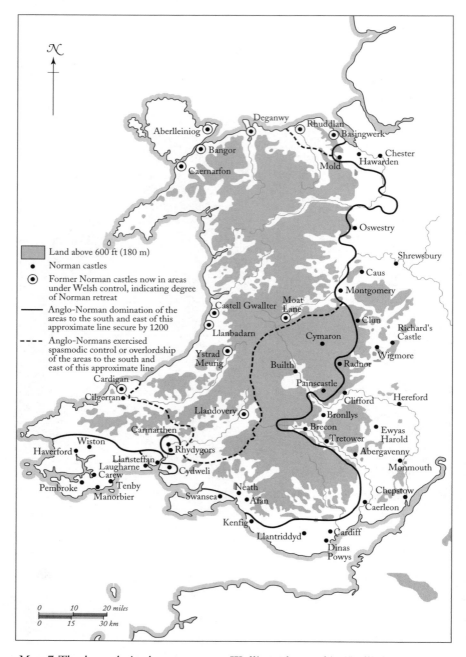

Map 7 The boundaries between *pura Wallia* and *marchia Wallie* by *c.* 1200

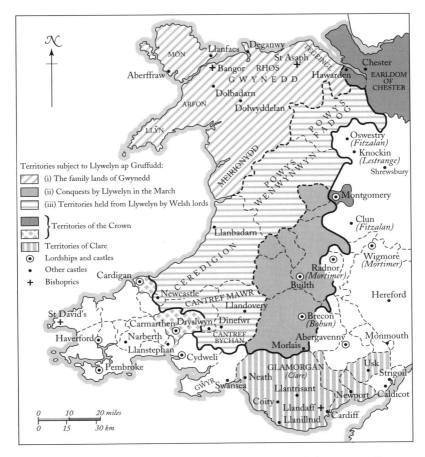

Map 8 The principality of Wales under the terms of the treaty of Montgomery, 1267

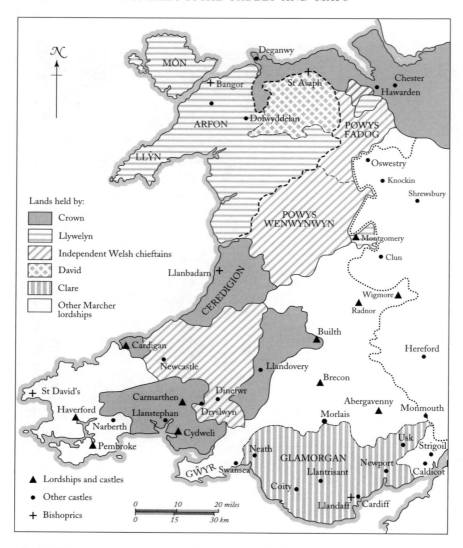

Map 9 Wales under the terms of the treaty of Aberconwy, 1277

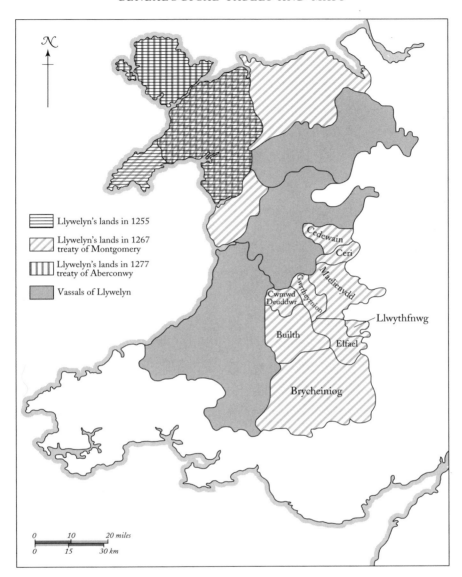

Map 10 The gains and losses of Llywelyn ap Gruffudd, 1255–77

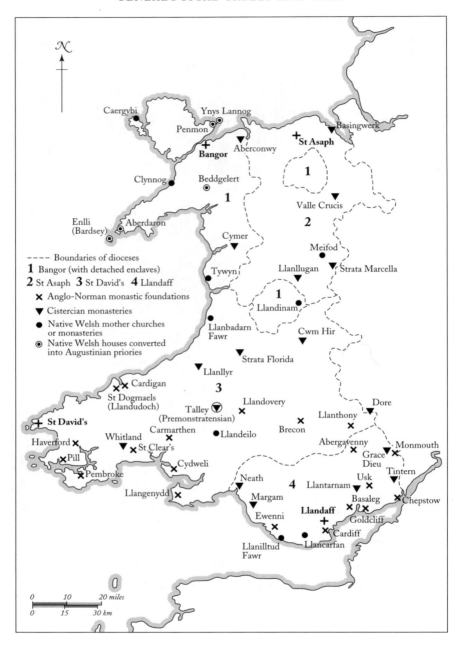

Map 11 The dioceses and monasteries of Wales *c.* 1250

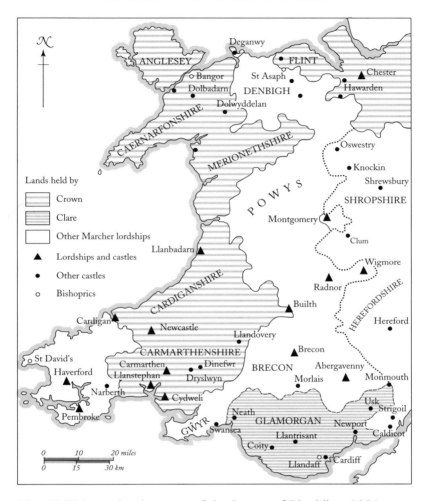

Map 12 Wales under the terms of the Statute of Rhuddlan, 1284

INTRODUCTION:
OUTLINES AND SOURCES

The history of Wales in the two centuries between 1063 and 1283 is in essence the history of its rulers and their systems of governance. Who and what they were, what they did, and the nature and extent to which they influenced and were influenced by those, and by things, around them, are among the questions that this book attempts to answer as it explores the key features of native rulership in medieval Wales. It is a book about people who, by their status, wealth and power came to dominate the social, political and economic life of medieval Wales, while having a decisive hand in shaping its religious and cultural life also. It is not possible, even if it is desirable, to write a full biography of a medieval person, even someone as powerful as a Welsh ruler. In the cases of those individual rulers who were written about, we may have a general idea of their character but little in terms of their personal appearance. There are no portraits, no death masks and no contemporary tomb effigies; but even if there were, they would need to be treated with circumspection, since it was customary to portray important figures as it was thought they ought to look, rather than as they actually were. This applies equally to written descriptions and contemporary estimations, particularly those penned by the bards and poets which tend to portray their subjects in an idealised way. Consequently, much of what we learn about the Welsh rulers comes to us by means of what they did and how they did it. It is how and why they reacted to events, pressures and problems that offer the best insight into what they were like.

Land, lordship and local acknowledgement were among the key determinants of a ruler's status but war was his badge of honour. The native rulers were a warrior elite who, unlike the majority of their subjects whose social and political horizon was bounded by the structures of local life – the village, its church and the *seigneur* – took a supraregional view of the world that involved kingships and kingdoms. By a process of expansion, definition and development, particularly in the agencies of coercive authority, they, like the rest of western Europe, worked towards creating coherent territorial principalities. The more successful rulers were those who most effectively wielded power, not just over the bond or peasant element of the population, but over the free or noble element also. By endeavouring to create an administrative infrastructure for their respective polities they were attempting to make real and tangible their power and authority. The exceptional among them succeeded in broadening their power by exercising a form of hegemony over the other native rulers of Wales.

Defining and evaluating the size of this exclusive aristocratic group of native rulers is difficult, if not impossible. Contemporary understandings inevitably change over the two centuries under study, and there are, moreover, no forms of record-keeping that are sufficiently standardised or consistent to offer appropriate norms. In truth, this period is poorly documented from a Welsh point of view so that historians are forced to depend heavily on the records generated by their enemies, the agents of the English state. Equally difficult is appreciating, let alone understanding, the disjointed nature of medieval Wales, particularly after the arrival of the Normans in 1066, the various kingdoms, territories and lordships that consisted native-controlled 'Welsh' Wales and Marcher Wales. The confusion in their size, number and name is eased somewhat by the twelfth century, after which a measure of stability is attained. Clearly, medieval Wales was not so much a country as a collection of regions and localities, of ever shifting boundaries, hegemonies and loyalties, so that their history is as much the history of their rulers.

Outlines

Wales was a fragmented land of many kingdoms and many dynasties, the principal divisions of which, at least by the middle of the eleventh century, were the four major territories of Gwynedd, Powys, Deheubarth and Morgannwg. Unlike Gwynedd and Powys, which had a history stretching back to the departure of the Romans, Morgannwg and Deheubarth were relatively new creations dating to the eighth and tenth centuries, respectively. Only three of these kingdoms survived into the twelfth century, Morgannwg falling by the wayside late in the eleventh, of which Gwynedd alone emerged enlarged and strong enough to dominate the Welsh political landscape in the thirteenth. There had, in the past, been various lesser kingdoms, principal among them Brycheiniog, Dyfed, Gwent and Gwynllwg, but most of these had gradually been absorbed by their more powerful neighbours or, more likely after 1066, had succumbed to alien conquest. Remarkably and exceptionally, the minor royal dynasties of Maelienydd, Gwrtheyrnion and Elfael, together making up the region known as Rhwng Gwy a Hafren (literally, between the rivers Wye and Severn), largely survived absorption by their Welsh neighbours in the twelfth century only to be conquered by the English in the thirteenth. The minor rulers of Arwystli and Meirionydd too enjoyed brief periods of independence when they either resisted or temporarily strayed from the control of their respective parent kingdoms of Powys (by annexation) and Gwynedd.

For much of the period under review, the rulers of these various kingdoms were selfishly engaged in their own, almost endless political and military competition. Rulers and kingdoms vied with each other for supremacy, pursuing objectives that were, for the most part, instinctual. Thus did successive rulers of Gwynedd make war on their native contemporaries, the rulers of Deheubarth and Powys in 1150–3 and in 1202, in order to annex, respectively, the bordering territories of Ceredigion and Penllyn. Arguably, it is not until the thirteenth century that there developed any real sense of a 'Wales', a Cymric nation of linguistically and culturally like-minded people who shared a common heritage. Whether it was due to a maturing self-awareness of themselves as a people alone that united the Welsh or simply the deepening of the shared experience of their being threatened from without, by Anglo-Norman lords and English kings, is open to debate. On the other hand, it was, in part, a Wales manufactured by war, fashioned by the ambitions of a ruler bent on uniting under his command the territories of his dissident Cymric neighbours whom he sought to make his vassals. It was a Wales that had at its territorial core the kingdom of Gwynedd and at its political heart a prince of Gwynedd, so that it was a Wales united less by idealism, much less the anachronism of nationalism, than by conquest and coercion from within. Nor was this competition confined to rivalry between kingdoms but it involved dynastic struggles within kingdoms also: between 949 and 1066 no fewer than 35 rulers were butchered at the hands of their compatriots. Membership of the dynasties of Deheubarth and Powys seemed to be among the most precarious, with some 14 of their number suffering death or maiming at the hands of their dynastic rivals between 1076 and 1160. Only when there emerged a leader of exceptional authority and skill could a kingdom transcend this internal violence and make its mark on the wider political stage. Consequently, the twin elements of territorial fluidity and political fragility predominated, so that political unity was invariably transient and ephemeral, achieved by military might alone.

On occasion, the balance of power in this fragmented land turned on the intervention of English kings, all of whom were concerned to maintain Welsh recognition of their hegemony without necessarily having to physically enforce it. At no time before the reign of Edward I (1272–1307) did the Crown contemplate the conquest of Wales, being content to visibly demonstrate its power by means of spasmodic, if mainly impressive, military expeditions. In all, 21 royal expeditions were launched in Wales between 1081 and 1267, some of the more successful being those led by William I (1066–87) in 1081, Henry I (1100–35) in 1114 and 1121, Henry II (1154–1189) in 1157–8, John (1199–1216) in 1211, and Henry III (1216–72) in 1241 and 1245–6. Arguably, besides Edward I, one king only may be said to have played more than just a passing part in Welsh affairs, namely Henry I. He was a dominant figure who manipulated the destinies of the dynasties of Deheubarth, Gwynedd and Powys, and was the first to establish significant royal territorial holdings in Wales. Apart from their dynastic wrangling, royal intervention generally caused the native rulers some of their periods of greatest turmoil, in that they almost inevitably led to disruption and destruction or, in some instances, their demotion, and in the worst cases, their death. Equally tumultuous were the periods when royal rule was at its weakest, as in the reign of Stephen (1135–54), at its most indifferent, as in the reign of Richard I (1189–99), or at its most distracted, as it was for short periods in the reigns of John and Henry III in 1215–17 and 1258–65, respectively. These periods enabled the more enterprising Welsh rulers to reshape, to their advantage, the map of political power in Wales.

The Crown's generally fitful interest in Welsh affairs before the mid- to late thirteenth century meant that the balance of power in Wales was more often likely to depend on the emergence of outstandingly able or ruthless native, and after 1066, Marcher leaders. The demise of Morgannwg in the 1080s and 1090s at the hands of Marcher barons serves to highlight the new and permanent element that was introduced to the history of Wales by the coming of the Normans. While it might be argued that they came to Wales as much allies as enemies, taking advantage of domestic squabbles to side with one dynastic faction against another, they were, above all, conquerors, freebooting barons intent on carving out for themselves territorial enclaves in this region of the Anglo-Welsh frontier or March. The Marchers' free-enterprise and land-grabbing expeditions along coasts and river valleys, staking their claim by erecting earth and timber castles as they went, transformed the power structure in Wales. By dint of their conquests, the eastern and southern parts of Wales were occupied by Marcher lordships that ranged in size from great earldoms like Pembroke and Glamorgan to lesser entities like Brecon and Gower. Indeed, great Marcher families like Clare, Braose and Mortimer were no whit less dynastic in outlook than their native counterparts with whom they contended for control of Wales. It was the conflict arising from this political, territorial and jurisdictional division between Marcher lords and native rulers, a pattern established that was to last in its basic outlines throughout the twelfth century and for most of the thirteenth, that provided the native rulers, who had constantly to live on the edge of conquest, with some of their sternest challenges.

Before 1063 only four native rulers had been able to extend their power over a substantial part of Wales: Rhodri Mawr (d. 878) and Gruffudd ap Llywelyn (d. 1063/4) of Gwynedd, and Hywel Dda (d. 950) and Maredudd ab Owain (d. 999) of Deheubarth. Whether any of them had a sense of unity or were merely war-leaders seeking domination, is open to debate. Indeed, what exactly *Wallia* or *Cambria* meant, in conceptual terms, to the Welsh of the period is not easy to answer.

A country geographically and politically fragmented, the first largely dictating the outlines of the second, did not make for easy internal communications, and in the absence of an accessible heartland which might serve as a focus for unity, it was almost inevitable that loyalties would be intensely local. That said, there is sufficient evidence from contemporary literature to suggest that the Welsh were self-aware and that they tended to express their sense of identity by looking back to the past when, as 'Britons', their ancestors had ruled the whole island of Britain. In the opinion of Michael Richter, 'it is in the two centuries before the Edwardian conquest of 1282–3 that the Welsh people experienced an enlargement of their view of the world, when gradually they came to know each other as fellow-countrymen by being fellow-sufferers'.[1] Their coming together was indeed a slow and painful process, made harder by the petty squabbling that not only bedevilled relations between the nation's political leaders, but also marred family relationships within their respective dynasties.

After 1063, two rulers only succeeded in extending their hegemony over the greater part of Wales: Llywelyn ab Iorwerth (*c.* 1194–1240) and his grandson Llywelyn ap Gruffudd (1247–82). That both hailed from Gwynedd reveals the extent to which this kingdom, with its naturally defensive core of Snowdonia, realised its potential to be the most powerful element in Welsh dynastic politics. The key to the success of the two Llywelyns, besides their military muscle, was in bringing to heel the other native rulers within a political framework that tolerated but excluded the Marcher lords, while simultaneously seeking acknowledgement of the English Crown of their status as the undisputed masters within a separate and unitary principality. Coexistence and cooperation with their Marcher neighbours and royal overlords became as much a feature of their policies as conflict and conquest had been. Consequently, under their capable and enlightened leadership, the prospect of creating an united native polity gradually turned into a practical proposition and was, briefly, realised between 1267 and 1277.

The credit for establishing Gwynedd's primacy in Welsh affairs is due, primarily, to the work of two earlier rulers, Gruffudd ap Cynan (*c.* 1075–1137) and his son Owain ap Gruffudd or, as he is more commonly known, Owain Gwyned (1137–70). They withstood the external pressures of Marcher ambition and royal intervention while repairing the dynastic fissures within that regularly threatened to tear their territorial power apart. Between them, they created a stable and prosperous kingdom by strengthening their hold on church and state and by wisely acknowledging English suzerainty. They were also responsible for originating and promoting the idea that a ruler of Gwynedd possessed authority over Wales as a whole, and, as if to emphasise the fact of their primacy, to Owain Gwynedd goes the credit of being among the first of his countrymen to cultivate a diplomatic friendship with a foreign ruler, Louis VII of France (1137–80).[2]

The composite kingdom of Deheubarth, formed by the enforced merger of three lesser kingdoms, Ceredigion, Dyfed and Ystrad Tywi, had its share of talented rulers during this period, namely Rhys ap Tewdwr (*c.* 1081–93) and his grandson Rhys ap Gruffudd, popularly known as the Lord Rhys (1155–97). Between them they kept alive a polity which might otherwise have disintegrated long before it actually did so in the early thirteenth century. By sheer force of personality they held together a kingdom that had been manufactured by military might and political will but which was subject to almost overwhelming pressures as much from within as from without. Crushed and dismembered by the Anglo-Normans after the killing of Rhys ap Tewdwr, it was left to the Lord Rhys to resurrect the kingdom in the second half of the twelfth century, only for it to implode after his death amid a complex tangle of domestic squabbles. Thereafter, its territorially embarrassed princelings, Maelgwn ap Rhys (d. 1231), Rhys Gryg (d. 1233) and Rhys ap Maredudd (d. 1292) principal among them, became subject either to the rulers of Gwynedd or England depending on the prevailing political situation.

Geographically locked between the native kingdoms of Gwynedd and Deheubarth on the one side and the alien Marcher lordships on the other, Powys was surrounded by hostile powers willing and eager to seize on any moment of weakness. Its rulers had the unenviable task of maintaining a balance of power that required a political skill and dexterity which only the most talented possessed and in Madog ap Maredudd (*c.* 1132–60) the Powysian dynasty had found its champion. During his twenty-eight year rule, Powys entered a period of prosperity and relative stability which was shattered only on his death with the partition of the kingdom into Powys Wenwynwyn (or southern Powys) and Powys Fadog (northern Powys). Although gravely weakened as a result of this partition, particularly in the case of Powys Fadog which suffered further dynastic subdivisions in 1236 and 1269, senior segments of the Powysian dynasty continued to play a role in national affairs. Two of the most significant, by reason of their talent and instinct for survival, hailed from Powys Wenwynwyn, namely, Owain Cyfeiliog (1160–97) and his grandson Gruffudd ap Gwenwynwyn (1216–86). Between them, they managed to keep alive the hopes and aspirations of their dynasty, and their success may be measured in as much as their principality was the only one to survive the Edwardian conquest.

Sources

The Welsh ruling elite of the later Middle Ages, living in the period between the mid-tenth and the end of the thirteenth century, are more elusive than their English or continental counterparts. Chronologically, geographically and familially, the sources simply do not have a great deal to say about the medieval rulers of Wales much before the thirteenth century, or much beyond the borders and dynasty of Gwynedd. Consequently, Llywelyn ap Gruffudd alone, the last native ruler of a largely united Wales, has been able to command sufficient source material for the kind of book, some 664 pages long, that is relatively commonplace on chronologically comparable rulers in England such as Henry III and Edward I.[3] Indeed, unlike its English counterparts, the magnum opus that is Professor J. Beverley Smith's *Llywelyn ap Gruffudd Prince of Wales*, is a recent one, being published in 1998. Although its author was surprised that his book was 'the first attempt to make extensive use of the source materials in a study centred on the prince', we can but envy the rich source material available to our English colleagues such as Professor Michael Prestwich who initially thought, sometime back in the late 1960s, that Edward I was simply 'too large' a subject for a biography.[4] In the event, his magisterial biographical volume on Edward came to a not inconsiderable 618 pages and is as vital a work today as when it was published. It is unlikely that books on this scale can or will be written on the Welsh princes, which is why some scholars have adopted a new approach, namely the collaborative biography. This technique has resulted in separate studies of two twelfth-century rulers, Gruffudd ap Cynan (1996) and, in Welsh, Rhys ap Gruffudd (1996), and though they are not biographies in the traditional sense but more a focused study of particular aspects of their respective reigns, they have proved to be very effective.[5] That this approach may prove to be the way forward for similar works on Welsh rulers who reigned before the mid-thirteenth century depends on the use made of the available source material which, though far from considerable, is not inconsequential.

If England is rich in twelfth- and thirteenth-century chronicles, Wales is not. The principal narrative sources for the history of the Welsh princes are the *Brut y Tywysogion* or *The Chronicle of the Princes*. Compiled sometime in the second half of the thirteenth century by anonymous monastic scribes and copyists, the *Brut* is based on earlier material which survives in more than one version and is, therefore, like the *Anglo-Saxon Chronicle*,[6] itself a useful peripheral source for Welsh affairs, a multiple source. Taking their name from the manuscripts from which they are identified, the two most important vernacular variants of the *Brut* include Peniarth Ms 20 and the Red Book of Hergest. A third and closely related version, the *Brenhinedd y Saesson* or *Kings of the Saxons*, is a composite source the first half of which, up to and including the year 1197, represents an independent variant that incorporates material from English annals, but which after 1198 follows almost exactly the Peniarth Ms 20 version. They have been edited and translated in a series of volumes by Thomas Jones and published by the University of Wales Press for its History and Law Series (Cardiff, 1952, 1955 and 1971).

That the twelfth-century redactions of the *Brut* have a Deheubarth provenance is well attested and the portions of the chronicle that refer to the events surrounding the lives of its princes are thought to hail from the cathedral church of St David's and the monasteries of Llanbadarn Fawr and Strata Florida. Consequently, the *Brut* has a great deal more to say about Deheubarth and its princes than about their rival counterparts in either Gwynedd or Powys. That there was an annalistic tradition peculiar to Gwynedd is suggested by the survival of a tract known as *O Oes Gwrtheyrn Gertheneu* (*From the Age of Vortigern*) which consists of a series of chronologically arranged notes recording events in north Wales.[7] Unfortunately neither it nor the other chronicles say very much on the more significant events such as the rise to power of Llywelyn ab Iorwerth which, as A.D. Carr rightly pointed out, is 'surely a worthy theme for the historian of the Welsh princes'.[8] Two further chronicles of importance are the Latin *Annales Cambriae* and *Cronica de Wallia* (the latter covering the period from 1190 to 1266). Both are thought to be closely related to the lost Latin exemplars upon which the versions of the *Brut* are based. Imperfectly published in 1860 by J. Williams ab Ithel (Rolls Series), a new edition of the *Annales* is currently being undertaken. The *Cronica de Wallia*, on the other hand, was not published until 1946, some seven years after its discovery in Exeter Cathedral Library. The value of each of these chronicles together with a discussion of their textual problems is provided by Thomas Jones in 'Cronica de Wallia and other documents from Exeter Cathedral Library MS 3154', *Bulletin of the Board of Celtic Studies*, 12 (1946–8), 17–44, and by Kathleen Hughes in 'The Welsh Latin Chronicles: Annales Cambriae and Related Texts', *Proceedings of the British Academy*, 59 (1973), 233–58.

Few historians would question the value of these chronicles as sources for pre-conquest Welsh history since they were written by Welshmen who would have had a greater understanding and appreciation of Welsh affairs than their English or European counterparts. However, they are not without their problems for they were written and translated in the second half of the thirteenth century by monks far removed from the time they were describing and, although some of the evidence they used and copied from may date from an earlier time, a lost Latin archetype, we cannot be sure of the accuracy of their transcriptions or where hindsight has influenced the text. Nor are they, and this applies to other contemporary sources also, unbiased or objective, being often subject to reworking in the interests of politically dominant dynasties and institutions. Again, when different versions of the *Brut* are compared for information they can occasionally prove contradictory, though this can sometimes be a benefit by offering a different perspective. Therefore, although Professor J.E. Lloyd was not far short of the truth when he said that the *Brut* is a 'sober, pedestrian chronicle, occasionally waxing eloquent, but as a rule content to record the simple facts', it can be demonstrated that some of the facts are perhaps not so simple to interpret, especially in those instances where the *Bruts* 'wax eloquent' and the distinction between fact and opinion becomes blurred.[9]

If the rulers of Gwynedd did not benefit from frequent reference in the native *Bruts*, they did at least attract the interest of English kings and, by implication, their clerks who were responsible for compiling royal records. Consequently, these records, particularly those dating from the thirteenth century, are rich sources for many aspects of Welsh history including the ruling princes. Among the more useful records, besides the calendars published for the History and Law Series, are *Calendar of Ancient Correspondence concerning Wales* (Cardiff, 1935) and *Littere Wallie* (Cardiff, 1940) edited by J.G. Edwards, and *The Welsh Assize Roll, 1277–84* (Cardiff, 1940) edited by J.C. Davies. The native rulers were no whit less productive, albeit on a much smaller scale, in issuing charters, letters and other acts, the sum total of which the History and Law Series has pledged to publish. In the meantime, historians will have to make do with a recently issued but no less valuable *Handlist of the Acts of Native Welsh Rulers 1132–1283* (Cardiff, 1996) edited by K.L. Maund.

Fortunately, a fair number of princes attained sufficient eminence or infamy to attract the attention of English and continental chroniclers. Among the more important of the twelfth- and thirteenth-century chroniclers were Orderic Vitalis (d.*c.* 1143), Herbert of Bosham (d. 1186), Roger of Howden (d.*c.* 1201), Ralph of Diceto (d.*c.* 1203), Ralph of Coggeshall (*fl.* 1210), Roger of Wendover (d. 1236) and Matthew Paris (d. 1259) and, to a lesser extent, Robert of Torigny (*fl.* 1150–80s) and Gervase of Canterbury (*fl.* 1160–90s).[10] Their usefulness lies in the fact that they were well-informed contemporaries with a sound knowledge of much of what they wrote while some were closely connected with, or employed by, the English royal court or, in Bosham's case, as chaplain to Archbishop Thomas Becket. Matthew Paris, for example, makes an important reference to Llywelyn ab Iorwerth's stroke in 1237, an event which escaped the pens if not the notice of the native chroniclers. The odd nugget of valuable information notwithstanding, Paris and his contemporaries were foreigners, both English and French, with little, or at best peripheral, knowledge of Welsh affairs and much of the information they supply on Wales is often incidental and occasionally distorted. Indeed, Robert of Torigny is a good example, visiting England but twice, in 1157 and 1175, so that his judgement on Welsh affairs may lack authority. The same cautionary note must be applied to those few anonymously written monastic annals and chronicles of the reigns of various English monarchs that make reference to Wales and its princes. On the other hand, monastic cartularies are a rich and sober source of information on church property and related matters which might involve the princes often in some conveyance, dispute or damage. Taken in conjunction with the evidence culled from the native chroniclers, these various sources do at the very least provide some rounding in the picture of the native rulers of Wales.

The twelfth-century renaissance witnessed the beginning of one of the great periods of vernacular, or non-Latin, poetry, and in Wales therefore the works of the court poets or *Gogynfeirdd* (poets of the princes) cannot be ignored for, archaism and hyperbole apart, if used with caution they provide much historical information not forgetting valuable social and political perspective. In a fitting tribute to their work, the University of Wales Centre for Advanced Welsh and Celtic Studies at Aberystwyth is in the process of editing the works of the *Gogynfeirdd* in seven Welsh-language volumes, four of which have been published. Close on forty court poets have been identified and the majority of their work can be found in the following principal manuscripts: National Library of Wales MS Peniarth 1, 'The Black Book of Carmarthen', (*c.* 1250); MS Peniarth 3 (*c.* 1250–1300); MS NLW 6680B, 'The Hendregadredd

Manuscript', (*c.* 1300–30). As the dates of their composition suggest, the texts of the poems survive only in later copies so that they must be approached with a degree of circumspection, though in the majority of cases it can be shown that they were faithfully reproduced from the originals. The most useful guide in English to their works, though sadly lacking an index, is J.E. Caerwyn Williams, *The Poets of the Welsh Princes* (2nd edn, Cardiff, 1994).

Of equal if not greater importance were the literary compositions of writers who were not content just to record events in annalistic form but were keen to describe their experiences, travels and opinions, especially of those they knew and others they had met. Two such writers – Walter Map and Gerald of Wales – tower above their contemporaries and both were either wholly or partly Welsh. Walter Map (d.*c.* 1210) served God and the Crown in a number of capacities during his long life. He was a cleric by vocation but a royal clerk by profession, but above all he was a scholar who left behind him a rich catalogue of tidbits of information written under the apt title of *De Nugis Curialium* or *Courtier's Trifles* in *c.* 1181–2.[11] Hailing from what is today Herefordshire in England but was then very much a part of Welsh-speaking Wales, the Welshman Map, a sometime student in Paris, served King Henry II loyally for nearly twenty years between *c.* 1170 and 1189. During his time in and around the king and the court, he met several foreign dignitaries of whom Rhys ap Gruffudd (d. 1197) of Deheubarth was one. That he wrote of this Welsh prince is strongly suggested by a piece entitled 'Of the King Appollonides', in which he deliberately used a pseudonym in order not to be too direct in criticising a living contemporary. He was less circumspect when writing of the departed and vented his spleen on Gruffudd ap Llywelyn (d. 1063), the outstanding ruler of a largely united Wales, whom he ridicules as a bloodthirsty tyrant. Composed for the delectation of the Angevin King Henry and his court, 'The *De Nugis* is not only very entertaining; it is a rough inventory of the mental furniture of a learned and witty 12th-century clerk'.[12]

The writings of Gerald of Wales are perhaps among the most frequently used and potentially the most valuable sources for the history of twelfth- and early thirteenth-century Wales. The significance of his volumous works lies in the fact that they originated in the mind and emanated from the pen of a contemporary who knew well the people and country he was describing. As the son of William de Barri, an Anglo-Norman lord of Manorbier, and Angharad, the grand-daughter of Rhys ap Tewdwr (d. 1093), king of Deheubarth, Gerald was a product of the twelfth-century March who lived his life torn between two worlds never fully reconciling himself to either, though in his heart, one might suspect, he was more Anglo-Norman than Welsh. Thus, being of mixed race but noble parentage, holding a respected position in the church and, by virtue of his contacts, with the courts of Welsh rulers and English kings alike, Gerald was well placed to comment on the political, social and religious scene. He knew well his kinsman Rhys ap Gruffudd and was acquainted with many of the leading Welsh and Anglo-Norman nobility of his day. Among his many works, the most significant in respect to Wales and things Welsh are his *Itinerarium Kambriae* [*The Journey through Wales*] (travelled in 1188 but written in 1191), *Descriptio Kambriae* [*A Description of Wales*] (1194) but there is much also to be gained from the following selected works *De Rebus a Se Gestis* [*Autobiography*] (1208), *Speculum Duorum* [*A Mirror of Two Men*] (1216), *De Jure et Statu Menevensis Ecclesiae* [*The Rights and Status of St David's*] (1218) and *De Principis Instructione* [*The Instruction of a Prince*] (1218).[13]

Unfortunately, the princes did not share in the good fortune that attended Gruffudd ap Cynan of Gwynedd (d. 1137), of whom a biography was written, a Welsh translation of a Latin original, some thirty years after his death. Approved, if not commissioned, by his son and successor Owain Gwynedd (d. 1170), the *Historia Gruffud vab Kenan* is the only near-contemporary biography to be written for a Welsh prince, or at least the only one to have survived.[14] There is some evidence dating from the seventeenth century to suggest that biographies were composed for the Gwynedd dynasts Llywelyn ab Iorwerth (d. 1240) and his son Dafydd (d. 1246): they were known to the eminent antiquaries Edward Lhuyd and Robert Vaughan of Hengwrt and were thought to be preserved in Corpus Christi College, Cambridge but that the manuscripts have subsequently been lost.[15] Loss, destruction, accident and sheer bad luck together with the good intentions of the unwitting and the unweary has conspired to reduce much of our written history to priceless fragments. Nevertheless, from the evidence that does survive historians can, at the very least, begin to reconstruct the lives and careers of men who played such a dominant role in the history of Wales until the end of the thirteenth century.

Notes

1. M. Richter, 'The Political and Institutional Background to National Consciousness in Medieval Wales', in *Nationality and the Pursuit of National Independence*, ed. T.W. Moody (Belfast, 1978), 38.
2. H. Pryce, 'Owain Gwynedd and Louis VII: The Franco-Welsh Diplomacy of the First Prince of Wales', *WHR*, 19 (1998), 1–28.

3. M. Prestwich, *Edward I* (London, 1988); D.A. Carpenter, *The Reign of Henry III* (London, 1996).

4. J.B. Smith, *Llywelyn ap Gruffudd*, ix; M. Prestwich, op. cit., xi.

5. N.A. Jones and H. Pryce, *Yr Arglwydd Rhys* (Caerdydd, 1996); K.L. Maund, ed., *Gruffudd ap Cynan: A Collaborative Biography* (Woodbridge, 1996).

6. The most recent edition is that translated and edited by M. Swanton and published in London in 1996.

7. See J. Rhys and J. Gwenogvryn Evans, eds, *The Text of the Bruts from the Red Book of Hergest* (Oxford, 1890).

8. A.D. Carr, *Medieval Wales*, 6.

9. J.E. Lloyd, 'The Welsh Chronicles', *PBA*, XIV (1928), 370.

10. Ralph of Diceto, *Radulfi de Diceto Decani Lundoniensis Opera Historica*, ed. W. Stubbs (2 vols, Rolls Series, 1876); Matthew Paris, *Chronica Majora*, ed. H.R. Luard (7 vols, Rolls Series, 1872–83); Roger of Wendover, *Chronica*, ed. H.O. Coxe (4 vols, English Historical Society, 1841–4).

11. Walter Map, *De Nugis Curialium* (*Courtiers' Trifles*), ed. and trans. M.R. James (Oxford, 1983).

12. Ibid., xix.

13. Gerald's *Speculum Duorum*, ed. M. Richter, Y. Lefevre and R.B.C. Huygens, trans. B. Dawson (Cardiff, 1974); *Journey & Description*; *Autobiog.*

14. *Mediaeval Prince.*

15. R.T. Gunther, *Early Science in Oxford 14: Life and Letters of Edward Lhwyd* (Oxford, 1945), 371.

chapter one

FAMILY, DESCENT AND INHERITANCE: THE PRINCES AND THEIR PRINCIPALITIES

Who and what were the Welsh princes? Put simply, and as their title implies, they were men of status and of power. In a hierarchical and stratified society where status was important, theirs was the most important of all, for by birth, lineage and blood they were royal. Their power too was derived in large part from their royal status but was dependent also, as befitted a warrior caste, on their courage in combat and leadership on the battlefield. Heroic in deed, dynastic in ambition and rulers by intent, the princes were the elite of a privileged aristocratic class. Yet in spite of these shared characteristics, it is difficult to categorise the Welsh princes as a group, for although they were royal and they were rulers, they were not necessarily equal. Most were rulers of a single kingdom; some, by dint of conquest, more than one; but the exceptional among them were able to extend their hegemony over the greater part of Wales. However, such successes could usually be measured in the space of a generation since the gains made by one ruler were, more often than not, lost by another. This continual shifting of the dynastic and political balance of power is reflected in the use by contemporaries of a bewildering array of titles to address or describe their rulers. This is perhaps unsurprising in a period spanning a little over two centuries, 1063–1283, since change is inevitable and, in respect of the rulers of medieval Wales, the evolution in the nomenclature of their authority may usually be taken as a fair reflection of the winners and losers in the dynastic battle for supremacy, for while some prospered and increased their power, others suffered a diminution in theirs. However, while we may refer to them as princes, contemporaries were not so consistent in their use of the title, so that some justification, and definition, is necessary. Consequently, it is in terms of their identity, status and title, individual and territorial, together with a discussion of their kinship, descent and inheritance, that this chapter is concerned.

Kings, lords and princes: the nomenclature of authority

The nomenclature of authority was important to contemporaries since a man's status and power was regulated by law and custom, so that the title he assumes can be taken as a public recognition of one and public expression of the other. Indeed, their titles provide virtually the only evidence of the way in which the rulers of native Wales viewed themselves and, in what was evidently a conscious and calculated move, it was their way of interpreting their status for the outside world. This had not always been so since for much of the period before the tenth century, the rulers of Wales had no, and often did not use, any formal or consistent titles. It is not until the native law texts were assembled during the twelfth and thirteenth centuries that the issue of titular nomenclature was seriously addressed, with the result that a measure of definition and hierarchy was gradually introduced into the titles of native rulers. According to those who framed the Welsh laws, Latin-educated jurists who were familiar with concepts of royal office and royal government, supreme power was vested in the title and office of king or *brenin* (*rex*). Kingship was compounded of military, civil and religious authority, varying in proportion and strength according to the qualities and fortunes of individual kings. The chief court or *prif lys* was the seat of the king's power and it was from here, together with its itinerant satellite courts, that he ruled his subjects.

However, from about the middle of the twelfth century a change can be discerned, the reasons for which have yet to be properly investigated, for as J. Beverley Smith has pointed out, 'the evidence which survives hardly provides the means for any elaborate study of the Welsh princes' titles',[1] so that only a cursory examination can be attempted here. The nature of the change in nomenclature can most closely be followed in the chronicles, both English and Welsh, the poetry, charters and even in some of the romance tales of the period since these sources, despite their often later and copied provenance, reflected far more vividly the reality of daily political life than the precepts of the native laws. Where once the rulers of dynasties had been described as kings they were now called princes (*tywysog, princeps*) or even lords (*arglwydd, dominus*). The change was neither immediate nor absolute for there continued to be apparent inconsistencies in the application of titles, an example of which may be instanced from the three versions of the *Brut y Tywysogion* or *The Chronicle of the Princes* reporting on the death of Maredudd, ruler of Deheubarth in 1155. The *Brut* [Peniarth Ms 20] calls Maredudd 'lord of Ceredigion and Ystrad Tywi and Dyfed', the *Brut* [Red Book of

Hergest] calls him 'king', while the *Brenhinedd* does not ascribe him any title, he is merely 'of Ceredigion and Ystrad Tywi and Dyfed'.[2] Of course, there is no guarantee that the titles employed by the various editions of the *Bruts* in respect of the rulers of twelfth-century Wales are anything other than later embellishments, for the chronicles as we have them today are essentially late-thirteenth-century copies in Welsh of lost Latin originals.

Commenting on the death of Maredudd's grandfather Rhys ap Tewdwr in 1093, the English chronicler John of Worcester was moved to declare that 'from that day kings ceased to rule in Wales'.[3] Nor was this merely empty rhetoric for the Welsh chroniclers appear to have been in agreement, stating with unaccustomed unanimity that with the death of Rhys 'the kingdom of the Britons fell'.[4] Thereafter, from 1094 to 1137, titles of any description, let alone that of king, are almost entirely absent from the texts of the *Bruts*. Indeed, in contrast to the chroniclers of old who were apt to use the terminology of kingship more freely, those of the twelfth century appear reluctant to accord the title of *brenin* or king to rulers, often sons of kings, whose patrimonies were either much reduced or facing extinction. Henceforth, the tenth and eleventh-century *brenhinoedd* or kingdoms of Ceredigion, Dyfed, Gwent, Morgannwg, Gwynedd and Powys referred to in the *Bruts*, were to be replaced in the twelfth, by those of Deheubarth, Gwynedd and Powys, along with a host of lesser lordships, while the title 'king' was given to only four rulers after 1137: Gruffudd ap Cynan (d. 1137) and his son Owain (d. 1170) of Gwynedd, Maredudd ap Gruffudd (d. 1155) of Deheubarth, and Madog ap Maredudd (d. 1160) of Powys.

The contrast in the titles employed by the Welsh chroniclers between the eleventh and latter half of the twelfth century is quite marked; the title of king was gradually giving way to those of lord and prince. This may reflect the changed political conditions of the twelfth century, a result of piecemeal Anglo-Norman conquest and the spread of feudal influence, for the Welsh rulers would have been nothing more than pale reflections of their Angevin neighbour, King Henry II (d. 1189), had they retained the increasingly meaningless title of king. The late T. Jones Pierce suggested that the change may have been due to pressure exerted by Henry II on the leading rulers of Wales to drop the title of king thus enabling him to assert the principle of the English Crown's superiority and its political overlordship.[5] The Welsh chronicles would seem to support this assertion, for after 1155 the title is applied but once more to a native ruler, Owain Gwynedd, and then only at his death in 1170.[6] On the other hand, David Crouch has argued that the abandonment of kingship was a 'native decision' and that the Welsh were not 'forced into it'.[7] In stark contrast to their counterparts in Wales, the English chroniclers, with one notable exception, Ralph of Diceto, seem to have taken a different view since they were according native rulers like Rhys ap Gruffudd (d. 1197) of Deheubarth regal status consistently calling him variously, *rex Walensium* [king of the Welsh], *rex Sutwalliae* [king of south Wales] or simply *rex* [king Rhys].[8] Once only is he acclaimed *rex Walliae* or king of Wales in the late-thirteenth-century Annals of Tewkesbury.[9] So why was Rhys so called by contemporary observers from across the Severn who, from their experience of European kingship, knew perfectly well, or should have known, what regal status entailed. A clue to their attitude on the nature of Rhys' regal status is afforded by Roger of Howden who consistently styles Rhys *regulus* which may be translated as petty or little king, thus strongly suggesting the superiority of Angevin kingship over that of its Welsh vassals.[10] This accords well with the view that Rhys and his fellow rulers, at the behest of Henry II, set aside all pretensions to regal status in return for confirmation of their landholdings. It seems that during the twelfth century the native chroniclers were tending increasingly to acclaim only their greatest rulers *brenin* or *rex* and then only as an epithet of greatness to be dispensed at death as a mark of respect and for past deeds should they warrant titular distinction. By the thirteenth century this practice had ceased completely and the title of king is henceforth only to be found in the texts of the Welsh laws, or at least in those copies that have survived.

Gerald de Barri (d. 1223), as he should more properly be addressed, though known to posterity as Gerald of Wales, or in Latin, *Giraldus Cambrensis*, was in no doubt as to what they were and how they should be addressed. Being related to some of the native rulers, he either knew well or knew of the others, there was no dispute in his mind but that the greatest of them were princes, and it was with great pride and by means of his mixed ancestry that he declared that he was 'sprung from the princes of Wales and from the barons of the Marches'.[11] His eloquent testimony bridges the gap somewhat between the views expounded by native writers and the opinions expressed by their English and continental counterparts. Of course, we have no way of knowing whether Gerald's definition of the title, dignity and authority of 'prince' matches that described by the native chroniclers or that used by the native rulers themselves. Certainly in the surviving, though admittedly late and often copied, charters, letters and other acts issued by the Welsh rulers it is as princes that they present themselves, the styles of which vary and were intended to imply a personal, in terms of status, a political, in terms of an ill-defined leadership of the Welsh people, or a territorial authority. Thus was Rhys ap Gruffudd of Deheubarth styled or referred to by contemporaries between 1165 and 1197 as Prince Rhys (*Principis Resi*), Rhys, prince of south Wales (*Reso principi Suthwalliae*) and Rhys prince of the Welsh (*Resus Walliarum princeps*).[12] It is important to note that the adoption of the title and style of prince did not necessarily mean a dimunition in status and power for as J. Beverley Smith has said in respect of Owain Gwynedd he 'did not cease to be king of Gwynedd in order to be prince of Gwynedd, . . . he chose to present himself as 'prince of the Welsh' (*princeps Wallensium*).[13]

If the changing nature of the relationship between the Crown of England and its native vassals, the rulers of Wales, was, arguably, at the root of the change in their nomenclature in the twelfth century, in the thirteenth its cause was as much the ambition of the princes of Gwynedd as pressure exerted by successive English kings. In their efforts to extend their hegemony over native Wales, the princes of Gwynedd were seeking to define the nature of their relationship with the other native rulers whom they attempted to make their vassals. Their success in this endeavour can be measured in respect of the progress they made via the reigns of Llywelyn ab Iorwerth (1194–1240) and Dafydd ab Llywelyn (1240–6), towards the defining moment, as encapsulated in the terms of the Treaty of Montgomery of 1267, in which Llywelyn ap Gruffudd asserted his right, with the cooperation of a reluctant king of England, Henry III (d. 1272), to the exclusive use of the title 'prince of Wales'. Equally grudging in their recognition of Llywelyn's hegemony was the native aristocracy, the elite of whom, the rulers of a dismembered Deheubarth and a sundered Powys, were forced to set aside any pretension to royal status and accept their lordly vassalage. This is reflected in the *Brut y Tywysogion* which shows a marked tendency to restrict to a few and thereafter during the thirteenth century, to reduce the use of the title in so far as the 'princes of Wales' mentioned in 1216 had become the 'barons of Wales in 1240 and the 'magnates of Wales' in 1256.[14] In the opinion of David Walker, modern writers, unsurprisingly, 'find it easier to avoid concepts of rank', preferring instead to refer to those rulers outside of Gwynedd, particularly from the early thirteenth century, either as 'princelings' or 'of the lineage of princes'.[15] In spite of having muddied the waters of nomenclature, there is no doubt that the title 'prince' remains a useful generic term to describe the native rulers of medieval Wales. It also has the added advantage of being a title with which we, today, are familiar and is the one most consistently applied by contemporaries between 1063 and 1283.

The Wales of the princes

Cambria is called Wales . . . It is two hundred miles long and about one hundred miles wide. It takes some eight days to travel the whole length, from the mouth of the River Gwygir in Anglesey to Portskewett in Gwent. In breadth it stretches from Porth-mawr, that is the Great Port, near St. David's, to Rhyd-helyg, the Welsh for Willow Ford, called Walford in English, this being a journey which lasts four days. Because of its high mountains, deep valleys and extensive forests, not to mention its rivers and marches, it is not easy of access.[16]

Thus was Wales described by one who knew it well. Writing in the last decade of the twelfth century, Gerald of Wales had not long completed a journey along the length and breadth of a land in which he was born and which he proudly called home. Nor was his knowledge confined to the geography of Wales: he knew well enough much of its often bloody history and the resulting political divisions of the country:

From time immemorial Wales has been divided into three more or less equal parts. When I say equal I mean in value rather than in size. These are Gwynedd, or North Wales; South Wales, called in Welsh Deheubarth, which really means Right-Hand Wales, a sub-section of which, containing seven cantrefs, has been given the name of Demetia or Dyfed; and Powys, which is the middle and stretches eastwards.[17]

Although he was of mixed race, Anglo-Norman and Welsh, and had been brought up in the Anglo-Norman colony of south Pembrokeshire, located in Dyfed, he knew well some of the ruling princes of his day, one of whom, the Lord Rhys of Deheubarth, he called cousin. In his twin-treatise on Wales and the Welsh, appropriately entitled *The Journey through Wales* and *The Description of Wales*, Gerald of Wales admits to the problems of making sense of much of what he had to impart to those of his readers not familiar with either the country or its people. How much more difficult for us today who are removed from the period by the space of some seven centuries. That Gerald succeeded in reaching his audience is due in large part to his intuitive style of writing the cornerstone of which was the care that he took in explanation and definition. Thanks largely to the efforts of Gerald and others like him who wrote so vividly of the country and its people we are able, with their guidance, to reconstruct a picture of Wales and the Welsh during a crucial period in their history.

As Gerald of Wales ably pointed out, the Wales of his time is hard to define. Its territorial extent varied according to the ebb and flow of war, so that its shape was largely dictated by invasion, conquest and settlement.

This had as much to do with aggressive Anglo-Saxon and later Norman and Anglo-Norman *conquistadores* as with the Welsh themselves for they were a divided people and, in a land where local and regional identities were strong, prone to violent dispute. It was a land of multiple-kingship which because of 'its high mountains, deep valleys and extensive forests, not to mention its rivers and marches', did not make for unified control or a unified development. Thus, for example, the Wales encountered by the earliest Normans who made their way to the fringes of the country soon after 1066, consisted of a number of separate kingdoms each of which, though they varied considerably in size and strength, had its territorial identity, cultural traditions, ruling dynasty and, most precious of all, its independence. Consequently, unlike its near neighbour England, Wales did not, until late, experience that process of political coalescence which might lead to the emergence of a single kingdom and kingship.

In terms of their size, strength and longevity, Gerald of Wales was correct to state that the most powerful kingdoms in twelfth-century Wales were Gwynedd, Powys and Deheubarth but this had not always been so. On the eve of William the Conqueror's victory at Hastings, the kingdom of Morgannwg too was as large, if not as powerful, and its relatively rapid crumbling in the face of enemy attack may have been due as much to the ferociousness of the Norman onslaught as to its own internal weaknesses. Certainly, the royal dynasty of 'Gwlad Morgan' was under pressure from a rival in the shape of the emerging dynasty of Gwent which had survived attempted suppression in 1030 to stake its claim to independent rule by the 1060s. However, an equally pressing threat to the survival of Morgannwg came not from within or from without, in the shape of Norman *conquistadores*, but from the Welsh of Deheubarth. War between kingdoms and their dynasties posed as much of a threat to their continued existence as did alien conquest, and it was the result of conflict with the dynasty of Deheubarth that the last king of a largely united Morgannwg, Caradog ap Gruffudd, was killed in battle in 1081. Political confusion followed his death and by the early 1090s the kingdom collapsed amid competing dynasts and Norman intruders.[18] If competition between Deheubarth and Morgannwg dominated native politics in the south for a short period in the late eleventh century, in the north, conflict between Gwynedd and Powys endured for a remarkably long time, lasting throughout the twelfth and thirteenth centuries. Gwynedd's military strength and superior resources eventually prevailed in as much as the truculent rulers of a divided Powys had largely succumbed, certainly by the 1220s, to the hegemony of their bitter rivals.

Evolution of the native principalities and princely authority

If territorial disputes between kingdoms were common, so were those within kingdoms, particularly in cases where smaller units had been reluctantly absorbed into larger ones. Absorption betokens expansion which, in turn, fuelled dispute, for in the acquisition of additional lands the sins of envy, greed and rivalry were bred. Contraction too posed problems, for in times of conflict kingdoms might lose territory which only added to dynastic stresses and strains as there was less land to go round. Apart from arguments over who should rule the kingdom, the most serious disputes involved claims by competing members of the same dynasty to particular regions or localities, which, if allowed to continue, would inevitably lead to partition. The kingdoms or principalities which had most to lose by such disputes were those with the most land, and the means to acquire more, namely Gwynedd, Powys and Deheubarth.

Dynastic stamina, geography and good fortune played significant parts in Gwynedd's survival, longevity and extended hegemony in the two centuries after the arrival of the continental *conquistadores*. Protected by natural barriers such as the rivers Clwyd, Conwy and Dyfi, the mountain ranges of Snowdonia, Cader Idris, Berwyn and Clwyd, Gwynedd was able to withstand all but the most determined attempts to subdue it. Certainly, Gerald of Wales was awestruck by his first sight of Snowdonia which seemed to him 'to rear their lofty summits right up to the clouds'.[19] To him, Gwynedd was 'the rudest and roughest of all the Welsh districts. The mountains are very high, with narrow ridges and a great number of very sharp peaks all jumbled together in confusion'.[20] If such terrain presented potential enemies with a daunting prospect it proved equally intimidating for a ruler bent on welding it together into a coherent polity.

Gwynedd is a kindom naturally divided by the Conwy so that the area to the west is designated Gwynedd Uwch Conwy, and that to the east Gwynedd Is Conwy. The first formed the central heartland of the kingdom, which, with the possible exception of Meirionydd, retained its cohesiveness for much of the period under review. It was from this secure base, backed by the fertile grain-producing areas of Anglesey and Lleyn peninsula, that the rulers of Gwynedd struck out to extend their hegemony south and east. To this they added, by naked aggression in 1202, the territory of Penllyn which they took, and retained, from Powys. The latter, Gwynedd Is Conwy, also known as the Perfeddwlad or middle country, was frequently subject to attacks by enemies from across the Dee, the earldom of Chester, or from the south by the rival dynasty of Powys. As if to make more difficult the task facing the rulers of Gwynedd, they had also to snuff out the independent tendencies of lessser dynasties who claimed the territories of the Perfeddwald, namely Rhos and Rhufoniog and Tegeingl, as their own. This they did during, and periodically after, the 1120s by enticing these would-be dynasts into their protection, intially imposing upon them a loose hegemony that took account of their sensitive positions, which gradually turned into full assimilation.

Meirionydd posed rather more of a problem, not so much from any claim to dynastic independence by an indigenous family, but by the lofty pretensions of cadet branches of the Gwynedd dynasty itself. Between 1241 and 1256 the sons of Maredudd ap Cynan ab Owain, cousins of the ruling prince, succeeded in establishing a sub-kingdom in Meirionydd only to be absorbed once more by their dynastic seniors. Nor was Meirionydd free from the predatory raids of others, being the subject of at least two attempted annexations by Powys in the 1110s and Deheubarth in 1177–8. In fact, accommodating the *membra regis* of Gwynedd, a problem shared by other dynasties also, proved more than a little difficult since satisfaction with their lot was rarely the end result of parcelling out selected areas of the patrimony. This was shown in 1252 when Dafydd ap Gruffudd (d. 1283), younger brother of the ruler Llywelyn II (k. 1282), registered his discontent at having been invested with courtly office without territory. He was eventually found a small corner of the kingdom, in the Lleyn peninsula, over which to exercise his lordship, but as J.B. Smith pointed out, 'Lordship over Cymydmaen hardly satiated Dafydd's ambitions, and by 1253 he had taken his first steps towards securing what he would regard as an appropriate portion of the inheritance'.[21]

If dynastic rivalry and segmentation posed problems for Gwynedd, they proved almost fatal for Powys. Thrice partitioned by dynastic rivalry, in 1160 (permanently as Powys Wenwynwyn and Powys Fadog), 1236 and 1269 (in Powys Fadog only), the kingdom was never able to repair itself so that its component parts were regularly subjected to attempts at assimilation or annexation. It was, in the opinion of J.E. Lloyd, 'the weakest of the realms of Wales',[22] a kingdom possessing few natural barriers that was early forced into retreat from the fertile English borderlands even before the arrival of the Normans. In view of their weak strategic position, the rulers of Powys had, it seems, little choice but to develop a flair for diplomacy. Pressured from the north by Gwynedd and from the east by Anglo-Saxon and later Anglo-Norman invaders, the dynasty seemed fated either to be the willing but subservient ally of the foreigner, or the unwilling vassal of Gwynedd. A little luck and the genius of individual rulers notwithstanding, that they periodically did both while being able to maintain a large measure of independence for long periods, even in partition, is remarkable. That a degree of elasticity characterised the dynasty is almost inevitable given the segmentation that occurred over a century. Indeed, at one point in the thirteenth century, no less than eight members of the dynasty exercised their rule in areas of pre-1160 partition Powys that, in themselves, did not amount to much in landed terms and even less in political terms.

Her boundaries too were anything if not elastic, and as they changed so did the capacity of her rulers to exercise their power. Nevertheless, by dint of tradition, descent and inheritance, Powys had become one of the territorial mainstays of medieval Wales, a geopolitical bloc which, unlike Deheubarth, partition later in the twelfth century could not alter. The rulers of Powys worked tirelessly to define and maintain the integrity of their principality and for short periods, most notably in *c.* 1102–16 and again in the mid to late 1190s, they exercised a supremacy in Welsh politics that belied their political divisions and strategic weaknesses. In attempting to extend and define their power the princes had, like Gwynedd, to overcome the independent tendencies of dissident minor dynasties that clung to their patrimonies with rigour. The independent spirit of the ruling dynasty of Arwystli was remarkably resilient – it was as king of Arwystli that Hywel ab Ieuaf (d. 1185) made grants of land to Haughmond Abbey between *c.* 1143 and 1151[23] – successfully resisting several attempts by Gwynedd to annex its remote and inaccessible mountainous terrain before succumbing to that part of Powys ruled by Gwenwynwyn ab Owain Cyfeiliog (d. 1216) in 1198. Princely rule in Powys, in whichever segment that existed in that space and time, was not easy, but nor was it impossibly difficult. The various family branches regularly allied together in the face of common threats, as seven of eight of them did in 1282 against Edward I, and in spite of Powys Wenwynwyn being the larger and stronger of the partitioned parcels of the former kingdom, its rulers resisted all attempts to crush and annex the component parts of its weaker neighbour Powys Fadog. In fact, by deft political manoeuvring, one part of Powys (Wenwynwyn) at least managed to outlast all its rivals, surviving into the fourteenth century as a principality-cum-Marcher lordship.

The problems facing the rulers of either Gwynedd or Powys were as nothing compared with those confronting the would-be rulers of Deheubarth. As its name suggests, Deheubarth (literally, southern region) was a composite kingdom, a 'ramshackle realm' as the late Gwyn A. Williams called it,[24] created by the enforced merger of the former sub-kingdoms of Dyfed (modern Pembrokeshire) and Seisyllwg, which was itself a fusion of two even older petty-kingdoms, Ceredigion and Ystrad Tywi (modern Ceredigion and Carmarthenshire). Created piece-meal sometime between the tenth and eleventh centuries, the kingdom of Deheubarth (it included during the late eleventh century the sub-kingdom of Brycheiniog) was a territorial and social conglomerate more prone to fracture than it was a mature and united political unit. Unsurprisingly, it was torn by rivalry and dissension, and bedevilled by the fractious effects of local particularism and patriotism. The difficulties of ruling it effectively were highlighted by Gerald of Wales who was of the opinion that

> although South Wales was by far the largest region, it was much the least attractive, for it was ruled by a great number of local chieftains, called 'uchelwyr' in Welsh, who were in constant rebellion and hard to control.[25]

It was not so much their hostility towards the ruling prince that made the *uchelwyr* 'hard to control' as their hostility for each other. The pro-Deheubarth scribes of the twelfth-century redactions of the *Brut* realised the futility of trying to disguise the mutual hatred felt by the 'disorderly folk from Dyfed' for the 'men of Ceredigion' and this 'even though they were of the same race'.[26] This was a society where kinship and the almost 'tribal' ideal of the kindred and the bloodfeud was a more power-ful influence in shaping loyalties and dictating actions than local or regional patriotism. Where the two coincided to a significant degree, as in the artificially created kingdom of Deheubarth, the stage was set for strife. Kinstrife exacerbated by regional discord played its part in Gruffudd ap Rhys' (d. 1137) ill-fated attempt in 1116 to unite his subjects in common cause against the all-conquering Anglo-Normans. He failed, according to the *Brut*, because among his followers from Dyfed 'there were hearts hostile to the men of Ceredigion because of the outrages which they had formerly committed against them and against their kinsmen'.[27]

Clearly, a significant number of the *uchelwyr* of Deheubarth were unwilling participants in the empire-building of their princes, yet if the latter were ever to succeed in wielding power within this royal conglomer-ate they had first to overcome the powerful forces making for disunity. In fact, in so far as Deheubarth can be said to have had any unity it rested solely in the person of the prince, his dynastic claim, his peripat-etic court and his military household. To judge from the reaction of contemporaries at the news of the death of the ruler of Deheubarth in 1093, it seems that they too believed this to be the case. Hence, 'when Rhys ap Tewdwr, king of the South, was slain by Frenchmen who were inhabiting Brycheiniog . . . fell the kingdom of the Britons'.[28] That Rhys was thought to be all that stood between Deheubarth and destruction is amply testified by the *Brut* which states that

> After his death Cadwgan ap Bleddyn plundered Dyfed on the Calends of May. And within two months of that, the French overran Dyfed and Ceredigion – what was not in their power before that – and made castles in them and fortified them.[29]

If the old conception of the king-prince as the personification of a 'tribal' folk had yet to fade completely from the minds of contemporaries, we need not doubt that with the king-prince personally rested the fate of his people and his kingdom. The native chroniclers make plain the disaster that struck the kingdoms of Powys in 1160, Deheubarth in 1197 and Gwynedd in 1282 after the deaths, by fair means and foul, of their respective rulers Madog ap Maredudd, Rhys ap Gruffudd and Llywelyn ap Gruffudd. Some poets too were prone to wax less lyrical at the passing of undoubtedly strong and talented rulers lest chaos reign in their stead. Gruffudd ab yr Ynad Coch's celebrated and oft-quoted elegy on Llywelyn ap Gruffudd sums up perfectly the utter despair felt by contemporaries who now lay in a hopeless *limbo patrum* awaiting either deliverance or destruction.[30] In truth, the continued existence of the native kingdoms relied almost entirely on the political and military talents of their rulers, all of whom fought hard to hold their territories together in the face of fierce attacks by neighbouring Welshman and invading Anglo-Norman alike.

This was no mean feat, for as Gerald of Wales indicates elsewhere in his treatise on Wales, the most important sub-division of a kingdom or *gwlad* (country) was the *cantref* which, he explains, was 'a word made up from *cant* meaning hundred and *tref* meaning vill, . . . a term used in both Welsh and Irish for a stretch of land which contains a hundred vills'. In Gerald's estimation 'South Wales contains twenty-nine cantrefs, North Wales twelve and Powys six' or, presuming he was including those areas conquered and incorporated into the English border shires, 'fifty-four cantrefs in all'.[31] Although the *cantref*, at some earlier time, had possibly been based on such a unit as a hundred *trefydd* (townships), roughly equating with an administrative division of a shire with which he was familiar in England, they were not so strictly defined in the Wales of the late twelfth century. Rather they were lordships, territories which commanded the patriotic loyalty of their inhabitants, sometimes to the extent that their ruling families proved too independent or disruptive. The *cantrefs* of Arwystli, Cedewain, Meirionydd and Tegeingl boasted dynastic families of their own and they did not take kindly to their annexation by Powys and, in respect of the latter two, Gwynedd.

Meirionydd and Arwystli were perhaps among the more intractable regions of Wales to overcome and it was only after much time and effort had been spent, and blood spilt, in their conquest, that they were finally absorbed into their respective polities.

Although not referred to in Gerald's work as often as the *cantref*, the *cwmwd* or commote represented a further sub-division which, like the *cantref*, was early more a political and dynastic unit than an administrative one. Only as a kingdom evolved into a more complex and sophisticated neo-bureaucracy did the commotes, more than the *cantrefs*, assume an administrative capacity within an organised state. Here could be found the *llys* or local court to which all the inhabitants of that district, free and unfree, would render their submission, offer their service and pay their dues either in cash or in kind. Gerald of Wales, however, makes no mention of these local courts, for him the ones that matter are the royal courts of Aberffraw, Dinefwr and Mathrafal, each of which lay at the heart of the kingdoms of Gwynedd, Deheubarth and Powys respectively. Here would be found, when they were not travelling the kingdom, the rulers of Wales, be they called kings or princes, together with their nobility, served and maintained by the labour of the peasantry.

To the people who lived in these territories they were more than just administrative or geographical 'divisions', they were real places where they lived, worked, worshipped and died. Not unnaturally there developed in some a deep love of country, in others a strong bond of local or regional loyalty, still more might be drawn to their birthplace by reason of some indefinable sentimental attachment, but in all there evolved some sense of communal identity. The princes tended to express this 'love of country' in terms of their kingdoms rather than focus on any one district; the poet-princes Hywel ab Owain Gwynedd (d. 1170) and Owain Cyfeiliog (d. 1197) delighted in 'lovely Gwynedd' and 'Powys land' respectively. Less exalted but no less patriotic was Ieuan ap Sulien (d. 1137), a churchman of distinction and son of the distinguished Sulien (d. 1091), twice bishop of St David's, who celebrated his 'love of country' in a poem dedicated to his homeland or *patria*, the *gwlad* of Ceredigion. Even when praising others the court poets were wont to sneak a reference or two to their birthplaces like Gwynfardd Brycheiniog who refers to the 'parish of Llanddewi where I worship' in his poem to St David's (*Canu y Dewi*).[32] These 'patriotic' attachments to region, locality or community were often deeply rooted and not easily dislodged, a fact which early impressed itself on those princes with ambitions to unite and rule the sometimes disparate elements that made up their kingdoms.

Ironically, a key factor that made for greater unity, though it was long in the making, was alien invasion and conquest. Wales had long been subject to the pressure of foreign invaders like the Vikings and the Anglo-Saxons, but the incursions of the Normans and later Anglo-Normans, and the growth in the power of the English state, added a new and more threatening dimension to their political existence. If the princes themselves appeared slow to appreciate the danger posed by these foreigners, the native *literati* were not. War brought forth great men to whom, in the opinion of the chroniclers and poets, the Welsh people owed a huge debt for maintaining a focus for patriotic resistance. Leaders of the calibre of Gruffudd ap Cynan (1075–1137), Owain Gwynedd (1137–70), Llywelyn ab Iorwerth (1194–1240) and Llywelyn ap Gruffudd (1247–82) of Gwynedd, Madog ap Maredudd (1132–60) and Owain Cyfeiliog (1160–97) of Powys, Rhys ap Tewdwr (1078–93) and Rhys ap Gruffudd (1155–97) of Deheubarth were eulogised by those who saw in their efforts to counter Norman and Anglo-Norman domination the means to give credence to the ancient prophecies that foretold of Welsh success against the foreign invaders. The thirteenth-century *Black Book of Carmarthen* contains some of the best examples of native vaticinatory prose, much of which is a great deal older than the volume into which it was copied. The following extract from a poem by an unknown bard expresses perfectly well contemporary thoughts and feelings.

> *The Welsh will triumph, excellent will be their leader.*
> *Everybody will get their rights.*
> *The natives will administer their own cities by the time-hallowed days.*[33]

Vaticinatory verse had long been a powerful medium for propaganda, and it was with this aim in mind that community and leaders alike were urged by the poets to resist the insurgents and the forces making for change, thereby hoping to invoke the appearance of the so-called redeemer-heroes of popular myth – Cadwaladr, Cynan and, later in the twelfth century, Arthur – who would deliver them from oppression. Indeed, so strong was the theme of the mythical deliverer or *Y Mab Darogan* (the son of prophecy) in native culture that the 'foreign invaders' were themselves irresistably drawn into its ambit. Living cheek by jowl with the Welsh inevitably left its mark on the invaders and no more so than on the son or grandson of a Breton settler in Gwent, Geoffrey of Monmouth (d. 1155). By pillaging, borrowing and copying from the literary and oral cultural and historical traditions of the Welsh, he did more than anyone to popularise the myths and legends of his adopted country. Perhaps his most spectacular and enduring success in this respect was in giving shape and form, and added importance, to the ancient legend of Arthur which Breton-inspired model of the redeemer-hero the Welsh came to adopt as their own. Ironically, some of the most potent native vaticinations can be found in Geoffrey's book *Historia Regum Brittaniae* [*History of the Kings of Britain*] (*c.* 1136) such as the following verse-extract purported to be from Merlin himself:

> *Cadwaladr shall summon Cynan and shall make an alliance with Albany.*
> *Then the foreigners shall be slaughtered and the rivers will run with blood.*[34]

As one of the foreigners threatened with slaughter, we can but wonder how Geoffrey viewed such prophecies. Needless to say, his sympathies were not entirely with the Welsh, though he never lost his fascination for them or their culture.

If the likes of Cadwaladr, Cynan and Arthur, not forgetting the now-lesser known folk-heroes Owain and Hiriell, served to inspire the Welsh, they did so as national heroes. Whether in the commotes of Cemais and Cedewain or Tegeingl and Talgarth, the communities that lived in these far-flung corners of Wales shared a sense of history and communal myth, and were as likely to be entertained by the same itinerant bardic masters and story-tellers as they were to delight in their poems and stories. Theirs was a shared culture which transcended political differences and enriched regional or local lore so that despite themselves the Welsh, through their bards and poets, and their daily use of a common language and law, were reminded at every turn of their fellowship. The coming of the Anglo-Normans served gradually to dull the differences between the natives while at the same time sharpening the racial, linguistic and cultural divide between themselves and the foreigners. This had the effect of contributing both to their will to resist and to a growth in patriotism which found its clearest expression in the thirteenth century. In his quest for power, Llywelyn ap Gruffudd (k. 1282) posed unashamedly as the deliverer of his people by encouraging and making use of the myth-makers while fanning the flames of growing anti-English sentiment. It was a policy which met with some success as the chronicles and poems of the period can amply testify. The poet Dafydd Benfras (k.*c.* 1258) had nothing but contempt for the 'foreign, alien-tongued people',[35] while the *Brut* for the year 1256 stated that

> the gentlefolk of Wales, despoiled of their liberty and their rights, came to Llywelyn ap Gruffudd and revealed to him with tears their grievous bondage to the English; and they made known to him that they preferred to be slain in war for their liberty than to suffer themselves to be unrighteously trampled upon by the foreigners.[36]

If the princes appreciated and made use of such propaganda, they were also hard-headed politicians, astute enough to realise that in the real world such sentiments counted for little. They survived because they proved to be as adaptable as the Anglo-Normans whom they imitated and from whom they borrowed.

Status, descent and inheritance

According to the native lawbooks there were three grades of men in Welsh society: royal (*brenin*), noble (*breyr*) and villein (*bilain*). Needless to say, the simplicity of this threefold division of native society is typically rigid in its legal definition which, in reality, hides a more complex truth that hardly admits to the evolutionary forces at work in the diversification of that society. Nevertheless, taken to their limit, these broad categories reflect well the thinking of contemporaries for whom the idea of status and the protection of that status was crucial to an aristocratic society. The villeins or bondmen (*taeogion*), the ruled, may have been the numerically superior class but in all other respects they were inferior, occupying as they did the base of the social, political and economic pyramid. Its summit, not unnaturally, was occupied by the aristocracy, freemen (*bonheddigion*) for whom the line between those of royal and those of noble blood was clearly drawn. In law, each had his status (*braint*) for which a sliding scale of compensation payments was worked out in respect of such things as damage to property or insults to their person. Indeed, in respect of his 'person', a man's *braint* was rarely defined in isolation but depended as much on his standing as an individual as on that of his family, for in Welsh society the extended family or kindred was a fundamental concept. Such were the familial bonds of obligation that in certain circumstances, as, for example, in the killing of a man, the perpetrator and his kindred, extending even to fifth cousins, would be liable for the compensation payment or *galanas*. Rarely would there be any difficulty in identifying the more distant elements of a kindred, for as Gerald of Wales observed, 'Even the common people know their family-tree by heart and can readily recite from memory the list of their grandfathers, great-grandfathers, great-great-grandfathers, back to the sixth or seventh generation'.[37]

Clearly, status and kinship were of fundamental importance in Welsh society and nowhere more so than in the ownership, transmission and inheritance of land. 'The Welsh people are more keen to own land and to extend their holdings than any other I know', observed Gerald of Wales.[38] In his opinion they were hardly to be trusted, 'So prone are they to this lust for possession, from which I may say they all suffer, that they are prepared to swear that the land which they happen to occupy . . . is their own freehold and has always belonged to their family, even when they and the rightful owner . . . have publicly sworn an affidavit about his security of tenure'.[39] Kin-title to and kin-control of land was guaranteed only after a family had occupied the land by unbroken descent over four generations. Thus by 'kin and descent' this land was legally recognised as the paternal inheritance (*treftadaeth*) so that the permanent interest of the kindred, as opposed to the rights of an individual proprietor, predominated, making its outright alienation almost impossible. The transmission of the paternal inheritance was more narrowly defined, being confined to a smaller kindred unit extending as far as second cousins. The paternal inheritance passed first to sons, then to first cousins, and finally to second cousins, though surviving members of an older generation, particularly those who claimed a common great-great-grandfather, retained some claim. However, having insured against the alienation and possible disbursement of land outside the kindred there was nothing to prevent its division within. Partible inheritance (*cyfran*) ensured that if there were many sons or heirs the property would be shared equally between them. The danger inherent in operating such a system was obvious to Gerald: 'Quarrels and lawsuits result, murders and arson, not to mention frequent fratricides'.[40]

Socially these laws had much to commend them but politically they spelt possible disaster. The ownership of land implies some form of power, and those in whom was vested the power to own land were either royal or noble in status. Their land holding invariably involved lordship since theirs was a land in which others lived and over whom they exercised their authority. Therefore, these were more than simply units of land, but units of political power presided over by rulers who had at their disposal military as well as economic resources commensurate with their status. In such circumstances, partible inheritance had the potential to destroy not only the integrity of existing units of land, and the accumulation of additional ones, but the political power that went with them. However, in a society where the principle of division seemed paramount there remained at least one essential element that was indivisible: kingship. The land might be divided and the power might be dissipated but the title and authority of kingship, the dignity of which had a special legal status, devolved undivided to those who succeeded by hereditary right. Of course, this does not mean that royal successions went unchallenged, for although succession by hereditary right need only to be based on royal blood, neither law nor custom offered much in the way of precision in specifying who was or who was not eligible. In so far as the ruling elite derived their status from their kindred, the dynasty, rather than any individual, was heir, in which case sons, nephews and even cousins might be eligible to succeed. In effect, a 'kingship of status' rather than a 'kingship of inheritance'.

Family: kinship and kin-strife

Should a claimant's royal credentials ever be questioned he need only turn to his genealogy to prove his 'right to rule'. The guardians of a man's status, his rights and his privileges were, what Gerald of Wales called, the 'bards, singers and jongleurs' who, in their role as reciters (*datgeiniaid*), kept geneaolgies of their royal, and no doubt noble, patrons. This they did, according to Gerald, in 'old manuscripts' which they could recite from memory 'going back from Rhodri Mawr (d. 878) to the time of the Blessed Virgin Mary'.[41] Although the part-Welsh Gerald felt 'that genealogies so protracted and remote [were] ridiculous',[42] the ruling elite evidently did not: for them, proof of their genealogical descent was a means of legitimising their rights to kingship. It is important to remember that in early Welsh society, kingship implied little in the way of governmental or legal responsibility, for the king was, primarily, a warrior and the leader of a war-band. Therefore, in a warrior society, these bards or poets fulfilled an important social function in that their declamations gave meaning to the heroic ideals to which all, royal and noble, aspired, thus upholding the privileged position of the aristocratic order. Membership of this order was determined by descent, so that lineage was not a matter of mere interest but of real import, particularly for those of royal blood for whom it was the only prerequisite for kingship. Of course, possession of an impressive genealogy might prove a claimant's 'right to rule' but it was not, in itself, a guarantee of success. The native chronicles are full of references to the 'kin-strife' that attended a disputed succession, much of which resulted in bloodthirsty and spine-chilling acts of ruthless barbarity. Three examples of kin-strife may be instanced from the *Brut* for one year alone, 1125: 'In that year strife was bred between Morgan and Maredudd, sons of Cadwgan ap Bleddyn, and in that strife Morgan slew with his own hand Maredudd his brother'.[43] Sympathy for Maredudd's plight is tempered somewhat by the realisation that earlier that year he had stood by and did nothing while his son 'Gruffudd ap Maredudd ap Bleddyn slew Ithel ap Rhiddid ap Bleddyn, his first-cousin, in the presence of Maredudd his father'.[44] Nor was the royal dynasty of Powys alone in its blood-letting: in Gwynedd, too, murder was afoot when

> a short while after that, Cadwallon ap Gruffudd ap Cynan slew his three uncles, namely, Goronwy and Rhiddid and Meilyr, sons of Owain ab Edwin: for Angharad, daughter of Owain ab Edwin, was the wife of Gruffudd ap Cynan, and she was mother of Cadwallon and Owain and Cadwaladr'.[45]

A swift murder was sometimes a blessed relief:

The following year [1130] Iorwerth ap Llywarch was slain by Llywelyn ab Owain in Powys. Soon after that, Llywelyn ab Owain was deprived of his eyes and his testicles by Maredudd ap Bleddyn. At the close of the following year [1131] Meurig was deprived of his two eyes and his two testicles.[46]

Such cruel treatment of one's kin was enough to convince many foreign commentators of the brute insensitivity of the Welsh being often held up as an example of their base-brutality. It was not so much revulsion at what they did but the fact that it was done to their kith and kin, some of whom were but children. As Gerald of Wales admits, the act of blinding and castration was not peculiar to the Welsh, but was a widely used practice to render impotent one's enemy. Citing an example 'in a place called Chateauroux' in France, Gerald used the story of a man's blinding, castration and long imprisonment to demonstrate the folly of thinking that success naturally attended every act of this sort. Taking hostage the only son of the castellan who had dealt so cruelly with him, the blind man threatened to kill the boy unless 'the father had first cut his own testicles off'. There then followed a pantomime in which the castellan attempted to deceive the man into thinking that he had done as he was bid:

> In the end he [the castellan] pretended to agree, and had himself hit a might blow in the lower part of the body, to give the impression that he had mutilated himself. All those present groaned lugubriously. The blind man asked the castellan where he felt most pain, and he replied, falsely, that it was in his loins. Thereupon the blind man stepped forward to throw the boy over. The father was struck a second blow, and this time he said that the worst pain was in his heart. The blind man did not believe him, and he dragged the boy forward to the very edge of the parapet. The third time, to save his son, the father really did cut off his own testicles. He shouted out that it was his teeth which hurt most. 'This time I believe you,' said the blind man, 'and I know what I am talking about. Now I am avenged of the wrongs done to me, in part at least, and I go happily to meet my death. You will never beget another son, and you shall certainly have no joy in this one'. As he said this, he hurled himself over the battlements and plunged into the abyss, taking the boy with him.[47]

Gerald's vivid story of revenge could likely be replicated in the courts of the Welsh princes. In a competitive environment stoked by ambition and riven by dynastic rivalry, violence within the family was not the stuff of myth but an ever present danger. They were men of violent emotions and if they were not mutilating each other they were either imprisoning or exiling their kinfolk. Nor was this behaviour confined to memory by the time of Gerald's death in 1223, for less than a quarter of a century later Llywelyn ap Gruffudd's ascendancy as sole ruler of Gwynedd in

1255 was marked in battle with, and the defeat of, his brothers. Having wrested control of Gwynedd from his brothers, Owain, Rhodri and Dafydd, with whom he had shared the patrimony since the death of their uncle Dafydd in 1246, Llywelyn imprisoned the first, exiled the second and sought to restrain the third. Being the eldest of the three did little to earn the rulership of Gwynedd, since Owain and he spent the best part of twenty-five years in close confinement.

Clearly, royalty was an obligation not for the faint-hearted since an heir to a Welsh crown needed more than simply pedigree, status and seniority to succeed; strength of character, martial courage, ruthless politicking and not a little luck, were among some of the essential ingredients. Ever to the fore with his opinions, Gerald of Wales had no doubt as to the cause of this apparent ruthless disregard of one brother for another:

> [A] serious cause of dissension is the habit of the Welsh princes of entrusting the education of each of their sons to a different nobleman living in their territory. If the prince happens to die, each nobleman plots and plans to enforce the succession of his own foster-brother and to make sure that he is preferred to the other brothers.
>
> It follows that you will find that friendships are much warmer between foster-brothers than they are between true brothers.[48]

This revealing insight into the upbringing of royal children is rare, for in truth we know little of the domestic side of life in the households of the princes. That the Anglo-Norman-raised Gerald got it partly right, is suggested by the native chroniclers who make reference to ambitious noblemen who sometimes preferred murder to waiting for the prince to die a natural death. In 1106 the *Brut* relates the case of Hywel ap Goronwy who 'was slain through treachery by the French . . . It was Gwgan ap Meurig, the man who was nurturing a son of Hywel's and in whom Hywel placed greater trust than in anyone who wrought his betrayal'.[49] However, no matter how compelling the evidence it must not be thought that dysfunctional family relationships were the absolute norm. In the early to mid-twelfth-century household of the dynasty of Deheubarth the virtues of friendship, brotherly love and mutual cooperation seem to have prevailed. In spite of having left at least four sons to contest the headship of the dynasty, the heirs of Gruffudd ap Rhys (d. 1137), Anarawd (d. 1143), Cadell (disabled 1151; d. 1175), Maredudd (d. 1155) and Rhys (d. 1197), seemed content to accept the authority of the eldest among them, and so it continued over the next twenty years with power devolving to each in turn as death and disability took their toll.

Indeed, to suggest that the native aristocracy was bereft of family sentiment would be far from the truth. Although there is ample evidence to support their depiction by Gerald of Wales as 'vindictive by nature, bloodthirsty and violent',[50] there is much to commend them in the literature of the period which does more than hint at their capacity to enjoy affectionate relationships both in and outside the family. Life, love and emotion figure prominently in the romance tales of the Mabinogion and poetic verse of the bards the writing and public performance of which was sponsored by the aristocracy. Even Gerald admits to the Welsh being among the most hospitable hosts he had encountered in so far as

> Guests who arrive early in the day are entertained until nightfall by girls who play to them on the harp. In every house there are young women just waiting to play for you.
>
> The whole family waits upon the guests, and the host and hostess stand there making sure that everything is being attended to. They themselves do not eat until everyone else has finished. If there is a shortage of anything, it will be they who go without.[51]

Perhaps the most revealing glimpse of expressive emotion is to be found in the sober pages of the chronicles which recorded in unusual detail the reaction of Owain Gwynedd (d. 1170) on hearing of the death of his beloved younger son Rhun (d. 1146):

> And when the news of his death reached Owain, he fell into so great a sorrow that neither the splendour of sovereignty nor the entertainment of bards nor the solace of courtiers nor the sight of costly objects could raise him from his . . . sorrow and grief.[52]

And yet, the means by which Owain was consoled in his hour of grief lend weight to the charge levelled against the ruling elite by Gerald, for only when news had been brought that a castle had been taken and its garrison either slain or made prisoner did 'joy arose in him and he laid aside all his grief and his sorrow for his son'.[53] Nor must we forget that within five years of suffering the unfortunate death of his beloved son, Owain Gwynedd, in the words of the chronicles, proceeded to deprive 'Cunedda ap Cadwallon, his nephew, his brother's son, of his eyes and testicles'.[54] His youth notwithstanding, Owain was determined to eliminate by any means rivals to his favoured surviving son Hywel whom he intended would succeed him. On the other hand, Owain's love for his wife Cristin was such that when he was encouraged to set her aside, on·penalty of excommunication, because she was his first cousin and thus within the prohibited degrees of consanguinity, he refused to give her up.

Dynastic succession

Inevitably, multiplicity of eligibility was a source of instability which is why the rulers of the late twelfth and thirteenth century, principally Owain Gwynedd, the Lord Rhys (d. 1197) of Deheubarth, and Llywelyn ab Iorwerth of Gwynedd (d. 1240), attempted to clarify the situation by manipulating the laws to suit their own purpose.[55] For them, a designated heir or successor (*edling*), publicly acknowleged during their respective lifetimes, was essential if they were to pass on intact their inheritance in territory and authority. To appease the 'royal members' (*aelodau brenin* or *membra regis*), that is, the ruler's remaining sons and his near kinsmen, each was usually provided with an estate located within the bounds of the kingdom. Henceforward, the status of these 'royal members' was to be determined not by their membership of the royal kindred but in terms of the status of the lands bestowed upon them. Territory taken in war and added to the kingdom was usually retained by the ruler and bestowed on his heir-designate since these lands were his by right and outside the control of the kindred, but also they might be too stategically important to entrust to someone of an independent mind. Thus did the Lord Rhys nominate his eldest legitimate son Gruffudd to be his *edling* at the expense of his first born but illegitimate son Maelgwn. That there was no distinction in native law between children born in or out of wedlock served only to complicate matters. The result was friction between Maelgwn and Gruffudd during the closing years of their father's reign and open conflict after his death. By 1201 Gruffudd was dead and the integrity of the kingdom shattered, as Maelgwn attempted to assume control in the face of counterclaims to the succession by his brothers and nephews. This was not simply a quarrel among the co-heirs of the Lord Rhys over their respective territorial shares of the kingdom, but rather a conflict within the royal kindred to secure Deheubarth in its entirety. The resulting fragmentation of Deheubarth was due, in large part, to the fact that no one of the contenders was able to secure an ascendancy.

Disputed succession and territorial fragmentation was a fact of Welsh political life during the twelfth and thirteenth centuries. After the death of Madog ap Maredudd in 1160, Powys irrevocably split into two kingdoms, Powys Wenwynwyn (southern Powys) and Powys Fadog (northern Powys). The same occurred in Deheubarth after the death of the Lord Rhys in 1197, although here the territorial dissolution of the kingdom was on an altogether more massive scale continuing through much of the following century. Gwynedd too suffered being sundered at the death of Owain Gwynedd in 1170, reconstituted under his grandson

Llywelyn ab Iorwerth in the 1190s only to be undone again at his death in 1240. His attempt to secure the integrity of the kingdom for his heir-designate called for a fundamental rethinking of the nature and status of his patrimony, and himself as its ruler. In styling himself 'prince of Gwynedd' (*princeps Northwallie*) Llywelyn was providing a clear affirmation of his right to rule as a single jurisdiction the patrimony which was to be an integral royal estate or principality (*principatus*). He further legitimised his position, and that of his principality, by insisting on his claim to be recognised as the heir and successor of Owain Gwynedd and Gruffudd ap Cynan (d. 1137). This continuity of succession provided also a much sought-after antiquity which could be used to uphold his right to set aside indigenous native lordship to *cantref* or commote in favour of treating them as administrative districts and their lords as his provincial governors. This was by no means easy, for status and kinship were no less important to a ruler of a single cantref or commote than they were to a ruler of many, so that the interests of the kindred rather than any one man were being set aside by Llywelyn. Despite his failure to secure Gwynedd for his heir-designate, Llywelyn's attempt did at least provide a model for his successors, most notably his grandson Llywelyn ap Gruffudd.

The two Llywelyns, grandfather and grandson, ensured that alongside land and lineage, lordship and leadership in war were to be the key determinants of their royal or princely status. Principally by means of war the princes of Gwynedd extended their direct authority over Powys and Deheubarth and became princes of the Welsh. The old concept of multiple kingship or princeship was replaced by the concept of a single principate for an enlarged kingdom or principality which was united politically. Through lordship the princes became the instrument of law, order, security and prosperity. They offered their subjects protection, justice and political unity in return for their obedience, loyalty, personal service and their conscription in war which was no less invaluable than their support in peace. Indeed, a prince's lordship or *tywysogiaeth* was limited only by what his subjects and the English king were prepared to tolerate and by his own energy and resources. The Llywelyns had succeeded in imposing a degree of political and territorial unity unparalleled in the recent history of the people, certainly not since the death in 1063/4 of Gruffudd ap Llywelyn. Where once the royal courts of Dinefwr and Mathrafal had vied with that of Aberffraw for primacy, the royal court of Gwynedd alone became the principal centre of power, its prince the richest of all, its rewards greater but with competition all the keener. It is perhaps the final irony that having achieved a single, unified state, the title to which was universally recognised and

the principle of succession to which was well established, the most powerful of the Welsh princes, Llywelyn ap Gruffudd, had only a daughter to
succeed him.

Notes

1. J.B. Smith, *Llywelyn ap Gruffudd Prince of Wales* (Cardiff, 1998), 283.
2. *BT. Pen.*, 58; *BT. RBH,* 132–3; *B. Saes.*, 156–7.
3. *The Chronicle of John of Worcester*, iii, *The Annals from 1067 to 1140*, ed. P. McGurk (Oxford, 1998), 64.
4. *BT. Pen.*, 19; *BT. RBH*, 32–3; *B. Saes.*, 84–5.
5. *Medieval Welsh Society*, 27–8.
6. *Ann. Camb.*, 53.
7. D. Crouch, *The Image of Aristocracy in Britain 1000–1300* (London, 1992), 86. See also, idem, 'The Slow Death of Kingship in Glamorgan, 1067–1158', *Morgannwg*, xxix (1985), 35–6.
8. Robert de Toringy, *Chronica Roberti de Torigneio*, ed. R. Howlett, in *Chronicles of the Reigns of Stephen, Henry II, and Richard I* (4 vols, Rolls Series, 1884–9), IV, 251; Roger of Howden, *Chronica Rogeri de Houdene*, ed. W. Stubbs (4 vols, Rolls Series, 1868–71), IV, 21; Gervase of Canterbury, *The Historical Works of Gervase of Canterbury*, ed. W. Stubbs (2 vols, Rolls Series, 1879–80), I, 544; Anon., *Gesta Regis Henrici Secundi*, ed. W. Stubbs (2 vols, 1867), I, 162; II, 87, 97.
9. *Annales Monastici*, ed. H.R. Luard (5 vols, Rolls Series, 1864–9), I, 55.
10. Roger of Howden, *Chronica*, II, 133.
11. W.S. Davies, ed., 'Giraldus Cambrensis: De Invectionibus', *Y Cymmrodor*, xxx (1920), 22.
12. Giraldus Cambrensis, *Opera*, ed. J.S. Brewer, J.F. Dimock and G.F. Warner (8 vols, Rolls Series, 1861–91), I, 43, 57, 77, 203, 208, 216; IV, 10, 152; VIII, 216; *Monasticon Anglicanum*, ed. W. Dugdale. Rev. edn by J. Cayley *et al.* (6 vols in 8 parts, 1817–30), V, 632–3.
13. J.B. Smith, *Llywelyn ap Gruffudd*, 283.
14. *BT. RBH*, 207, 237, 247.
15. D. Walker, *Medieval Wales* (Cambridge, 1990), 92.
16. *Journey & Description*, 220.
17. Ibid., 221.
18. D. Crouch, *Morgannwg*, xxix (1985), 20–41.
19. *Journey & Description*, 194.
20. Ibid., 182.
21. J.B. Smith, *Llywelyn ap Gruffudd*, 68.
22. Lloyd, *Wales*, II, 650.
23. K. Maund, *Handlist*, 2.
24. G.A. Williams, *When Was Wales?* (Harmondsworth, 1985), 34.
25. *Journey & Description*, 221.
26. *BT. Pen.*, 42.
27. Ibid.
28. Ibid., 19.

29. Ibid.
30. *Guide to Welsh Lit.*, I, 154–5.
31. *Journey & Description*, 223.
32. *DWB*, 330.
33. Elissa Henken, *National Redeemer: Owain Glyndwr in Welsh Tradition* (Cardiff, 1996), 40.
34. Ibid., 39.
35. R.R. Davies, *Wales*, 317.
36. *BT. Pen.*, 110.
37. *Journey & Description*, 251.
38. Ibid., 261.
39. Ibid.
40. Ibid.
41. Ibid., 223.
42. Ibid.
43. *BT. RBH*, 111.
44. *BT. Pen.*, 49.
45. *BT. RBH*, 113.
46. Ibid.
47. *Journey & Description*, 142.
48. Ibid., 261.
49. *BT. RBH*, 49–50.
50. *Journey & Description*, 233.
51. Ibid., 237.
52. *BT. Pen.*, 55.
53. Ibid.
54. *BT. RBH*, 131.
55. See J.B. Smith, 'Dynastic Succession in Medieval Wales', *BBCS*, 33 (1986), 199–232.

chapter two

CONFLICT OR COEXISTENCE: *MARCHIA WALLIE* AND *PURA WALLIA*

. . . a certain man called William the Bastard, leader of the Normans, and with him a mighty host, came against him [Harold]; and after a mighty battle and a slaughter of the Saxons, he despoiled him of his kingdom and of his life, and he won for himself the kingdom of the Saxons.[1]

Recorded for posterity by the chroniclers of the *Brut*, the events connected with the battle of Hastings were of little immediate concern to the Welsh. Beyond hearing of, and some no doubt rejoicing at, the news of the death of King Harold, a former enemy responsible for the defeat and, indirectly, for the murder of their king, Gruffudd ap Llywelyn (d. 1063/4), the Welsh had little cause to take note of an event so distant from their own land. They had problems of their own, not the least of which was their tendency towards internecine warfare – a fault exacerbated by the disintegration of the temporary union of Welsh kingdoms after the death of Gruffudd. Yet within a few short years of Hastings the Welsh were to confront a greater threat to their political independence and way of life than they had ever faced from King Harold and his Saxons. They were to face a people, the Normans, who, according to a contemporary historian, the Shropshire-born monk Orderic Vitalis (d.*c.* 1140s), were 'a warlike race . . . moved by fierce ambition to lord it over others'.[2] The scene was set for bitter conflict, for no whit less warlike than the Normans, the Welsh were, in the words of Orderic, 'proud of their ancient independence, refusing all tokens of submission to the Normans'.[3]

Conflict

Under the leadership of King William I (d. 1087), the Normans were effectively organised as a professional fighting force which consisted, for the most part, of three ranks: mounted knights, archers and heavy infantry. If we are to believe the detailed depictions of the Bayeux Tapestry, the majority of Norman troops appear to have been generously provided for in terms of defensive mail armour, kite shields and weaponry. The cavalry was by far the most important element in Norman battle tactics, and it was the cavalry's use of its mobility added to the shock-value of the charge which unsettled and usually scattered their enemies. Together with their castles and siege engines the newcomers were, in military terms, technologically more advanced then the Welsh and thus better prepared for the struggle that lay ahead. Nevertheless, despite their tactical advantage and having overcome England and the English in little more than six years after Hastings, William and his Norman 'conquerors' were to find Wales and the Welsh a more difficult proposition. Quite apart from the fierce resistance of the natives, the Normans had to contend with a country which proved wholly unsuited for their methods of warfare. Couched in thick woodlands, riven by mountain ranges, cut by deep river valleys and generously besprinkled with marshlands, Wales favoured the defender. The invader was largely denied the element of surprise and mostly inhibited in the deployment and use of cavalry. The mounted charge was much less in evidence, as was the set-piece battle; there were to be few Hastings-like confontations here.

To the new king, not unaturally, Wales was regarded as a frontier country, or *March*, as poor and unattractive a land as he might care to find west of the rich fertile plains of the English lowlands, and as such the Welsh were to be contained rather than conquered. In this respect, William was setting no new precedent but following closely the policies pursued by his Saxon predecessors who sought, above all, to stop the Welsh raiding the counties of the west of England. This they hoped to achieve either by force of arms or by acts of submission, and though both were employed periodically by William, his policy was essentially defensive, relying for its success on the use of the castle. Consequently a line of mainly earth and timber castles stretching from Chester in the north to Hereford and Gloucester in the south were erected to mark the frontier and behind which rampart the Normans might feel reasonably secure. There is every justification in likening William's policy to that adopted by the eighth-century kings of Mercia, Aethelbald (d. 757) and Offa (d. 796), who between them fortified their frontier with Wales by building massive earthworks, Wat's Dyke and Offa's Dyke respectively, the last of which stretched more than seventy miles from north to south. However, unlike the probably unmanned dykes of Mercian England, William was astute enough to realise that the success of his policy depended as much on the castles as on the men who garrisoned them. These were the men to whom he turned for support and of whom he expected much, not only to police the frontier but to build and maintain the fortifications also.

Three powerful new earldoms were established on the frontier at Chester, Shrewsbury and Hereford, and to each King William appointed men he could trust to keep the Welsh occupied and in check. Besides defending the frontier from attack, the earls – first Gherbord of Flanders but later Hugh of Avranches (d. 1101) at Chester, Roger of Montgomery (d. 1094) at Shrewsbury and William fitzOsbern (d. 1071) at Hereford – were charged with the task of attempting the conquest and settlement of adjacent Welsh territory. This they were to effect either by themselves or by encouraging lesser men to do so on their behalf. Among the more successful of these 'lesser men' was Robert of Tilleul (d.*c.* 1093), 'the exemplar of the swashbuckling Norman warrior',[4] who visited his ruthless passion for war on the Welsh for the best part of fifteen years. Given free rein by his lord and cousin Earl Hugh to pillage and purge at will, Robert's devastating campaigns all but conquered the Welsh in north Wales. So successful was he that he soon attracted the eye of the king who took it upon himself to encourage Robert, giving him licence to take and hold of the Crown as much territory as he could capture from the rulers of Gwynedd east of the river Conwy. By 1073 he had established a castle at Rhuddlan, by which name he was henceforth to be known, to which was added by 1086, a borough, church and even a mint. Robert's success and ambition was such that having overcome the remainder of Gwynedd and ejecting its ruler from the territory west of the Conwy, he secured from the king recognition of his gains together with the right to hold the kingdom on terms similar to those extended to the native ruler of Deheubarth, Rhys ap Tewdwr (d. 1093), for which 'royal privilege' they each rendered an annual rent of £40. In the event, Robert did not live long to enjoy his new-found status and power: he was, according to Orderic Vitalis, killed in combat by a Welshman named *Grithfridus rex Guallorum*, whom historians are generally agreed is to be identified as Gruffudd ap Cynan.[5]

FitzOsbern and Roger of Montgomery too had their 'satellites', men who, for the most part drawn from their dependants and tenants in Normandy, were prepared to do their bidding for a share of the spoils. Foremost among them were Warin the Bald, Reginald de Bailleul and Picot de Say, loyal confederates of Earl Roger, and FitzOsbern's principal adherents Walter de Lacy, Ralph de Tosny and Turstin fitzRolf. Although nowhere near as successful as Robert of Rhuddlan, they were nonetheless warriors of comparable ability and ruthlessness who between them carved up a sizeable slice of south and mid Wales stretching from Oswestry in the north to Chepstow in the south. In all but a few cases, these were men used to the rigours of border warfare, having learnt their trade on the hotly contested frontiers of Normandy. Men like William d'Eu, whose own home lay full square on Normandy's north-eastern frontier, exchanged one frontier for another in the hope of bettering their lot. His reward was thirty-two ploughlands within the castlery of Chepstow together with a long-running and bitter dispute with his neighbouring landowners for a further eighteen. Certainly there was greater scope for expansion in Wales than in Normandy where, unlike in the former, the frontiers had achieved a degree of clarity and relative stability which precluded opportunities for aggrandisement, if not the need for war in their defence. As bitter and protracted as was the border warfare in Normandy, Wales was not a soft option: the risks were as great if not greater, not that this deterred the newcomers from taking up the challenge, and they did so in ever increasing numbers.

Yet it must be remembered that the so-called invasion and conquest of Wales, if such terms can be used without qualification, in the first twenty years of William's reign was engineered, conducted and led by possibly no more than two dozen knights, the three earls included, who between them may have commanded a force amounting to but a few hundred followers of whom a fair proportion were not even Norman. Therefore, unlike William's invasion of England in 1066, the 'invasion' of Wales was neither planned nor coordinated either by a king preoccupied in consolidating his victory over the Saxon-English or by Norman adventurers selfishly engaged in carving out for themselves pockets of Welsh territory. Nevertheless, although it is probably true to say that the Normans 'did not set out self-consciously on a conquest of Wales',[6] that there was an invasion of sorts and that contemporaries living in Wales may have been aware not only of the concept but also of the actuality of what it entailed, is inferred in the correspondence of Bishop Urban of Llandaff (d. 1134). In writing to Pope Calixtus II in c. 1119, Urban was quite candid in his assessment of the decline of the wealth and authority of his church which he put down to 'the savagery of the natives and the invasion or incursion (*incursio*) of the Norman people'.[7] Although incursion, which has a sharper and briefer aspect than is suggested by the use of the word 'invasion', best describes Norman efforts in Wales during the Conqueror's reign, at the time of writing Urban might be forgiven for believing that an invasion, and a successful one at that, had in fact taken place. In the half-century since the Norman's arrival, the kingdoms of Gwent, Gwynllwg, Morgannwg and Deheubarth had all but been extinguished, and but for a few scattered territories, the south had been almost completely overrun and settled. In the final analysis, it matters not if we prefer incursion to invasion, or vice versa, the end result for those at the sharp end was much the same, a brutal bloody conflict which hardly hints at the popular adoption of a chivalric code by warriors elsewhere in Europe. In Wales, very often, and in the best (or worst) traditions of a frontier society, no quarter was given or asked.

Norman nominee that he was, it is hardly surprising if Bishop Urban, formerly a priest in the diocese of Worcester before his promotion in 1107, should heap the blame for the savagery that characterised the conflict in Wales on the Welsh. Savage they certainly were, the native chroniclers leave us in no doubt of that, but to suggest that the 'savagery' was confined to the Welsh would be to do them a disservice: it was practised equally by the Normans, often to a degree that shocked their contemporaries. Orderic Vitalis writes with undisguised horror at the blood-lust of William fitzOsbern who 'caused the ruin and wretched deaths of many thousands'.[8] But even his tyranny pales into insignificance when compared with the practised barbarity of his fellow Marcher Earl Robert of Shrewsbury (d.c. 1130s), who 'harried the Welsh brutally for four years'.[9] Not that this prevented him from securing an alliance with his former foes once the spectre of a king angered against him hove into sight; the Marchers were anything if not practical. Almost inevitably, the Welsh March attracted, and appealed to, a certain type; men who, if Orderic is to be believed, included among their number a psychopath or two, but in general were energetic risk-takers, individualists moved as much by the spirit of adventure as by ambition. That said, it is difficult to escape the conclusion that during the Conqueror's lifetime, and for some time after, Wales was left to the warmongers, the greedy and the brutal, of whom only a few came with permanent settlement in mind much less any thoughts of coexistence. 'Pride and greed', according to a near contemporary 'were the incentives that drove the marcher lord, Robert [of Rhuddlan] to unrestrained plunder and slaughter'.[10] In such circumstances, the so-called conquest of Wales was a long drawn out process, a piecemeal affair, covering the best part of two centuries.

Without wishing to overstate the impact the Normans had on Wales and the Welsh in the first thirty years of conflict and settlement – there are but three references to them in the native chronicles before 1093 – it is worth noting the reaction of a contemporary, the priest-poet Rhigyfarch ap Sulien (d. 1099), who graphically expressed his fear and loathing for the foreigners in a poem composed during the last decade of the eleventh century and entitled, appropriately, *Lament*. 'One vile Norman', he states with pardonable exaggeration, 'intimidates a hundred natives with his command and terrifies them with his look'.[11] Indeed, his despair at their continued presence and oppression in the country is evident elsewhere in his poem in which he laments, 'Why have the blind fates not let us die? . . . O [Wales] you are afflicted and dying'.[12] Nor can his emotional outburst be dismissed simply as hyperbole since the chroniclers too speak of 'the Britons being unable to bear the tyranny and injustice of the French'.[13] Further afield, contemporaries elsewhere in Europe who had suffered a similar fate at the hands of the Normans – England, Spain and Sicily – concur in charging them with cruelty and terror calculated to overawe or crush those they subdued. Their infamy was such that even a half-Norman monk writing in England, William of Malmesbury (d.c. 1143), removed from the events and people he was describing by some sixty years and over one thousand miles, was able to relate with authority the story of the Norman conquest of southern Italy and Sicily. Its chief architect was Robert Guiscard (d. 1085) on whose tomb at Venosa was etched the following inscription: 'Here lies Guiscard, the terror of the World' (*Hic iacet terror mundi Giuscardus*).[14] Unfortunately for the 'Britons', there were Guiscards aplenty in Wales, and the devastation wrought by these unwelcome newcomers had undoubtedly made their mark on a Welshman whose clerical cloth and sheltered life at Llanbadarn Fawr and St David's afforded him little protection from their worst excesses.

The native rulers may have been spared the daily sufferings inflicted by the newcomers on the rank and file and they were no doubt less intimidated either by their commands or looks, but royal blood or not, they were no less vulnerable to the depredations and slaughters of their foes. In 1093, Rhys ap Tewdwr, 'king of the South, was slain by Frenchmen',[15] in a skirmish somewhere in Brycheiniog. His death opened up south Wales to a crop of new men like Bernard de Neufmarché (d.c. 1125), the man most likely responsible for killing Rhys, Arnulf de Montgomery (*fl.* 1090–1110), who seized and imprisoned his son Hywel, and Robert fitzHamo (d. 1107) who established themselves in Brecon, Pembroke and Cardiff respectively. Rhys' counterpart in the north, Gruffudd ap Cynan, fared no better: he is thought to have suffered the ignomy of capture and imprisonment, for upwards of sixteen years, at the hands of 'he who was . . . the root of all evil',[16] namely Hugh of Avranches, earl of Chester. Yet for all their perceived cruelty there is evidence to suggest that the Normans may have earned the grudging respect of the Welsh in so far as Robert of Rhuddlan's description by Gruffudd ap Cynan's biographer, as 'a renowned, valiant baron of strength' or the *Brut*'s encomium on the Conqueror at his death as a man of 'exceeding great glory . . . being favoured with fame and innumerable victories'.[17] This is perhaps less surprising given the fact that a native ruler was more likely to be killed by his countrymen or murdered by members of his own family than to die at the hands of a Norman. Setting aside their natural bias and shorn of their propaganda, even the most prejudiced chronicler would have been hard pressed to explain away the cruelty practised daily by members of his own aristocratic class while deploring it in others.

Undeterred by tales of hardship on the Welsh borders, it was not long ere a second generation of *conquistadores* arrived to stake their claim to a share of the spoils. Having secured a foothold during the reigns of Norman and Angevin kings, Marcher families like Braose, Clare, Clifford, Corbet and Mortimer, to name but a few of the more powerful, established themselves, and around them the March and its distinctive society began to take shape. Few of the original eleventh- and twelfth-century Marcher families managed to survive beyond two or three generations, one of the rare exceptions were the Mortimers, of whom it has been said, 'to have survived for over three centuries as Marcher lords was a political and biological feat'.[18] Their survival was due in large part to their preparedness to use any means to secure their position, be it murder or assassination. Indeed, few could match the conduct of the Braose family in this respect especially as perpetrated in the so-called massacre of Abergavenny castle in 1175. Planned and executed by William de Braose, lord of Builth and Brycheiniog (Gerald of Wales suggests his innocence in the matter), and his uncle Phillip together with their loyal confederate Ranulf Poer, their aim was to exact revenge for the murder, some months earlier, of their kinsman Henry, son of Milo fitzWalter by the Welsh lords of Upland Gwent led by the paramount chief of the district Seisyll ap Dyfnwal. Accompanied by his son Geoffrey and his leading men, Seisyll was lured to the castle on the pretext, ironically, of hearing a royal ordinance as to the bearing of arms for the better protection of the king's peace in the Marches. Without the slightest suspicion of what their hosts had in store for them they were murdered to a man, after which the perpetrators made for the court and homes of the slain to complete their work: neither man, woman nor child was spared either death or incarceration. Unsurprisingly, the native chroniclers solemnly concluded that 'from that time forth, after that treachery, none of the Welsh dared place trust in the French'.[19] Nor was this mistrust misplaced, certainly not in the case of the Braose clan, for as the chroniclers were to report some twenty-two years later, in 1197:

> In that year Trahearn ap Fychan of Brycheiniog, a brave eminent man and of gentle lineage, with the niece of the Lord Rhys . . . as his wife, came incautiously to Llangorse, to the court of his lord, William de Braose, and there he was seized and imprisoned. And as a pitiful example and with unusual cruelty he was bound by his feet to the tail of a strong horse, and he was thus drawn

along the streets of Brecon as far as the gallows; and there his head was struck off and he was hanged by his feet; and he was for three days on the gallows.[20]

Life on the frontier was not for the faint-hearted; Marcher society was made up of tough, hard-nosed, rugged individuals who lived with the constant fear of attack and an almost precipitant prospect of a violent death. In such circumstances it is hardly surprising to find them resorting to what we might consider outrageous practices like decapitation as a means of terrorising their foes into submission.[21] We are reliably informed by Matthew Paris (d. 1259) that in 1231 Hubert de Burgh (d. 1243) had the heads of those responsible for raiding his lordship of Montgomery severed, bagged and sent to the king. Nor was this the action of a lone Marcher cold-bloodedly exacting revenge; it was a practice apparently condoned and encouraged by the Crown. In 1233, Richard de Minton claimed from the Crown a generous bounty of a shilling per head for 57 severed heads of Welshmen captured or killed while raiding Strattondale near Montgomery. Motivated no doubt by this financial incentive and in proving their prowess in killing Welshmen, a troop of English cavalry in Henry III's army on campaign in Wales in 1245, returned from one encounter with the severed heads of almost one hundred of the enemy. In fairness to the Marchers, the Welsh too practised decapitation but they did so on each other and not, as far as is known, on their Marcher neighbours. They were, if Matthew Paris is to be believed, as ruthless if not more so than their Marcher counterparts in this respect, for in 1258 the Welsh were reported to have decapitated everyone living within several towns captured during a series of raids.

Non-combatants too had reason to fear for their safety, as illustrated by the callous attitudes adopted on campaign by William the Atheling (d. 1120), son and heir of King Henry I, and his ally Owain ap Cadwgan (d. 1116), the maverick prince of Powys, whereby they

> pledged one another that not one of them would spare one person, neither man nor woman, neither boy nor girl, but whomsoever they caught they would not let any go, but kill or hang him or cut off his members.[22]

Nor did tempers improve or attitudes change with time, as may be gathered by Llywelyn ab Iorwerth's (d. 1240) devastating raids in 1231 on the towns of Montgomery, Radnor, Hay and Brecon during which many 'gentlefolk' (taken to mean clerics, women and children) who had taken refuge in churches were killed.[23] Perhaps the most poignant and stark reminder of what this form of warfare meant for the individual is provided by Robert Vieuxpont's treatment of his hostage, Rhys ap Maelgwn, 'an excellent boy not yet seven years old' whom he caused to be hanged at Shrewsbury in 1212.[24] It is as well to remember that it was with men like these, and their families, that the princes first came into contact, that it was they and their ilk who provided the Welsh with their first 'Marcher' experience, and in whose circle they continued and company they kept, as family and friend as much as foe, for the next two centuries.

To dwell on Norman successes would be to do the Welsh an injustice. The Welsh had to come to terms with the newcomers and they did so, sometimes reluctantly but oftentimes willingly. After the initial shock of suffering a number of heavy defeats, indeed some so serious that it looked as if Gwynedd and Deheubarth would go the way of Gwent and Morgannwg, the Welsh recovered sufficiently to fight the enemy on more-or-less level terms. They too learnt the art of castle-building, siege warfare, with its associated technology, and the techniques employed in conducting modern campaigns with trained archers, footsoldiers and well-armoured horsemen. Their resistance took its toll on the new-comers and a list of the slain reads like a who's who of the distinguished men of the March: Robert of Rhuddlan (k.*c.* 1093), Hugh, earl of Shrewsbury (k. 1098),[25] William of Brabant (k. 1110), Richard fitzGil-bert of Clare (k. 1136), Payn fitzJohn (k. 1137), Letard 'Little King' (k. 1137), Stephen fitzBaldwin (k. 1152), Henry fitzHenry, son of King Henry I (k. 1158), Henry, son of Milo fitzWalter (k. 1175), Ranulf de Poer (k. 1182), Stephen Bauzan (k. 1257), Patrick de Chaworth (k. 1258) and William de Valence the Younger (k. 1282). The list of those captured is equally impressive: William, earl of Gloucester (captured and released 1158), Robert fitzStephen (captured 1166; released 1169), Phillip fitzWizo (captured 1193) and William de Braose (captured 1228; executed 1230).

The undistinguished too suffered many hundreds of casualties; not for them capture, honourable imprisonment and ransom, but death, often cruelly applied. This is well illustrated by the events surrounding the battle of Cymerau in 1257 in which the Welsh 'captured the barons and ordained knights' but 'slew more than two thousand of the host'.[26] Nor are the chronicles shy of furnishing such examples of wanton slaughter; some three thousand Normans and Flemings are reported to have been slain, burnt, drowned and trampled underfoot at the battle of Cardigan in 1136. Again, in 1263 the Welsh of Cedewain 'slew two hundred of the English, some in the field, others', those evidently fleeing and seek-ing shelter from the slaughter, 'in the barn of Aber-miwl'.[27] Given the almost inevitable imprecision and often exaggerated figures supplied by monastic scribes, who were themselves informed by word of mouth, the historian would do well not to dismiss them entirely for at the very least they are suggestive of contemporary scale and significance. Garrison duty may have been less dangerous than exposing oneself to the enemy on the battlefield but it was not without risk. The natives seemed particularly vindictive towards those who had dared resist them from battlemented walls and towers, and the chronicles leave us in no doubt what fate was likely to befall the garrisons of those castles taken by the Welsh in siege or assault. In taking the castle of Hugh de Meules at Talybont (near modern-day Pontarddulais) in 1215, Rhys Ieuanc of Dinefwr (d. 1222) acted with accustomed ferocity when he put the entire garrison to 'fire and sword'.[28] It was a form of psychological warfare which often yielded spectacular results, for having taken the castles of Carnwyllion, Loughor and Talybont, Rhys Ieuanc 'made his way towards Seinhenydd, and for fear of him the garrison burned their town'.[29]

Besides their own fierce resistance, the Welsh struggle for survival was helped to some extent by the often indifferent attitude to Wales shown by successive kings of England who, with the exception of Henry I, whose active intervention in Welsh affairs might have set a precedent had his successors been disposed to follow it, were content to leave this Celtic fringe to their more adventurous comrades, the border earls, their followers and later settlers. Kings like the Conqueror, his son and successor Rufus and their descendant Henry II (d. 1189) involved themselves in Welsh affairs reluctantly and then only to restore the balance between native and Norman if the scales had tipped too firmly in favour of the Welsh. Despite the more interventionist policies of Kings Henry I (d. 1135) and, possibly, John (d. 1216), there was never any serious intention on the part of the Crown to conquer Wales; even Edward I (d. 1307) did not set out initially to eliminate Llywelyn or to entirely subdue Gwynedd, circumstances conspired to force the subjugation of 1282–3. Of course the Welsh were not to know this and they reacted accordingly, treating almost every royal campaign as the nemesis they believed it to be. Indeed, for them it was almost a question of adapt or die, but adapt they did with quite remarkable speed and efficiency which guaranteed for them a place in the new order. They learnt to fight the enemy on their terms, to erect and destroy castles, match them in open combat, to negotiate and to conciliate, but most important of all, to unite if the threat was sufficiently ominous. The native annalists had to wait until 1165 before they could proudly announce a coalition of princes united in their opposition to King Henry II's massive invasion of Wales.

[Henry] returned again to England and gathered a host beyond number of the picked warriors of England and Normandy and Flanders and Gascony and Anjou and all the North and Scotland. And he came to Oswestry, thinking to annihilate all Welshmen. And against him came Owain and Cadwaladr, sons of Gruffudd ap Cynan, and all the host of Gwynedd with them, and Rhys ap Gruffudd and with him the host of Deheubarth, and Owain Cyfeiliog and Iorwerth Goch ap Maredudd and the sons of Madog ap Maredudd and the host of all Powys with them, and the two sons of Madog ab Idnerth and their host.[30]

The gathering was quite unprecedented, but so it seems, if the chronicler is to be believed, was the scale of the menace. Once the threat had subsided so the coalition disintegrated, and within months of the abortive royal invasion many of the princes had either gone their own way or were at each other's throats.

The Welsh were fortunate also in that the disunity which damaged their cause was not an exclusively 'Celtic' phenomenon: the intermittent civil strife that beset England from time to time such as the short-lived rebellions against William Rufus in 1188 and Henry I in 1102, the protracted civil war of Stephen's reign, 1139–53 and the ongoing family strife that tore at the heart of Henry II's Angevin empire in 1173–4, 1183 and 1189, diverted attention away from Wales. In this way the Welsh princes became embroiled in English affairs and they found themselves in the unaccustomed position of being courted by dissident factions intent on humbling their king. Earl Robert of Shrewsbury's successful appeal to the sons of Bleddyn ap Cynfyn of Powys (d. 1075) to aid him against Henry I in 1102 led to an alliance which witnessed the sacking of settlements in Staffordshire. In 1141 at Lincoln, King Stephen faced a combined force of Welshmen and Anglo-Normans led in amity by earls Gloucester and Chester, and senior representatives of the dynasties of Morgannwg, Gwynedd and Powys. In taking his stand with the 'barons' against King John in 1215, at the behest of the Marcher family of Braose, Llywelyn ab Iorwerth (d. 1240) was able to enjoy the unique experience of humiliating a king of England. Perhaps the prince who most successfully exploited England's political discomfiture was Llywelyn ap Gruffudd when he allied himself with Simon de Montfort and the baronial movement. Taking advantage of the disruption caused as a result of the Barons' War (1258–65), Llywelyn manipulated Henry III into conceding the terms expressed in the Treaty of Montgomery 1267.

From conflict to coexistence: settlements and alliances

Politically, the Wales first encountered by the Normans consisted of a patchwork of kingdoms which, from time to time, might be drawn together under the control of a single powerful ruler like Gruffudd ap

Llywelyn who ruled an united Wales between 1055 and 1063/4, but such unity proved often to be a temporary abberation. No matter how laudable or sensible, as it seems to us, the political aims of men of vision and ability like Gruffudd, they were often defeated by the stubborn pride and fierce independence of the local ruling families. The Normans were able to take advantage of this disunity and mutual hostility to further their almost inexorable advance into the Welsh heartland. This they accomplished as much by invitation as by invasion or incursion, which might suggest that, initially at least, the Welsh had seriously underestimated the newcomers and the threat they posed. Not that they should be berated for this apparent lack of judgement: to contemporaries no doubt the Normans may have appeared little different from previous foreign foes bent on militaristic mischief.

Although it is known that by 1070 the Normans were firmly settled in some strength along the frontier, particularly in Herefordshire, it is not until 1072 that the native chronicles first refer to them infiltrating Wales proper, 'when Maredudd ab Owain was slain by the French and Caradog ap Gruffudd ap Rhydderch (d. 1081) on the banks of the Rhymni'.[31] Clearly, in some areas, their introduction to Wales in force was by invitation, by native dynasts determined to enlist the support of these newcomers in their petty but bloody squabbles and to exploit their military potential to that end. This was no new thing: Welsh rulers had long allied themselves with royal and noble factions in Saxon England either to effect political advantage for themselves or simply to aid the cause of those with whom they were in alliance. As early as 983 the chronicles were able to record an alliance between Hywel ab Ieuaf of Gwynedd (d. 985) and Earl Aelfhere of Mercia who between them defeated Einion ab Owain ruler of Dyfed (d. 984). In 1055, Earl Aelfgar had cause to be grateful to Gruffudd ap Llywelyn with whose help he withstood an attempt to have him exiled and deprived of his earldom of Mercia. Clearly, both sides stood to gain from these alliances, and although they worked in the short term, relations between Saxon and Welsh remained brittle. Both Hywel and Gruffudd met their end, either directly or indirectly, at the hands of their erstwhile allies, the former, in the words of an unforgiving native chronicler, 'slain through the treachery of the Saxons'.[32] In spite of the mutual distrust and hostility, Welsh rulers were not deterred from seeking to augment their forces with Saxon warriors, a number of whom were hired simply to act and serve as mercenaries. Hence Maredudd ab Owain's success in ravaging Glamorgan in 992 'by hiring Gentiles' (*kenedloed*)[33] to fight alongside his own host. Hiring mercenaries was a practice long followed in Wales, as elsewhere in Europe, and among the foreigners who could be found serving Welsh masters were Saxons, Scots, Vikings and, often in large numbers, Irishmen.

The Normans too soon became embroiled in the domestic disputes that characterised relations between competing members of the various Welsh dynastic families. Having already employed Norman mercenaries in 1072, Caradog ap Gruffudd turned to using them again in 1081 when, according to Gruffudd ap Cynan's biographer, supported by 'his men of Gwent, the men of Morgannwg, and many Norman cross-bowmen',[34] he fought the rulers of Gwynedd and Deheubarth, Gruffudd ap Cynan and Rhys ap Tewdwr, respectively. Similarly, Owain ab Edwin (d. 1105), the would-be ruler of Gwynedd, is credited by contemporary chroniclers with the dubious distinction of introducing the 'French' to Gwynedd.[35] Who these Normans-for-hire were, whence did they come and, more importantly, whom did or had they served, is not known for certain. Nor do we know the means or methods by which the native rulers were able to contact or recruit them. They are only ever referred to in general terms by the native chroniclers who almost always dismiss them in a word as either *y Freinc*, the French or *Nordmannyeit*, the Normans. Equally intriguing is the question of what happened to them once they had discharged their military functions. Were the best and most loyal of them allowed to settle in the territories they had helped acquire for their princely employers? It is perhaps difficult to accept that wandering bands of masterless men, particularly lowly 'cross-bowmen', were allowed simply to roam either England or Wales in search of commission. These were men scorned even by their own kind, like the anonymous scribe of the *Gesta Stephani* who refers to their cruel (*crudelitatis*) and sacrilegious (*sacrilegi*) conduct in war, and Orderic Vitalis to whom they were nothing but *pestilentes homines*.[36]

On the other hand, it has been argued that the so-called feudalisation of England was in its infancy and that the ties of service and bonds of allegiance between lords and their vassals were not as rigid or as formal as was once thought. Certainly, by 1066 there is a clear distinction made between the land or fief-holding vassals of the duke and his leading followers, the *milites* or *mediae nobilitatis*, and those who served for wages, the *gregarii* or *stipendiarii*. It is possible that the majority of those hired by the Welsh hailed from this latter group and that their service was consented to by Norman lords, some of whom might already have established themselves on the frontier, eager to earn the trust and goodwill of grateful native rulers. It is only in alliance that the Normans are identified by means of their leader, as in the case of Robert of Rhuddlan (or Tilleul), who consented to help Gruffudd ap Cynan in his bid to win the throne of Gwynedd in 1075:

he [Gruffudd] besought him [Robert] for help against his enemies who were in possession of his patrimony. And when Robert heard who he was, and for what he had come, and what his request was, he promised to support him.[37]

We can only guess at the reason behind Robert's willingness to aid his erstwhile foe, but if the part-English monk William of Malmesbury is to be believed, it was in the Normans' nature to be 'always ready to use guile or to corrupt by bribery', especially 'when force fails'.[38] Indeed, if the Welsh princes thought they could hire and fire the newcomers at will, they were mistaken. The Normans were not merely mercenary soldiers in search of the next commission, they were as much settler and trader as soldier, and they determined to establish roots and to play their part in the life of the locality, preferably in the role of master. Nor could they easily discard those with whom they had formed alliances, as Owain ab Edwin found to his cost, for having achieved his purpose and secured his position in Gwynedd he wanted rid of his Norman allies who, it seems, were reluctant to leave.

> And since the men of Gwynedd could not suffer the laws and judgements and violence of the French upon them, they rose up against them a second time, with Owain ab Edwin as leader over them, the man who had previously brought the French to Anglesey.[39]

Once established, the Normans were difficult to dislodge, and although the natives of Brycheiniog, Gwent, Gwynllwg and Gwynedd scored notable successes in throwing off 'the rule of the French' in 1096 and 1098 respectively, so that 'the inhabitants stayed in their houses unafraid', it was, as the *Brut* makes clear, a victory tempered by the knowledge that they would be back: 'And when they had failed to have their will in aught, they returned home . . . The castles, however, still remained intact, with their garrisons in them'.[40] The castle was, and remained, the primary of unit of conquest and domination, a fact readily acknowledged by the Welsh.

Without imminent prospect of alliance or commission, and if guile, bribery and promises failed, the Normans resorted to their primary method of having their will in Wales: war. The invaders followed the natural lines of entry into the country by river valley and coastal plain and as they went they erected castles to safeguard their conquests. As their occupation became more permanent these early earth and timber castles were replaced by more sophisticated stone structures that, in turn, gave rise to the fortified towns and boroughs which, together with their churches, were created to supply the temporal and spiritual needs of the garrisons. The essential details of conquest, colonisation and domination elude us but enough is known to suggest that in many cases, but by no means all, the unit of penetration appears to have been the *cwmwd* or commote, sometimes the *cantref* (a grouping of two or more commotes), territorial divisions created, if they existed at all, for ease of princely administration long before the Normans arrived. This certainly seems to have been the case in respect of the *cantrefi* of Tegeingl, Rhos and Rhufoniog and the commotes of Cynllaith, Edeirnion and Iâl, conquered and detached from Gwynedd and Powys respectively, which are referred to as Norman lordships in Domesday Book.[41] Here the newcomers may have found a pattern of authority which suited their needs since the subjugation of a clearly defined and long established commote or *cantref* is thought to have carried with it certain rights, possibly even quasi-regal in character, which devolved to them by right of conquest. As much by process of osmosis as by adoption and adaptation, the newcomers may well have assumed the powers of *arglwyddiaeth* or lordship once exercised by their predecessors but upon which they purposely grafted their own customs and feudal institutions.

The extent to which native customs and institutions survived conquest and to which Norman feudal institutions and practices predominated, might vary considerably between lordships so that there never developed or existed an integrated and uniform system of government in, and governance of, the March. Although the March, or more properly the Marches of Wales, was nowhere near as homogeneous either jurisdictionally or institutionally as was once thought, it, or they, did share much that was held in common, and in respect of this, and because the March(es) defied simple definition, later commentators tended to refer to the bundles of rights and powers assembled by the Marcher lords as the 'liberties of the March' (*libertas Marchie*). These so-called liberties enabled the Marcher lords to act independently of each other and largely of the Crown also. In the well-worn phrase coined by the fifteenth-century chief justice of England, John Fortescue (d.*c.* 1476), 'The king's writ does not run in Wales'.[42] Nor was he far from the truth, for the Marcher lords could make war, negotiate peace treaties and build castles without royal licence, judicially they had the freedom to dispense their justice in their courts, some had exchequers while others possessed highly sophisticated administrative machinery staffed by officials some of whom sported familiar titles as sheriff, steward or bailiff. The true character of the powers and position enjoyed by the typical Marcher lord is best summed up in the phrase of a contemporary, to the effect that he behaved 'as if he were king and justiciar'.[43] In short, within his lordship the lord's authority was absolute; his was a kingdom in miniature.

At the heart of every commote or *cantref* was the local *llys* or court which acted as the focal point for jurisdictional and administrative purposes and where the newcomers would invariably choose to site their castle. Their reason for doing so may have had something to do with the utilisation of pre-existing patterns of native authority or else they simply wished to underline their mastery of the territory by usurping the symbolic power-base of their predecessors. Where the pattern of native authority was not so well defined, either unitarily or institutionally, the newcomers simply improvised and created their own *dominia* and *patriae*, which most often owed their existence, as much as their name, to the castle around which they were formed and to which they looked for administration and protection. Hence, for instance, contemporary reference to 'the lordship of the castle of Brecon',[44] an example which may be multiplied from across *marchia Wallie*. Even where native territorial units existed they might either be distorted and overlaid by a new territorial pattern or else swept away and replaced completely. As the newcomers settled and secured their grip so we see the emergence and development of the terminology and institutions of feudalism. By the second half of the twelfth century, contemporaries could refer in concrete terms to the palatine earldoms or counties of Glamorgan and Pembroke, to the honours of Carmarthen and Monmouth and the baronies of Roche and Llanstephan. Within each the customs, services and obligations of feudalism were established, shaped and moulded during the twelfth and thirteenth centuries.

As a rule, much of the conquered territory was situated in the rich fertile and agriculturally productive lowlands, so that by the beginning of the twelfth century the newcomers were powerfully planted in much of the coastal lowlands of Gwent, Glamorgan, Gower and Pembroke and along the wide valleys of mid and north-east Wales, such as at Brecon and Radnor, and the settlements along the Dee. Here they established manors, agrarian communities that prospered from exploiting the rich soil, woods and fisheries, and towns where weekly markets served to stimulate the local economy through trade. The Normans had little interest in settling in the highland, scrubland and thickly wooded regions which were left to the Welsh to inhabit. In this way lordships were divided between the upland Welshry and the lowland Englishry, territorial and racial divisions which were ruthlessly maintained. In some areas the Crown pursued a conscious policy of colonisation, the most well known being that encouraged by Henry I (d. 1135) in southern Pembrokeshire. The large number of Flemings who settled there were, according to Gerald of Wales, 'a brave and robust people, but very hostile to the Welsh and in a perpetual state of conflict with them'.[45] The blame for this hostility between the races is put firmly on the Flemings whom Gerald accuses of 'behaving so vindictively and submitting the Welsh to such shameful ill-treatment'.[46] Nevertheless, numerically speaking, far more English colonists were attracted to Wales than any other racial group, and nor were they represented by a single class, there being both plebian and common English among the settlers.

Despite differences in race and class, the single most important factor that linked and united these colonists was their fear and distrust of the natives whom they had displaced. Unsurprisingly, the Welsh were demonised by the settlers, who regarded them with such suspicion as to encourage tales of their barbarity and depravity, which propaganda served only to widen the gulf between them. Their destructive and vindictive nature was said to extend even to the despoliation of the church, something the Normans and their settler communities would never contemplate. Of course, this is far from the truth. In 1073, having already ravaged Ceredigion and Dyfed earlier in the year, the Normans may well have been the 'gentiles' referred to in the chroniclers responsible for the pillage of the cathedrals of St David's and Bangor. Even the half-Welsh Gerald of Wales (d. 1223) was prepared to admit to the faults of his countrymen in this respect, describing how the king's troops, in the campaign of 1165, 'had burnt down certain Welsh churches, with their villages and churchyards'.[47] Predictably, the Welsh reacted with bitter recrimination, 'swearing that they would never in future spare any English churches'.[48] The truth, of course, hardly squares with Gerald's biased opinions, for there is ample evidence to show that both Welsh and Norman visited their savagery on church and churchman alike, often without regard for the latter's racial origin.

As one might expect, the issue is far more complex than the evidence suggests, for by the standards of their own time many such men, both Norman and native, were regarded, and behaved, as devout Christians. The curious paradox to our modern way of thinking is that where the majority were utterly ruthless they were also excessively pious. Even Robert of Rhuddlan, 'the warlike marcher lord' described by Orderic Vitalis, who 'harried the Welsh mercilessly' to the point where 'some he slaughtered . . . on the spot like cattle [while] others he kept for years in fetters, or forced into a harsh and unlawful slavery',[49] was not above giving generously of his wealth to the monks of St Evroul, a monastery situated in the heart of Normandy. Nor was his piety assumed, for he was one among many who not only endowed monasteries and churches but founded them also. Religious benefaction and monastic foundation was as much a part of the Marcher psyche as war and plunder, and after the one came the other. By the end of the eleventh century no less than five religious houses of the Benedictine order had been established in Wales, their monks transplanted from Norman mother houses. By the end of the following century they had been joined by an additional 26 houses from five different religious orders which between them accounted for a considerable slice of Welsh territory. Although few in number, the impact of these Norman monks and their secular brethren, the parish priests and bishops, on Wales, its princes, its people and its institutions was every bit as significant as that of their warrior compatriots. Conquest takes many forms, and in refashioning and remaking the native church the Welsh might have been forgiven in thinking that the Normans intended their subjugation not only in this world but the next also.

By the second half of the twelfth century the Normans, or Anglo-Norman as we may legitimately refer to them, having been resident in England for some time, had carved out for themselves a significant slice of the country so that their territories or Marcher lordships added a new dimension to the old divisions and rivalries between the native principalities. No longer could the princes of Gwynedd, Powys and Deheubarth vie for supremacy without taking into account the reaction of their new and unpredictable neighbours. Their intervention might tip the balance in favour of one or other of the principalities or else extinguish all three if support from the Crown were forthcoming. On the other hand, to suggest that the lords of the March acted in concert in any consistent fashion or were wholly united in their opposition to the Welsh would be to ignore the truth. The initial unity of purpose which characterised their early penetrations into Wales soon gave way to dissension and rivalry once they had established themselves with any degree of permanence. Thus it was that in 1147, the native chroniclers could record an alliance between Cadell ap Gruffudd (d. 1175), ruler of Deheubarth, and William fitzGerald (d. 1174), a Marcher lord from Pembroke, to make war on the lord of Wiston, Walter fitzWizo, himself a Marcher lord of long-standing. This underlines the fact that among the more important changes in the twelfth century was that the Anglo-Norman settlers in Wales were no longer newcomers but residents. Their presence led to greater intercourse with the Welsh whereby firmer political, economic and social ties were forged.

At the end of a century of conflict, *c.* 1070–1170, the battle honours were shared almost equally between the Welsh and the newcomers; both had enjoyed victories and suffered defeats but neither had established an overwhelming supremacy in the country. As D.G. Walker concluded, 'in the end, they [the Normans] did not achieve a conquest of Wales comparable with their devastating success in England, but they created a complex of Anglo-Norman lordships which permanently changed the political and social character of Wales'.[50] The line between *pura Wallia* and *marchia Wallie* had been drawn, and despite the natural ebb and flow of periodic conflict, it was to remain much the same for the remainder of the period before 1284.

Coexistence

Relations between the rulers of *pura Wallia* and *marchia Wallie* came to be rooted in mutualism and conducted on a less emotional level. Indeed, if truth be told, the princes had more in common with their Marcher counterparts than with their own non-noble compatriots, to the vast majority of whom it mattered not who governed them, native prince or Anglo-Norman lord, the daily grind was equally as difficult. True, there remained much mutual hatred and some bitter feuds, but increasingly during the twelfth and thirteenth centuries, the tendency was towards what has been termed 'armed coexistence' with the newcomers.[51] 'Armed coexistence perhaps, but coexistence nonetheless which, as we have seen, found its expression in the political and military alliances of the period.

Clearly, the century and a half after the arrival of the 'foreigner' in Wales was characterised by massive change, not least in the attitudes of the princes, the more perceptive of whom were brought to the realisation that their alien neighbours were here to stay and that some form of lasting accommodation had to be reached. This became more of a probability than a possibility from the mid-twelfth century when the political history of Wales entered a new phase with the advent of the superior and intelligent rule of Rhys ap Gruffudd, prince of Deheubarth (1155–97). He more than any of the princes understood that coexistence was the surest means of guaranteeing his independence, perhaps his very survival, and, if he spared them a thought, that of his ruling compatriots also. Here was a man prepared to replace the cut and thrust of the sword with that of debate, to abandon the rhetoric of conflict in favour of the language of diplomacy. Coexistence was preferable to non-existence but not at any price; conciliation without humiliation was the preferred policy.

Having proved his mettle in war, he appeared to turn easily to the ways of peace, concluding an agreement with King Henry II in 1171 which recognised and confirmed his independent status albeit as a client of the Crown. It was in essence a personal understanding between two men that required periodic maintenance to repair inevitable breaches and which relied on them both to keep in check the more hot-headed members of their respective communities. This understanding lasted for an unprecedented eighteen years and it was only by reason of the untimely death of Henry II that it ended. The relationship between

Rhys and Henry's successor Richard I was anything but cordial. His 'alliance' with the Crown notwithstanding, it is in his dealings with his neighbours, the Marcher lords, that the prince of Deheubarth reveals his true 'cosmopolitan' nature tempered by political realism. Concerned to strengthen the foundations upon which rested his newly reconstructed kingdom of Deheubarth, he departed from the traditions of the past in order to encourage and promote good relations with the Anglo-Norman community of south Wales. This he did in part by protecting the captured alien boroughs of Llandovery and Cardigan, taken by him in 1163/4 and 1165 respectively, and by patronising the mercantile communities within them. Never before had a native ruler refrained from the ritual destruction of a plantation borough, which may be taken as a tacit recognition of their right to exist. Under his enlightened rule, communities of both races were given the opportunity to live side by side in amity and peaceful coexistence. It was an arrangement that appeared to work to the satisfaction of all concerned at least until the outbreak of war in 1189, at which point Rhys may have allowed the colonists to withdraw to the safety of England. Naturally, Rhys was not behaving entirely selflessly in allowing the communities of alien colonists to flourish: he was alive to the possibilities of what their trading expertise and contacts might do for him, and as their lord and patron he had a stake in their future prosperity. His care for his fledgling boroughs was noted by his kinsman and contemporary Gerald of Wales (d. 1223), who had recourse to speak with his princely cousin on behalf of the monks of the Benedictine priory at Llandovery who had fallen out with Rhys.

> And when I spoke to him on this matter, he replied that if we had known what manner of men they were and how evil was their living, we should most certainly never have uttered a word on their behalf; he said also that the burgesses of the castle were ready one and all to leave his town and to retire to England, for the sake of their wives and daughters whom these monks frequently and openly abused.[52]

Clearly, Rhys was concerned lest his colonists should leave the borough, which suggests that he had come to value their presence, perhaps even to depend on them. Certainly, John the reeve (*prepositus*) and Turstin his son, to name but two of the alien burgesses of Cardigan who elected to remain in the town after its conquest, apparently found life under their native patron not uncongenial. By the same token neither did the likes of Lambert of Flanders or Ailbrutus of Bristol raise any objection to trading with the newly Cymricised community with whom they formed close links. In fact, no less than nine burgesses of alien extraction appeared as witnesses to an undated charter (*c.* 1165–89) issued by Rhys to the town's Benedictine priory in which he confirmed its status as a cell of Chertsey abbey in Surrey.[53]

The monk, no less than the burgess, found Rhys a generous patron and it seemed not to matter if he were Norman or native, or whether he lived within or without his domain. As the community of Knights Hospitallers of Slebech could amply testify, Rhys' beneficence was truly astonishing for though made up entirely of foreigners and never having once come under his direct rule, they nonetheless benefited from grants amounting to moieties of at least two churches with their associated glebe, a vill, a mill and an unspecified number of landed acres in and around Ystradmeurig.[54] Of course, the fact that these grants involved property entirely within his domain (he could not do otherwise) rather than gifts of money or other 'moveable' wealth, suggests either that Rhys did not have the available cash or, more likely, was intent on drawing the community into a dependent relationship. That said, there is no reason to question the sincerity of his action for it fits into the emerging pattern of native appreciation for the continental church which by its very nature – it was an agressive form of piety – appealed to the warrior-like Welsh who very early turned away from sacking the monastic foundations of their enemies to patronising them. Gruffudd ap Cynan's (d. 1137) death-bed bequest to the Benedictine monasteries of Chester and Shrewsbury and Hywel ab Ieuaf's (d. 1185) grants of land to Haughmond abbey, Shropshire (*c.* 1140s), illustrate well that despite themselves, natives and Normans were drawing ever closer.[55]

Indeed, in some respects it might be said that the church, or more properly the essentials of Christian piety and grace, had the potential to transcend politics, perhaps even race, an opinion evidently shared by Orderic Vitalis who, despairing of the slaughter on both sides, declared that, 'It is not right that Christians should so oppress their brothers, who have been reborn in the faith of Christ by holy baptism'.[56] Well might Orderic be charged 'with the simplicity of outlook that was often the product of the cloister'[57] but there is no denying the fact that a *rapprochement* of sorts between the races had occurred in, and as a result of, the church. Well within a century of the arrival of the newcomers, the inmates of some monasteries, particularly of the Cistercian order, were sporting names like Cynan, Llywelyn, Maredudd and Seisyll which, when set alongside the names of their Anglo-Norman brothers, many of whom shared the same house, is suggestive of something more than mere coexistence but well short of racial integration. There were exceptions of course, such as at Margam where a list of some seventy monks known to have been inmates between 1147 and 1270 contains not a single Welshman. In truth, if, by the first half of the twelfth century, it is not unusual to find Welsh princes patronising Norman monks, it was the exceptional Norman lord who took it upon himself to become the benefactor of native clerics. Indeed, it was often the case that the church might preach the virtues of racial coexistence but in practice, some of its senior representatives were anything but conciliatory.

In the volatile world that was the March, peaceful coexistence had a short life. Relationships built up over many years might degenerate into war and destruction or else develop into peace and reconciliation, so much depended on those in power. In the first century of contact between the races the former condition had prevailed, alliances were made, promises given and agreements concluded, all to no avail. If Gerald of Wales is to be believed, the future bode ill for those disposed to peace and reconciliation for there was none to be had in a 'people who rarely keep their promises'.[58] He was speaking of the Welsh of course, as was his literary compatriot Walter Map (d.c. 1210), who was of the firm opinion that they were 'wholly unfaithful to everybody – to each other as well as to strangers' and were, in short, 'neglectors of peace'.[59] Both wrote at a time when Rhys ap Gruffudd of Deheubarth, the foremost native ruler of his day, was striving to prove otherwise. Nor was he alone in this, for as Gerald of Wales admits,

> In Gwynedd Dafydd ab Owain and in Glamorgan in South Wales Hywel, son of Iorwerth of Caerleon, maintained their good faith and credit by observing a strict neutrality between the Welsh and the English.[60]

If politics, economics and religion, perhaps even war, sometimes served as convenient mediums through which contact between the races might be made, marriage paved the way to racial integration. Among the earliest of these 'racial' marriages was that between Nest, daughter of Gruffudd ap Llywelyn (d. 1063/4) and Osbern fitzRichard, and another Nest, the daughter of Rhys ap Tewdwr (d. 1093) of Deheubarth, and Gerald of Windsor (d.c. 1136). That they may well have been forced marriages does not detract from the fact of their happening which set a precedent for future unions. Nor were such personal unions confined to the princely class; the fact that Einion ab Anarawd (d. 1163), a nephew of the Lord Rhys, had within his household a man named Walter ap Llywarch, while a nephew of Raymond le Gros was named Meiler fitzHenry, gives rise to the possibility of more widespread mixed marriages. Even if their names are simply the result of borrowing it is, nevertheless, indicative of wider social contacts.

Perhaps the first of the Welsh princes to fully embrace marriage as a tool with which to draw into closer union his Marcher neighbours was the Lord Rhys ap Gruffudd of Deheubarth. In seeking to make deeper the roots of his own power and that of his dynasty, his children were married into the Anglo-Norman aristocracy. His was a policy of inclusion rather than exclusion, hence the marriage between his son and designated heir Gruffudd (d. 1201) and Matilda (d. 1210), daughter of William de Braose. Second only to the Lord Rhys in terms of his territorial wealth and power in south Wales, the match was probably politically inspired for the benefit of both families. Their territories marched upon each other so that their long-term security depended on something more concrete than a negotiated peace. Similar considerations may have prevailed to influence Rhys to arrange the marriage of his daughter Angharad to William fitzMartin whose lordship of Cemais bordered his own. Evidently deeds and not simply words, were required to solidify the understanding between the prince and his erstwhile foes. Politics aside, the very fact that these marriages were arranged at all is significant for it went contrary to the traditions of the House of Deheubarth which had looked, almost without exception, to the dynasties of Gwynedd and Powys for its brides and grooms. Rhys had himself taken to wife Gwenllian, the daughter of Madog ap Maredudd (d. 1160) of Powys, and his marital infidelities thereafter were conducted only with native women.

Although love cannot be discounted entirely from being the cause of some marriages, political, social and economic, even dynastic, motives tended to predominate in their determination. For example, the professed aim of the marriage alliance between Rhys ap Maredudd of Dinefwr (d. 1292) and Ada Hastings was to end 'the major enmities and mortal wars between the kinsmen and ancestors' of the respective partners.[61] As common and accepted a practice as it was, some marriages might have served to cement alliances between native and Anglo-Norman but they did not always result in happy relationships. Betrayed by his wife's infidelity with his hostage William de Braose, Llywelyn ab Iorwerth (d. 1240) reacted in rage by hanging the hapless youth. His victim's rank and his wife's status as the natural daughter of King John (d. 1216) notwithstanding, Llywelyn cast aside the political implications of his rash action. If relationships between spouses sometimes failed bitterly, so too did those between parent and offspring. In 1248 the *Brut* records that 'Rhys Fychan ap Rhys Mechyll obtained his castle, namely Carreg Cennen, which his mother [Matilda de Braose] had treacherously placed in the hands of the French, out of emnity towards her son'.[62]

Wales was always much more important to the Welsh and to the Marcher barons than it was to the English Crown. Their lives, their struggles and their deaths contributed to its shape and development, and although the Crown might often encourage and sometimes sponsor the military enterprises of its vassals in Wales, it rarely intervened. Only when Wales developed a single dominant principality in the thirteenth century did English kings act more decisively, though they sometimes found the Marcher lords reluctant or duplicitous allies. The March had developed a life and law of its own and it followed a social code which remained in essence militaristic. The Welsh learnt to live with their Marcher neighbours and though there remained much mutual hatred and some bitter feuding, there were also alliances and, increasingly, intermarriage. It is instructive to note that in his treatise on Ireland, *Expugnatio Hibernica*, Gerald of Wales states that the Marchers may be considered Welsh 'by nation if not by descent' (*nacione Kambrensis non cognacione*).[63] This serves to highlight the complexities of Welsh and Marcher society and that, progressively, the distinction between the two was becoming ever more blurred. Despite the growth of national consciousness on the part of the Welsh, their relationship with their Marcher neighbours developed an intimacy that almost defies strict definition but which lay at the heart of what may be termed an Anglo-Welsh world.

Notes

1. *BT. Pen.*, 15.
2. Orderic Vitalis, *Historia Ecclesiastica*, ed. M. Chibnall (6 vols, Oxford, 1969–80), V, 24.
3. Ibid.
4. R.R. Davies, *Conquest, Coexistence and Change Wales, 1063–1415* (Oxford, 1987) 30.
5. *Historia Ecclesiastica*, IV, 140.
6. R.R. Davies, *Domination and Conquest: The Experience of Ireland, Scotland and Wales 1100–1300* (Cambridge, 1990), 3.
7. *Episcopal Acts relating to Welsh Dioceses 1066–1272*, ed. J. Conway Davies (2 vols, Historical Society of the Church in Wales, 1946–8), II, 617.
8. *Historia Ecclesiastica*, II, 320–1.
9. Ibid., V, 224–5.
10. Ibid., IV, 139–41.
11. M. Lapidge, 'The Welsh–Latin Poetry of Sulien's Family', *Studia Celtica*, viii – ix (1973–4), 91.
12. Ibid., 8–9.
13. *BT. Pen.*, 19.
14. William of Malmesbury, *De Gestis Regum Anglorum libri quinque*, ed. W. Stubbs (2 vols, Rolls Series, 1887–9), II, 322. For a modern edition, see R.A.B. Mynors, R.M. Thompson and M. Winterbottom, eds (Oxford, 1998).
15. *BT. Pen.*, 19.
16. *Mediaeval Prince*, 75.
17. Ibid., 59; *BT. Pen.*, 18.

18. A.C. Reeves, *The Marcher Lords* (Llandybie, 1983), 41.
19. *BT. Pen.*, 71.
20. Ibid., 79.
21. For the examples given in this paragraph, see F. Suppe, *Military Institutions on the Welsh Marches: Shropshire 1066–1300* (Woodbridge, 1994), 21.
22. *BT. Pen.*, 44.
23. Lloyd, *Hist. Wales*, II, 674; F. Suppe, op. cit., 21.
24. *BT. Pen.*, 86.
25. Although Hugh met his death at the hands of Magnus, king of Norway, it is conceivable that the latter was acting in concert with Welsh allies.
26. *BT. RBH*, 249.
27. *BT. Pen.*, 113.
28. *BT. RBH*, 203
29. *BT. Pen.*, 90.
30. Ibid., 63.
31. *BT. Pen.*, 16.
32. Ibid., 9.
33. *BT. RBH*, 18–19.
34. *Mediaeval Prince*, 66.
35. *BT. Pen.*, 21.
36. *Gesta Stephani*, ed. and trans. K.R. Potter and R.H.C. Davis (2nd edn, Oxford, 1976), 230; *Historia Ecclesiastica*, II, 316.
37. *Mediaeval Prince*, 59.
38. Malmesbury, *De Gestis Regum Anglorum*, II, 306.
39. *BT. RBH*, 39.
40. *BT. Pen.*, 21.
41. R.R. Davies, 'Kings, Lords and Liberties in the Welsh March', *TRHS*, 29 (1979), 51.
42. Quoted in R.R. Davies, *TRHS*, 29 (1979), 42.
43. Ibid.
44. Ibid., 48.
45. *Journey & Description*, 141–2.
46. Ibid., 142.
47. Ibid., 202.
48. Ibid.
49. *Historia Ecclesiastica*, IV, 139.
50. D.G. Walker, *The Norman Conquerors* (Llandybie, 1977), 10.
51. R. Mortimer, *Angevin England, 1154–1258* (Oxford, 1994), 146.
52. *Autobiog.*, 85.
53. E.M. Pritchard, *Cardigan Priory in the Olden Days* (London, 1904), 144–5, 147–8.
54. W. Dugdale, *Monasticon Anglicanum*, ed. J. Caley, H. Ellis and B. Bandinel (6 vols in 8 parts, London, 1817–30), VI, i, 837.
55. *Mediaeval Prince*, 81; *The Cartulary of Haughmond Abbey*, ed. U. Rees (Cardiff, 1985), no. 1214.
56. *Historia Ecclesiastica*; D.G. Walker, *The Norman Conquerors*, 28.
57. Ibid.

58. *Journey & Description*, 256.
59. Walter Map, *De Nugis Curialium*, 183.
60. *Journey & Description*, 256.
61. *Litt. Wallie*, 92, 101.
62. *BT. Pen.*, 108.
63. *Expugnatio Hibernica* (*The Conquest of Ireland by Giraldus Cambrensis*), ed. and trans. A.B. Scott and F.X. Martin (Dublin, 1978), 150–1.

chapter three

CHALLENGE AND RESPONSE: ENGLISH KINGS AND WELSH PRINCES

Kings of England had long claimed lordship over Wales. Their aim, primarily, was the submission of their Celtic neighbours, the native rulers, from whom they sought to elicit at least an acknowledgement of their superior status or, failing that, the means to reduce them to obedience. At no point before the campaigns of the last quarter of the thirteenth century did Saxon, Norman or English kings seriously contemplate the total conquest and annexation of Wales. Domination and submission rather than conquest and assimilation, were the twin themes that characterised royal policy towards the Welsh. For their part, the Welsh rulers seem not to have objected unduly to either submitting or acknowledging the will of the English Crown, their objective always to retain the initiative in native affairs and, as far as possible, to maintain their personal and political independence, as much from each other as from the English king. This called for a delicate and deferential balancing act, a *modus vivendi* between the wearers of the crown and coronet, the success of which depended more on the latter than on the former who were required, it seems, to possess and exhibit in equal measure the characteristics ascribed the Lord Rhys ap Gruffudd at his death, namely 'a Ulysses for speech, a Solomon for wisdom, an Ajax for mind, and the foundation of all accomplishments!'[1] That few of the native rulers measured up to the exacting standards set by Rhys' annalistic admirers might explain why the relationship between kings and princes was, more realistically, characterised as much by violence, vitriol and vindictiveness as by accommodation, accomplishment and agreement.

Points of contact: Welsh, Saxon and Norman

From the period of the emergence of the early Welsh kingdoms onwards, contact between their rulers and those of Anglo-Saxon England appears to have been fairly regular. Episodes such as the murder, by strangulation, of Caradog of Gwynedd in 798 and the killing of Rhodri Mawr and his son in 878 notwithstanding, the likes of Cadwallon ap Cadfan of Gwynedd and Ithel ap Morgan of Glywysing evidently thought it to be to their advantage to come to some sort of agreement respectively with kings Penda (d. 655) and Aethelbald (d. 757) of Mercia. In this age of multiple kingship, neither Welsh nor English kings were in a position to dominate the other for long periods, and, when they did so, it was invariably an English king who held sway over his Cymric neighbours. However, the rise of Wessex and the gradual unification of all other English kingdoms under its hegemony changed this relationship for ever. The early seeds of submission evident in the time of Alfred the Great developed to the extent that submissions by Welsh rulers were almost routine by the end of the tenth century; it is evident too that by the time of King Edgar (r. 959–975) submission also meant the payment of tribute. Even a great prince such as Hywel ap Cadell (Hywel Dda) was obliged to adopt a policy of coexistence, despite, it would appear from the sentiments of the poem *Armes Prydain*, composed in *c.* 930, the opposition of many of his people:

> *Cynan leading the charge in each assault,*
> *Saxons facing Britons will groan, 'Oh God!',*
>
> *When their forces collapse on their beds*
> *In pain, blood staining foreign faces,*
> *At the end of each challenge, great plunder,*
> *Saxon will rush pell-mell to Caer Wynt . . .*
> *The Welsh will be compelled to make war.*
>
> *They will demand what Saxons are after,*
> *What right have they to the land they hold,*
>
> *Since Gwrtheyrn's time on us they trample:*
> *No right have they to our father's realm.*[2]

This mixture of violent opposition to English pretensions and the peaceful relationships implied by intermarriage and regular Welsh princely attendance at the English kings' courts was a constant theme until 1066. Even the outstandingly powerful Gruffudd ap Llywelyn could not ultimately escape English domination; his interference in English affairs eventually provoked decisive intervention by earl Harold Godwinesson. His devastating campaigns of 1062 and 1063, memorably recalled more than a century later by Gerald of Wales as being so ferocious that at their end the English 'left not one that pisseth against a wall',[3] resulted in Gruffudd's defeat and death. For the Welsh the writing was on the wall, and few of the more discerning leaders who succeeded Gruffudd to take their place at the head of their respective polities in a fragmented Wales, would have been left in any doubt of the consequences should the might of the English Crown be roused against them. Precedents had been set and the parameters governing the political relationship between the rulers of Wales and the ruler of England had been broadly established. All that was required was that some substance and definition be added to flesh out and clarify that relationship, a task that the Crown was more than willing to undertake to its benefit. Not that the clarification of relationships after 1066 should be seen simply as something characteristically English; rather it should be looked upon as a consequence of developing legal precision and literacy which was western European.

With the coming of the Normans, native contact with the courts of the kings of England, all but ceased for a time. As far as is known, neither William I nor his son William Rufus (d. 1100) maintained regular contact with the rulers of Wales. The Conqueror made but one visit to Wales, ostensibly in pilgrimage to St David's in 1081, during which he met, and imposed tribute upon, the ruler of Deheubarth, Rhys ap Tewdwr of Deheubarth (d. 1093), and no other. Although Rufus led two expeditions into Wales in 1095 and 1097, he failed to meet a single representative of the ruling dynasties. It is not until the early years of the reign of Henry I (d. 1135) that king and princes meet in any consistent fashion, by which time the Normans, or Anglo-Norman as we might fairly refer to them by this date, had been in Wales for over thirty years. Although Henry led two expeditions into Wales, in 1114 and 1121, his preferred method of dealing with the princes, almost all of whom he met at some time during his thirty-five-year reign, was to summon them to meet him, be that in England or on expedition to Normandy. Not that this deterred Henry from exploiting the opportunities which Welsh dynastic politics frequently afforded him, for although as Rees Davies has suggested, his mastery may not have been of an 'interventionist kind', which is itself an issue of considerable debate, his policies, nevertheless, 'ranged the whole gamut from cajolery to forfeiture'.[4] Arguably, it was almost entirely through the eyes of the men of the March that the Welsh viewed the Anglo-Norman world, and through their experience that the princes soon came to appreciate what it was to be Anglo-Norman. Consequently, it was the code and values of the March and its lords that early impressed itself on the native princes rather than any royal-inspired influence.

Understandably, for the Welsh, this tended to narrow their horizons and they reacted accordingly, treating Anglo-Norman kingship, though perhaps in Henry I's case less so, as a distant power to be reckoned with only occasionally and usually in times of grave crisis. In some respects they were right, for in truth, and unlike their Saxon predecessors, Welsh affairs were invariably of peripheral importance to the likes of the Conqueror and his successors, a factor which, arguably, remained a feature of their policy, with the possible exception of Henry I, until the reign of Edward I. This distinguishing fact was noted by Gerald of Wales who asked his readers to 'consider the English kings before the Normans came. They gave their whole attention to the island of Britain, and they made such a determined effort to subdue the Welsh that', he relates with pardonable magnification, 'they destroyed them almost to a man'.[5] On the other hand, 'the first three Norman kings have been greatly preoccupied with their possessions across the Channel', hence, in Gerald's view, their concern merely to contain the Welsh and, above all, 'to preserve peace in Wales'.[6] This is not to suggest that the Conqueror and his Anglo-Norman successors were either entirely ignorant of or wholly disinterested in Wales and its affairs, but that their aim, primarily, was to have their overlordship acknowledged by its rulers with the minimum of effort and expense. That they managed to balance successfully these mutually conflicting objectives was, according to Gerald, due in no small measure to the efforts of 'by far the greatest' of the Saxon kings in taming the Welsh. Consequently, 'It is to [Harold's] recent victories of the English over the Welsh, in which so much blood was spilt, that the first three kings of the Normans owe the fact that in their lifetime they have held Wales in peace and subjection'.[7]

Indeed, the attitude of both William the Conqueror and the native chroniclers has much to suggest that he and they considered the whole of Wales already subject, thus requiring little in the way of an active or interventionist policy. On the occasion of William's 'visit', or more properly 'expedition', to St David's in 1081, he is described by the native chroniclers as 'king of England and Wales'.[8] He is similarly dubbed but twice more, at his death in 1087 and in respect of his son's death in 1135. Without wishing to read too much into a title ascribed an eleventh-century king by a thirteenth-century native copyist who may or may not have been faithful to the original source, it is noteworthy that William alone, though possibly also his son Henry, is invested with this titular distinction.[9] There is no evidence to suggest that William himself used or was ascribed by English chroniclers such a title, but that Welsh scribes and copyists were capable of thinking in these terms, either at the time or later in the thirteenth century, is perhaps indicative not only of his perceived impact on Wales but also of a widely held belief that he claimed or behaved as if he were invested with the powers of kingship. That he claimed overlordship of Wales is not in dispute, and that he believed this to be his inalienable right by virtue of his succession to the throne of England, is highly likely. This would account for William's treatment of Rhys ap Tewdwr, king of Deheubarth, who, it seems, was compelled, probably on the occasion of the Conqueror's 'pilgrimage' to St David's, to swear fealty to him and, significantly, to render £40 per annum in tribute.[10] That William exacted the same from one of his own countrymen, Robert of Rhuddlan, who had all but conquered north Wales, indicated early his desire to establish firmly in principle his authority either to bestow, confirm or seize territory in Wales.[11]

There was nothing new in this; William was merely continuing what his Saxon predecessors had begun, but the manner in which he enforced his authority was compelling – demonstrably so. Well might the *Anglo-Saxon Chronicle* say of him at his death that 'Wales was in his control' and that he 'entirely controlled that race of men'.[12] No reigning Saxon king had ever penetrated so deep into Wales, either as 'pilgrim' or warrior, a fact which must have impressed itself on Rhys ap Tewdwr and others of his class. Even those Welsh rulers who viewed his progress from afar must have been affected by an expedition calculated to over-awe with what would surely have been an impressive display of royal, if somewhat raw, power. Certainly, the *Anglo-Saxon Chronicle* had no doubt but that William's expedition, at the head of a heavily armed force, was as much military as political in intent and one of its main achievements was the freeing of considerable numbers of, presumably Norman, captives.[13] This may suggest that the Welsh had met with some significant success in resisting the Norman onslaught which, captives aside, had been sufficiently grave as to warrant the personal attention of the king. On the other hand, William's expedition followed so hard on the heels of the battle of Mynydd Carn as to suggest a link between the two. The battle was fought between Gruffudd ap Cynan of Gwynedd in alliance with Rhys ap Tewdwr of Deheubarth, both of whom were seeking to win back their respective patrimonies, against a coalition of rulers led by the usurper-king of Gwynedd, Trahearn ap Caradog of Arwystli, Meilyr ap Rhiwallon of Powys and Caradog ap Gruffudd of Gwynllwg. The total annihilation of the coalition, together with its Norman allies (could these have been among the 'many hundreds of men' referred to in the *Anglo-Saxon Chronicle* as being freed by William)[14] resulted in a significant restructuring of the native polity henceforth to be dominated, in the south, by Rhys ap Tewdwr and, more precariously for a few years yet, in the north by Gruffudd ap Cynan. If his claim to overlordship of Wales was to have any meaning, William was com-pelled to act in some capacity even if it were merely to confirm Rhys ap Tewdwr's victory and his territorial gains. That a force of 'many

Norman crossbowmen',[15] and presumably some mounted warriors also, were involved in the battle and on the losing side, may have added to the sense of urgency that is suggested by his presence in the region.

Periodic expeditions were to become a cornerstone of royal policy in Wales and in all, some twenty-three were mounted between 1081 and 1282, though not all would meet with the success of the first. It was a costly exercise both in terms of expense and effort, and in its planning, organisation and execution ran the risk of failure, and not a little danger. Both Henry I and Henry II (d. 1189) suffered sobering experiences at the hands of the Welsh which, but for luck, could have resulted in their deaths. The native chroniclers relate with glee the first Henry's discomfiture at having been set upon in 1121 by a band of 'young men' sent 'to way-lay the king' on the orders of their ruler Maredudd ap Bleddyn (d. 1132) of Powys:

> And those young men met the king and his men; and with a great tumult and shouting they sent missiles and keen arrows amongst the host. And after some had been slain and others had been wounded, one of the young men drew his bow and discharged an arrow amongst the host; and without his knowing how it was going, it went right through the host until it reached the king; but because of the corselet and the armour that were about him it did him no harm, but the arrow recoiled. And the king had a great fright, exactly as though the arrow had gone through him.[16]

Or, as another chronicler put it, 'he felt an exceeding great terror' which is possibly how his namesake may have felt when caught in ambush in the woods of Hawarden in 1157.[17] The Welsh are said to have given Henry II 'a severe battle. And after many of the king's men had been slain, it was with difficulty that he escaped'.[18] It is likely that a senior member of the king's party, Henry of Essex, had wished that he too had been among the fortunate dead, for fearing his master killed and all was lost, he cast aside the royal standard, abandoned his fellow combatants and ran away. Subsequently tried for treason, defeated in a judicial duel and labelled a coward, the hapless Henry was forced to don the habit of a monk, spending the rest of his days safely ensconced within the walls of Reading Abbey.[19]

For kings no less than for their barons, there was a fate worse than death, defeat, humiliation and loss of prestige, since in mounting such expeditions English kings were engaged, aside from the often questionable military objectives, in a massive propaganda campaign calculated to overawe the enemy and, often without the necessity of combat, bring them to submission. The campaigns of William Rufus – 'the worst of kings' in the opinion of Walter Map[20] – were miserable failures which some contemporary chroniclers could not disguise.

[1095] . . . he ordered another army to be quickly called out, and after Michelmas travelled into Wales. And his army split and went all through the land, until on All Saints' [1 November] the army all came together to Snowdon; but the Welsh always went on ahead into the mountains and moors so that they could not be come at. And the king turned homewards because he saw that he could do no more there that winter.

[1097] . . . he travelled into Wales with a great raiding-army, and through some of the Welsh who came to him and were his guides, went deeply through that land with his army, and stayed there from midsummer well-nigh until August, and lost much there in men and in horses and also in many other things.[21]

The princes and Henry I

The expeditions of Henry I were a model of good practice, for in the thoroughness of their preparation and clearly defined aims lay the secret of his success. His campaign of 1114 was the most massive yet undertaken by an English king, requiring the service of many thousands of men drawn from across the realm, with contingents also from Scotland, Normandy and Wales itself, and organised into three armies. So struck were the rulers of Gwynedd and Powys with the scale of the campaign and the novel three-pronged strategy of attack that they submitted almost without demur. So convinced were the native chroniclers that Henry intended their complete destruction that they were freely using terms like annihilation and extermination – 'so that the Britannic name should never more be remembered'[22] – to characterise the nature of the royal expedition. Primarily punitive in deed and intent, Henry sought not conquest or destruction, though he did little to dissuade the enemy from thinking it, but the means whereby he might more thoroughly exploit his position as overlord and in so doing settle his Welsh affairs for some considerable time. That he succeeded is amply testified by contemporaries such as the scribe responsible for the Winchester variant of the *Anglo-Saxon Chronicle*: 'and the Welsh kings came to him and became his men and swore him loyal oaths'.[23] In effect, the native rulers had become, if they were not already, clients of the Crown, a position of dependence sufficiently vague as to defy close definition.

That he had recourse to mount a second punitive expedition is indicative more of the unstable and unruly conditions that pervaded native and Anglo-Norman politics and society in Wales than it is of any perceived failure on the part of the Crown to resolve outstanding issues in 1114. Henry adopted no new tactic or strategy, and nor did he initiate anything that might be construed as fundamentally innovative or inherently 'different' from that which he had used before. His aim, then (against

Gwynedd and Powys in 1114) as now (against Powys alone in 1121), was submission accompanied by an acknowledgement only of his superior status. Henry had no wish to formalise or 'constitutionalise' his relationship with the native princes, he had no need, for his dominion was such that though he demanded little of them in substantive terms, they were left in no doubt as to the nature of their subservient relationship with the king. To err was to incur the royal wrath and the instrument of punishment was the feudal host. Contemporaries were clearly in awe of Henry – 'a man against whom no one could be of avail save God himself'[24] – whom they credited with subduing the Welsh in as much as he had the power apparently either to invest or divest the princes of territory. That this 'territory' might include a patrimony or two – 'he gave Powys to Cadwgan ap Bleddyn' proclaimed the *Brut* in 1111[25] – suggests that Henry had aggregated to himself more power in Welsh affairs than any of his kingly predecessors.

The native rulers responded accordingly, submitting themselves to his will and judgement even to the point of acknowledging that he had the power, if not necessarily the right, to decide who should rule what. This was certainly the case in Powys where, for more than a quarter of a century, the king played the succession game like a political chessboard. Claimants to the rulership of Powys were supported and discarded with alarming regularity as the king sought to take advantage of the internecine warfare that threatened to tear the kingdom apart. In pursuing a policy dedicated to the art of divide and rule, in which native dynasts were set against each other in their quest of the king's bounty, Henry was early exploring a strategy that was to be perfected by his successors, most notably John and Edward I. No less than six members of the ruling family of Powys were seduced, in turn, by flattery, gifts, rewards and promises of support by that arch manipulator Henry, all but one of whom met a grizzly end at the hands of their familial competitors as a result. Elsewhere too the king managed to manipulate the family rivalries and influence the brittle politics within Gwynedd and in what little remained of native-held Deheubarth. Consequently, it is to him that Gruffudd ap Cynan looked for recognition of his claim to rule Gwynedd and from whom, according to his clearly impressed biographer, 'he got goodwill, affection' and, more significantly, a grant of 'the cantrefs of Llŷn, and Eifionydd, and Arllechwedd, along with their people and possessions'.[26] Equally, in the south, the dispossessed heir to the defunct kingdom of Deheubarth, Gruffudd ap Rhys ap Tewdwr, had cause to be 'grateful' to Henry for a grant of the commote of Caeo, a largely barren upland region comprising a fraction of his entire patrimony, which he held in tenure of the Crown.

The king was not averse to rearranging the political map of Wales or to promoting native interests if it suited him. In 1102, in the wake of the destruction of Deheubarth, he revived the ancient polity of Ystrad Tywi which comprised the lordships of Cantref Mawr, Bychan, Cydweli and Gower and installed his nominee Hywel ap Goronwy, scion of the house of Cynllibiwg, as its ruler. Hywel's 'reign', however, was shortlived; abandoned by an apparently disinterested or preoccupied king, he fell prey to 'the treachery of the French', his erstwhile allies, and in 1106 was slain on their behalf by one of his own countrymen, Gwgan ap Meurig.[27] For those princes who fell foul of the king, no less than for those who merely fell out of his favour, the consequences were such as to cause another nail to be struck in the coffin of native independence. Nor had time dimmed his reputation as the veritable hammer of the Welsh in so far as Gerald of Wales, writing near sixty years after the king's death (*c.* 1190s), was able to mark time 'from the subjugation of Wales down to the present day', this being, in his view, 'the final sub-jugation of Wales by Henry I, King of the English'.[28] It might not be politic today to make such extravagant claims on his behalf but there is no denying the impact his forceful and, arguably to some degree, inter-ventionist policies had on contemporary and near contemporary com-mentators and princes alike.

Anarchy and the 'national revival'

Yet if the use, or the threat of the use, of the sword as opposed to the taking of oaths was the key to Henry's strength and success it was, in other circumstances, the Crown's undoing, for under a lame, incompet-ent or distracted king it invariably failed. Such was Henry's successor Stephen, a king apparently bereft of both policy and direction in Wales, who failed to lead a single expedition and for whom the anonymous author of the contemporary chronicle, the *Gesta Stephani*, made excuses: 'when the Welsh were troubling the land in this fashion, it seemed to the king that he was striving in vain, pouring out his vast treasure to reduce them to peace; and so, advised by more judicious counsel, he preferred to endure their insolent rebellion for a time'.[29] Stephen's policy of entrusting Welsh affairs to lieutenants, who proved inadequate to the task, was a miserable failure that served only to exacerbate an already worsening situation. Freed somewhat from the restrictions imposed upon them by the able and supremely dominant Henry I, the native rulers took advantage of the king's death and Stephen's weakness to wreak havoc in the March, and within a few short years they had succeeded in turning the aims and objectives of royal policy on their head. In the words of the *Gesta Stephani*, the Welsh were now 'the stern masters of those before whom a little earlier they had bent compliant necks'.[30]

Clearly, in times of relaxed English dominance, the motivations and policies of the Welsh princes become more transparent. To all, recovery of lands lost to Anglo-Norman conquest was paramount, but to those few with the strength and means to do so, expansion was just as crucial as consolidation for the political and economic well-being of their kingdoms. In pursuing the first aim, the Welsh rulers showed a remarkable unity of purpose which resulted in a combined effort that saw them largely succeed in dislodging the Anglo-Normans from territories held, in some instances, for nigh on half a century. Thus did the leading members of the dynasties of Gwynedd, Deheubarth and Maelienydd combine in a series of successful attacks on Anglo-Norman-held Ceredigion in 1136–8. However, such unity was fragile and often only temporary, for once the Anglo-Normans had been ejected the Welsh hardly hesitated before resuming their attacks on each other; both between and within dynasties. Thus did the dynasty of Gwynedd take control of Ceredigion, traditionally part of Deheubarth, to which it had no prior claim and for which its success in this respect would not have been possible without the aid of the very dynasty it had so casually dispossessed.

Gwynedd's successful expansion at the expense of both Anglo-Normans and native dynasts was tempered by the difficulties its dynasty faced in attempting to consolidate its gains. Success had led to a glut of additional territory which contributed, in part, to unleashing those forces of dynastic envy and rivalry that threatened the very stability of the dynasty in its moment of triumph. Ironically, a strong king like Henry I might at least provide an external focus for hatred and envy that a weak king like Stephen could not. In responding to the curbing pressure of a threatening king, a native ruler might better channel dynastic dissent outwards and away from domestic matters. Gruffudd ap Cynan managed this reasonably successfully during Henry's reign, a feat his heir Owain could not repeat during Stephen's on account of the ambitious scheming of his brother and nephews. In stark contrast, the dispossessed dynasty of Deheubarth pulled together and supported each other over nearly twenty years without so much as a word raised in anger. Unlike Gwynedd which had maintained its territorial integrity during the difficult years of Henry's reign, Deheubarth had been broken and occupied so that its dynasts had little to lose and much to gain by uniting in a common cause against Anglo-Norman settlers. Freed from the suffocating restraint imposed upon them by Henry's rule, their whole energy was directed to the single purpose of reconstructing the kingdom of Rhys ap

Tewdwr, an aim made possible by the distraction of civil war in England and by Stephen's lack of resolve in Welsh affairs. In a striking display of opportunism that betokens a wider sense of political perspective, the Deheubarth dynasts were prepared to exploit rivalries among the Anglo-Normans in as much as they entered into temporary alliances with their foes.

In spite of the in-fighting and butchery, much less in evidence than the Crown could have hoped or expected, there is no doubting the resurgence in native power during the period of Stephen's reign. In fact, for all their quarrelling, the main focus of their actions remained the fight against the Anglo-Normans, some of whom, even without royal support, were making efforts to sustain or rebuild their lordships. Whether this constituted a 'national revival' in any self-conscious sense as claimed by J.E. Lloyd is open to doubt, as is the assertion by J. Le Patourel that there was during Stephen's reign a 'far-reaching collapse' of Anglo-Norman power in Wales.[31] Certainly it was in retreat, but to suggest that it collapsed is to inflate beyond what is reasonable the acknowledged successes achieved by the princes.

Defining relationships: crown and princes

In the face of this resurgence in native power it is to Henry II's reign that we must turn to appreciate the long-term problems facing the kings of England when dealing with their Welsh neighbours. Unlike his Norman predecessors, Henry hailed from Anjou, a region of France south of Normandy, and his territorial concerns were much wider than theirs. He became the ruler of a vast 'empire', so-called because it covered the greater part of France and the British Isles and consisted of a number of quite separate and independent territories of which the principalities of Wales formed but a small, almost insignificant, part. That Henry was forced to spend a proportionately greater amount of time and energy in dealing with affairs in Wales than any of his kingly predecessors was due in no small measure to the spirited and independently minded princes who resisted their Angevin neighbour at every turn. Their will to resist stemmed in part from the success they had enjoyed at the expense of their Anglo-Norman neighbours who, on account of the inability of the Crown under Stephen to support them, were thrown on the defensive. Although not as chaotic a reign as was once thought, there is no doubt that as a result of the civil war between Stephen and the supporters of the late king (Henry I's) daughter Matilda, the Crown had neither the time nor the resources, or indeed the will, to maintain, in any meaningful sense, its overlordship in Wales. Consequently, the period witnessed a resurgence in native power – the strengthening of Gwynedd, the stabilisation of Powys and the re-emergence, almost phoenix-like, of Deheubarth – which inevitably impacted on the Crown in so far as *pura Wallia* expanded while *marchia Wallie* contracted.

Henry II mounted and led four expeditions into Wales, in 1157, 1158, 1163 and 1165, the last of which is estimated to have cost in the region of an incredible £7,500, all of which, the last one especially, were deemed by some contemporaries to be singularly unsuccessful.[32] The difficulty of campaigning in Wales was well known to those born and bred in the March, like Gerald of Wales who was rarely shy of offering kings his advice. 'He [Henry] was unsuccessful in all three of these expeditions, simply because he placed no confidence in the local leaders, who were experienced and familiar with the conditions, preferring to take advice from men who lived far away from the Marches and knew nothing of the habits and customs of the inhabitants.'[33] With due respect to Gerald, his assessment of Henry's perceived failure is only partially correct, and then only in respect of the last expedition, for as one might expect from someone who was not privy to the king's intentions, his is an oversimplification of issues far more complex. Henry's aim was twofold: a return to the political and territorial balance of power that had existed in Wales prior to the accession of King Stephen in 1135, and the reassertion of the Crown's hegemony, lost in the ensuing civil strife of Stephen's reign, over the rulers of both *pura Wallia* and *marchia Wallie*. His expeditions, while ostensibly military in character and intent, though it is doubtful that he ever intended the conquest of Wales, were a means to that end and in respect of which he may be said to have been almost entirely successful.

Periodic expeditions or campaigns, no matter how impressive or well organised, were limited in what they could achieve. For example, in a reign spanning fifty-six years (1216–72), Henry III launched more expeditions against Welsh opposition, ten in all, than any other king before or after, but, arguably, achieved far less than any of them. Admittedly, they remained the ultimate sanction which, in the short term, might prove very effective but in the long term their contribution to the development of any meaningful, formal, even constitutional, relationship between the Crown and the rulers of native Wales was negligible. To wield the big stick without any form of reward or redress was bound to fail – a fact appreciated early by Henry I whose policy of pacification turned on making promises, few of which he ever intended to keep. In order to detach Iorwerth ap Bleddyn from his alliance with the rebellious earl of Shrewsbury, Robert de Bêlleme, the king promised the Welshman so much territory – Powys and virtually the whole of

Deheubarth comprising Ceredigion, half of Dyfed, Ystrad Tywi, Cydweli and Gower – that to keep to it would have made him the most powerful ruler in Wales. Needless to say, 'the king did not keep faith with him', and in a remarkably swift and ruthless volte-face the king turned on his newly recruited ally.[34] Summoned 'by deceitful means to Shrewsbury to be judged before the king's council', Iorwerth was adjudged 'according to their judgement guilty. And in the end, not by law but through might and power and violation of the law, they placed him in the king's prison' where he remained for seven years.[35] In return for the head of his fugitive son-in-law, Gruffudd ap Cynan was 'promised much good', as were Madog and Ithel, sons of Rhirid ap Bleddyn, if they would deliver the equally furtive Owain ap Cadwgan to the king's officers at Shrewsbury.[36] If, as the *Brut* would have it, 'it was the custom of the French to deceive men with promises', then Henry had turned it into an art form, yet he was not above fulfilling a promise if it suited his personal inclination or political purpose.[37] One such promise fulfilled was to his erstwhile foe Owain ap Cadwgan ap Bleddyn, whom he pledged to 'exalt' and 'raise up higher than anyone' of his kin and to 'reward . . . with worthy gifts'.[38] So taken was the king with Owain that he is reported to have said ,'Come with me and I will reward thee as may be fitting. And this I will tell thee: I am going to Normandy, and if thou wilt come with me, I will make thee a knight'.[39] Owain duly obliged and spent the better part of a year abroad and in doing so became the first Welsh prince to accompany a king of England on a continental mission.

If Henry I was a minimalist in respect of establishing or developing a more formal framework within which to regulate his essentially personal and flexible relationship with the princes, his namesake Henry II began his reign as a maximalist. He blundered onto the scene in the 1150s determined, it seems, to reduce the princes to a position of servile dependence. The tried and tested mechanisms and rituals of submission – military campaigns followed by parleys, pledges, hostages and tribute – were pursued with a will but it was the conciliar approach to settling the 'Welsh question' which had the potential to be innovative. Four councils were held between 1163 and 1177 – Woodstock (1163), Gloucester (1175), Geddington (1177) and Oxford (1177) – each devoted almost exclusively to Welsh affairs, an innovation in itself, and each attended by a gathering of native princes, Marcher barons and royal councillors. These were clearly intended to be great state occasions attended by the usual formalities and ceremonial one might expect when the king was sitting amid his senior councillors without whom he was apparently unwilling to act. Once, when asked to confirm the foundation charter of Battle Abbey to its incumbent abbot, the king replied 'I may not do so without a judgement of my court'.[40] In bringing together the rulers of *pura Wallia* and *marchia Wallie* the king was seeking consensus in delineating more clearly the limit and extent of their respective territorial and, to a lesser degree, political power while at the same time defining more closely his authority over them.

In the first, and least successful, of these councils he erred too far on the side of the Marcher lords, a fault he had largely corrected by the second and subsequent meetings, thus alienating the native rulers, particularly the Lord Rhys who was forced to cede much of his territory, and not for the first time, to Anglo-Norman lords whom he and his brothers had dispossessed some years before. The territorial issues aside, it was the apparent redefinition of their terms of allegiance that roused the princes to greater anger and indignation, for in forcing them to swear homage the king was, it seems, demanding more than the usual, and by this date routine, oaths of fealty. In the words of one who witnessed the gathering, Ralph of Diceto, 'Malcolm king of the Scots, Rhys prince of the southern Welsh, Owain of the northern, and five of the greater men of Wales did homage to the king of England and to Henry his son'.[41] According to the late W.L. Warren, they were 'required to demean themselves by accepting instead of their previous client status that of dependent vassalage'.[42] Yet in a society, both English and Welsh, based on personal dependence, subordination need not necessarily imply humiliation and powerlessness in either theory or practice. In rendering oaths of fealty – a personal oath of loyalty from a vassal to his lord – the princes had long ago accepted a subordinate position in their relationship with the Crown which did not, apparently, necessitate either grants of territory or incur other related 'feudal' incidents. That such grants had occurred and that some 'feudal incidents' were incurred serves only to obscure what was, in essence, an arrangement between individual kings and their native vassals the intensity, complexity or elasticity of which relationships varied enormously over time, circumstance and between the individuals concerned.

However, in the ceremony associated with homage, the princes might have been expected to bind themselves so rigidly to the king that they would have entered into a 'feudal' framework familiar to the Crown and its English and continental tenants but largely alien to themselves. True, the Welsh were not unfamiliar with the terminology and rituals associated with submission, or 'feudalism', which was as much a part of their social structure as that found in so-called feudal England or France, but that Henry II is acknowledged to have sought a definition of his overlordship which was, in the words of Rees Davies, 'novel in its precision and demeaning in its character'[43] suggests that much of what he intended was indeed alien and unpalatable to the princes. They would have become vassals of the Crown, pledging to render whatever service had been specified or was customary at the time. Unfortunately, only Ralph of Diceto and Robert of Torigny provide eyewitness accounts of the assembly at Woodstock and neither is forthcoming on the details attending the oaths rendered. Despite this, it is worth speculating on what transpired at Woodstock in as much as it seems to have caused the princes to set aside their bitter rivalry and unite in the face of what they perceived to be an ominous and common threat. It was usual for those rendering homage – the ceremonial acceptance of inferiority to a lord as a precondition for taking possession of land as his feudal tenant – to be publicly enfeoffed with property on pain of forfeiture if they failed in their duty to their feudal overlord. If Henry II intended that the princes' patrimonies, their kingdoms as opposed to any additional lands, were to be included in this public enfeoffment this would have all but admitted the king's right to direct or territorial lordship over each of them. If this was the case then it would have heralded a major shift in policy since, hitherto, the princes had not formally held their lands of this or any other king of England, their dependence on the royal incumbent had been personal not territorial. That this is what the king intended may be suggested by his treatment in 1158 of the Lord Rhys whom he stripped of his territories before 'his being allowed Cantref Mawr and another cantref, which the king chose to give him, and that whole and not divided'.[44] That Henry did not keep to his promise 'but gave him various portions within the lands of various barons'[45] indicated early the danger he posed to the princes. In such circumstances, their reaction in uniting to throw off 'the bondage of the French' is understandable.[46]

The response of Owain Gwynedd and the Lord Rhys

Henry's attempt to make real and tangible his overlordship in Wales may have spurred Owain Gwynedd to seek an alternative overlord in Louis VII of France whom he contacted through at least four diplomatic missions between the autumn of 1164 and the spring of 1166. In undertaking this diplomatic initiative, the first of its kind by a Welsh ruler, Owain was ably demonstrating his appreciation of the wider political and strategic situation in so far as it affected Henry II and, ultimately, himself. In one of his communications to the French court Owain proposed a military alliance:

> I vigorously entreat your clemency that you will inform me through the bearer of this present letter whether you are resolved to wage war against

him, so that in that war I may both serve you by harming him according to your advice and take vengeance for the war he waged against me.[47]

In seeking to establish independent political relations with the French king he evidently saw the possibility of bringing pressure to bear on Henry II from other quarters and the means whereby he might renounce his oaths of fealty and homage. Whether Owain intended to submit himself to Louis' 'conveniently distant' overlordship is another matter, and there are doubts in as much as his request to become one of the French king's 'faithful men and friends' is somewhat vague and technically ambigious, but it was a pretext sufficient for him to reject Henry's overlordship.[48] By 1168, relations between Louis and his Welsh 'vassals' had quickened and broadened to include not just Owain but, in the words of a contemporary, John of Salisbury, 'the other kings of Wales' which included, presumably, Rhys ap Gruffudd of Deheubarth and the 'five . . . greater men of Wales' referred by Diceto as having attended Woodstock.[49] According to Salisbury, the Welsh rulers dispatched an embassy to the French court which 'promised aid to the French king and offered him hostages' after which it 'departed under an obligation', the precise meaning and details of which are never spelt out.[50] It is interesting to speculate on whether Owain was fully cognisant of the wider implications of his becoming a vassal of the French Crown to whom Henry too owed allegiance in respect of his French territories. His kingship of England notwithstanding, Henry might have found himself on a par with one from whom he was attempting to wrest a more formal recognition of his superior status: the potential for the disruption of traditional bonds of allegiance and notional ties of overlordship was infinite. In the event, the Welsh were never obliged to test their new-found friendship with the House of Capet: circumstances quickly conspired to abort further contact between them. The conclusion of peace between Louis VII and Henry II at Montmirail in January 1169 followed by Owain Gwynedd's death in November 1170 served to sabotage their fledgling diplomatic and political relationship which, by 1174, was irrevocably severed by the decision of Rhys ap Gruffudd to aid his erstwhile foe Henry II rather than his late ally Louis VII when the armed struggle between Capetian and Angevin was resumed.

The dispatch by Rhys of his son Hywel Sais and some one thousand troops to Normandy is clearly evidence of a sea-change in Anglo-Welsh relations. Ever the pragmatist, Henry was willing to adopt a new approach in his dealings with the Welsh, with whom better relations were made possible in part by the death of Owain Gwynedd, but more as a result of the political maturity of Rhys ap Gruffudd who saw to it that, for his part, force and conflict would give way to diplomacy and conciliation. The king responded by seeking to enlist rather than alienate the native rulers, whom he preferred as willing allies than as unwilling vassals. On parleying with the king at Newnham, in the Forest of Dean, in September 1171, Rhys reaffirmed his allegiance to the Crown and promised tribute of three hundred horses and four thousand head of cattle, with the added pledge of twenty-four hostages as a sign of good faith. That Rhys failed to deliver the agreed tribute in full was not allowed to sour their good relations; indeed, as a gesture of his confidence and trust in Rhys' clientship the king respited the remainder until after he had returned from his expedition to Ireland. Herein may lie part of the reason for this *rapprochement*, for in seeking to control the Norman 'conquest' of Ireland, an adventure begun in 1169 and hitherto conceived and conducted very much as a private enterprise by a few hundred well-armed and motivated warriors the majority of whom had been recruited from among the Marcher communities of south Wales, Henry required secure lines of communication and safe passage for his army in this and in any future expeditions. True, Milford Haven was not the only port for Ireland but it suited Henry to recruit Rhys in whom he saw the potential for alliance and the means through which he might establish more than the mere semblance of stability in this far-flung corner of his empire.

It soon became clear to all concerned that the basis of their good relations was founded on more than mere gestures. Henry took the unusual, if not wholly unprecedented step, of confirming Rhys in all his possessions, much of which comprised territories he had conquered from Marcher lords – Clifford, Clare and fitzGerald – with whom he had been in dispute for nearly two decades. Their humiliation was Rhys' triumph and no amount of royal compensation – the fitzGeralds at least were given twenty librates of land in Devon[51] – could disguise the fact that the Crown had emasculated Marcher ambition in favour of promoting native cooperation. Where Henry had once attempted to marginalise the native rulers he now sought their acclimatisation and integration within the Angevin polity. The first steps in this process were taken in 1172 with the king's appointment of Rhys 'as justice on his behalf in all Deheubarth',[52] an enigmatic title of uncertain jurisdiction but one that was probably intended to carry with it some form of delegated royal authority, presumably over the other native rulers of south Wales, the majority of whom were closely bound to Rhys by deeply rooted familial and increasingly formal 'feudal' ties. That this is what was intended may, in large part, be evidenced from the next and subsequent steps taken by the king in settling his affairs in Wales, the fragmented political units of which had long posed serious problems for the Crown since there was no overall authority with which to make agreements. Consequently, it was 'by the king's counsel' that Rhys brought 'all the princes of the South' when he was summoned to attend Henry in council at Gloucester in 1175.[53] This approach to simplifying, and clarifying, the jurisdictional nature of native and Angevin politics was refined and applied across the political spectrum to include the lords and princes of north Wales when next the king met his Welsh 'vassals' in 1177. At the councils of Geddington and Oxford, the native rulers were required to swear the accustomed oaths of fealty and homage, but from Rhys of Deheubarth and Dafydd ab Owain Gwynedd, the two most powerful, considerably more was expected and demanded from the king. According to one contemporary chronicler they, and they alone, 'swore fealty and liege homage'[54] – where homage has been taken from several lords, there might be a chief liege lord, of whom the main estate was held – which immediately elevated them above their ruling contemporaries and over whom, in their respective spheres, they might be expected to exercise jurisdiction.

Where it is possible to agree with the opinion first expressed by W.L. Warren, that Rhys and Dafydd alone became vassals of the Crown, as understood and interpreted by the king, his court and their contemporaries, to suggest that this established anything approaching a constitutional relationship may be going too far. True, Henry was exercising the powers of a feudal overlord in conferring on both Dafydd and Rhys territory – Ellesmere and Meirionydd respectively – in return for oaths more solemn and binding than had been asked of Welshmen hitherto (including Woodstock), but 'there was little that was new and less that was permanent'[55] in this respect. The proof of this can be seen in the almost complete breakdown in relations between the princes, Rhys in particular, and the Crown on the death of Henry II in 1189. In taking to the field after nearly two decades of peace and before the new king, Richard I, had time to establish himself, Rhys was acknowledging the fact that his accord with the Crown had no institutional basis, that it was a personal contract between himself and Henry II which the latter's successor need not honour. This episode serves only to confirm the fact that to make concrete something that remained essentially fluid is to grossly misrepresent the nature and form of the relationships that were established between various princes and successive kings of England. Rarely did such bargains, accords and agreements, for this is what they were however we may wish to couch them in the language and terminology of feudalism, outlive either of the contracting parties. On the other hand, it can be argued that the seeds had been sown in respect of future developments in the sphere of Anglo-Welsh politics and the relationships resulting therefrom which might require some form of institutional framework. In addition, Henry, with the connivance of the most powerful native princes – the Lord Rhys and Dafydd ab Owain – had firmly planted the idea that some and not all of the native rulers could expect to be treated with distinction as sovereign lords.

Richard I and Wales

In respect of Welsh affairs Henry II had achieved no less, but certainly no more, than his kingly predecessors in so far as his authority was mediated through client rulers who took it upon themselves either to enforce or to dilute his commands. The sheer scale of his territorial interests meant that Wales would always be peripheral to his other political concerns which might explain the often rather fitful and apparently ad hoc way in which he dealt with the problems associated with native political ambitions. Preoccupied he might have been, but negligent he was not, unlike his son and heir Richard for whom Wales was an unwelcome irritant which, in a policy echoing that employed during Stephen's reign, he thought could be dealt with via lieutenants. That it failed was no surprise to anyone other than perhaps Richard himself, for though he might not have placed his overlordship of Wales high on his list of priorities, he continued to assume his natural right to it and expected, even demanded, that his native subjects respect it. However, respect alone does not guarantee peace and stablility, nor is it a one-way process as the Lord Rhys demonstrated when the king's lack of respect in his dealings with him impelled the aged prince to war. The breakdown in relations between prince and king shows not only the fragility of such relationships but how near the surface lurked distrust. Arguably, Richard's policies never amounted to anything more than a series of quick fixes designed to paper over the cracks which his hapless lieutenants were left to repair, if they could. That they could not enabled both princes and Marcher lords to fill the void.

To suggest that etiquette alone led to war in Wales after nigh on twenty years of peace is to oversimplify a more complex web of causes. With the ending of his accord with the Crown upon Henry II's death and the gross insensitivity shown him by Richard, the Lord Rhys probably felt that the best defence was attack, hence his decision to war. On the other hand, the king's attitude to, or treatment of, the native dynasts of Gwynedd and Powys played little part in their decision to resume hostilities. Rather, they were intent to settle some old scores with their Marcher neighbours whom they thought might be ripe for the taking now that the Crown had apparently loosened its grip. Despite the Crown's relaxation in respect of its dealings with Wales, there was no return to the anarchy of Stephen's reign since the Crown was not so much impotent as insensitive, both to the needs of its Marcher lords and to the problems of the princes. As Richard's justiciars Hubert Walter and Geoffrey fitzPeter demonstrated in their successful campaigns of 1196 and 1198, the Crown had the power to use force to intervene in Welsh affairs when it felt the need to do so. The Marcher lords may have been left to defend themselves but they were hardly the weak, distracted victims of Stephen's reign; rather they were the aggressors, freed of royal restraint and encouraged to fight, plunder and annex almost at will. The princes too were determined to take advantage of the Crown's indifference by attacking Marcher and native neighbours alike, and when possible, members of their own dynasty. As was the case in Stephen's reign, the absence of an external focus for conflict caused, in part, the rival members of the dynasty of Deheubarth to turn in on themselves, with fatal consequences for the kingdom. Gwynedd too suffered dynastic strife but here an exceptional figure emerged in the person of Llywelyn ab Iorwerth who succeeded in driving out or subjugating his rivals.

By the end of the reign, and in the short term, the battle honours were almost evenly shared between princes and Marcher lords, with both having made gains and sustained losses. On the other hand, in the long term, the military free-for-all had cruelly exposed the vulnerability of Deheubarth to attack from its Marcher neighbours and revealed the dangers inherent in dynastic politics if bitter rivalries were left unchecked. Equally important is the extent to which an ambitious Powys, keen to establish its primacy in native affairs given the dynastic strife besetting its rivals, had slipped into the shadow of a resurgent Gwynedd. Humbled in battle in 1198 by the forces of an indifferent Crown, the signs did not auger well for its ruler Gwenwynwyn ab Owain Cyfeiliog who was unable to compete with the increasing resources available to an ever expanding Gwynedd.

John, Llywelyn ab Iorwerth and the rise of Gwynedd

If Henry II and Richard I never truly came to grips with understanding either Wales, the Welsh or their affairs, though the former did at least reach an accommodation with them that lasted the best part of two decades, then the same cannot be said of John. A landowner of considerable status and standing in the March by virtue of his marriage in 1189 to the heiress to the earldom of Gloucester, through whom came Glamorgan and Gwynllwg, John had ten years' experience of Welsh affairs when he ascended the throne in 1199. His primary preoccupation during the reign of his brother Richard had been to maintain the hard-won peace established by his father by reaching a fresh accommodation with the princes, particularly the Lord Rhys of Deheubarth, with whom the new king had fallen out. That John failed was due primarily to the indifference of his brother the king, and the predilection of the princes for obstinacy. Nevertheless, he learnt valuable lessons which he put to good use during his kingship.

John sought and largely achieved what his predecessors had aimed: a clearer and firmer definition of his overlordship, founded on more tangible contracts than were possible with the mere recitation of words which, in spite of the solemnity surrounding their approbation, might be conveniently forgotten, deliberately misconstrued or blatantly ignored. Consequently, John initiated and introduced the first of his 'menacing innovations'[56] when he concluded the first known written agreements with the Welsh princes. In 1201 he signed a treaty with Llywelyn ab Iorwerth of Gwynedd, the terms of which are highly significant for they reflect the determination of the king to bring the premier native ruler firmly within the ambit of his power, to make of him, as it were, a natural feature of the prevailing political landscape. Llywelyn was required to swear fealty and, significantly, to do homage to the king as liege lord, the strongest bond in the feudal world. Strictly speaking, and we have no way of knowing how strict an interpretation either party placed on the oath rendered, those from whom kings demanded liege homage were men of status and consequence who invariably held their chief tenements or territories of him, rendering them, in effect, his tenants-in-chief. Thus were the nobility, the 'barons', bound to their king to whom they owed allegiance and from whom they received their lands, making for a relationship altogether more closely regulated and complex than had characterised that between the Crown and the princes hitherto.

In accepting John as his 'liege lord', and in the absence of any known grants of territory in addition to and as distinct from his patrimony, Llywelyn was, it seems, acknowledging his territorial as well as his personal dependence on the Crown. If Llywelyn did not intend that title to his patrimony should, henceforth, be adjudged his by virtue of the Crown's generous grant, then one can surmise from John's treatment of the Welsh prince's ruling compatriots – Maelgwn ap Rhys (d. 1231) of Deheubarth, Gruffudd ap Cynan ab Owain Gwynedd (d. 1200) and Gwenwynwyn ab Owain Cyfeiliog (d. 1216) of Powys – that John did. Within months of his accession (April 1199) and over a two-day period given over to Welsh affairs (3–4 December 1199), John had confirmed both Gruffudd and Gwenwynwyn in all their territorial possessions – much of Gwynedd Uwch Conwy centring possibly on the *cantrefi* of

Llŷn, Dunoding and Meirionydd, and southern Powys respectively – and in what they might win from the king's enemies. On Maelgwn ap Rhys the king conferred by charter the whole of Ceredigion (minus the commote of Is Hirwen) and the *cantref* of Emlyn in return for custody of the strategically important castle of Cardigan. His royal grant not-withstanding, it was left to Maelgwn to effect the king's munificence by force of arms and without, apparently, the active intervention of the Crown. If either Maelgwn or Gwenwynwyn took this to mean that they were free to act independently of the king, they were mistaken. In 1208 Gwenwynwyn fell foul of the king when he took it upon himself to attack the lordship of Blaen Llyfni which had recently been entrusted to the custody of a new lord. According to the *Brut*, he 'was seized at Shrewsbury by the king', imprisoned and his patrimony confiscated, his release was effected only on condition that he pledge henceforth to serve the king 'for himself and for his land' in respect of which he might be summoned to appear and answer in the king's court.[57]

His treatment was what one might expect of a tenant-in-chief being disciplined by his liege lord, which may have been the king's intention, for herein lie the roots of his policy in Wales to reduce or obscure the princes' status, no doubt a matter of conjecture then as now, and merge them into the feudal background, thereby becoming just some among the mass of his leading noble tenantry. There was nothing new in this; Welshmen of consequence had long been subject to the processes and pressures of integration, at court, in the church and in other ways such as in marriage, manners and custom, all of which was designed to pro-gressively weave them into the fabric of English politics and society, but John's particular talent was in turning 'process' into 'policy'. The princes were invited to meet with the king regularly, to attend his court and even to accompany him on missions and expeditions abroad. For their part the Welsh rulers tended to respond favourably since their increasingly regular and close contact with Marcher lords, the king and his court ensured that much of what they experienced was quickly learnt, imitated and assimilated. Nor, it seems, could they resist offers of marriage to members of the English royal family which were designed to lock them into a more intimate relationship with the king. Thus was Joan, natural daughter of King John, given in marriage to Llywelyn, a match which the latter had, until comparatievly recently, not even con-templated. Llywelyn's thoughts had turned on marriage with the widow of his uncle Rhodri (d. 1195), a daughter of Reginald King of Man, with whom he had been actively negotiating (via the Pope from whom he requested and got a papal dispensation) as late as April 1203 only some eighteen months before John promised him the hand of his daughter. It may be, as Sir John Lloyd put it, that 'the Manx alliance was not concluded when the specially advantageous match with the daughter of his overlord presented itself to Llywelyn as the more attractive alternative'.[58]

Marriage, family and friendship were never allowed to hinder John in his quest for power; rather they were a means to an end. Consequently, Llywelyn did not escape John's blatant assertion of royal suzerainty, for in committing himself in marriage and his political relationship with the king in writing, Llywelyn was making more concrete his ties and obligations of dependence. He had already, in September 1199 (within five months of the king's accession and fully two months before his native compatriots did so), tacitly submitted to the Crown by accepting John's protection and by acknowledging the king's confirmation of his lands in Gwynedd Is Conwy, but by the terms of the treaty of July 1201, which included the Crown's right to demand of his chief tenants or 'barons' (which might have included a fellow prince or two) oaths of fealty and the right of royal justices to hear certain cases within the bounds of his kingdom, Llywelyn was entering uncharted waters and, perhaps unwittingly, was contributing to enhancing the powers of royal overlordship. If, hitherto, the vassal status of Welsh princes and their nobility had been rooted in ambiguity then perhaps not for much longer, for in attempting to ensure that their fealty and homage would henceforth be shared between the premier Welsh prince and his overlord the English king, the Crown might succeed in establishing a framework in which the position of the premier native ruler, his noble underlings and princely compatriots could be more firmly placed, and the nature of which relationships could be more closely monitored and more easily regulated.

Thus were the native rulers rewarded with territorial grants and confirmations (Maelgwn ap Rhys, 1199), punished with imprisonment and territorial confiscation (Gwenwynwyn, 1208), summoned to swear oaths of fealty and homage (Woodstock, 1209) and 'invited' to serve on campaign against the king's enemies (Llywelyn in Scotland, 1209). This represented an intensification of lordship which carried with it the presumption of tenurial dependence, military obligation and judicial subjection. Not since Henry I had an English king exuded so much authority or exercised so much power and, by the same token, nor had the native rulers been so forcefully challenged. The Welsh, it seems, were to be denied, if it was ever seriously contemplated in royal circles, any semblance of statehood or notions of nationhood for though Llywelyn's subsequent reign was to represent a palpable advance in the powers of native overlordship, reaching its apogee in the short-lived principality of his grandson and namesake, it was to be the Crown's overarching lordship, here as elsewhere in the British Isles, that was ultimately to count. And so it transpired, for although John's achievements proved short-lived – he had to mount two devastating military campaigns against Llywelyn, whom he defeated, in defence of them in 1211 – his successors were able to build upon solid foundations. Well might an English chronicler conclude ten years after John's death that 'there is now no one in Ireland, Scotland and Wales who does not obey the command of the king of England; that, as is well known, is more than any of his ancestors had achieved'.[59]

A Welsh chronicler might have concluded the same for Llywelyn, for by the end of John's reign there were few, if any, among either the princes (better described by this date perhaps as 'princelings') or nobility who did not obey the command of *Lewelinus princeps Norwallie* who attained a position of supremacy in Wales 'more than any of his ancestors had achieved'. In some respects, Llywelyn's success in reducing and subjecting his ruling compatriots to his will owed something to the fact of his experiences at the hands of the king, in that what John was attempting to do to him was what he was doing to others. The partition of Powys in 1160 and fragmentation of Deheubarth after 1197 had, to some extent, rendered the regions and their rulers, particularly from the southern kingdom, either politically impotent or impaired leaving them ripe for subjection and exploitation. In 1216 the native chroniclers record the first known instance of a Welsh prince, Gwenwynwyn, having done homage to another, Llywelyn – a formal submission, moreover, that was committed to writing. It is reasonable to suppose that where Gwenwynwyn, the next most powerful native ruler to Llywelyn whom he vehemently opposed, had submitted, other less powerful rulers would have followed suit swearing fealty and owing homage to one whose overlordship was fast becoming, by its very proximity, more real and tangible than that of the king. Certainly, when Gwenwynwyn repented of his act of homage and defected to King John, Llywelyn did not hesitate in seizing the lands of his erstwhile vassal, the invasion of which was accomplished with the help, in the words of the *Brut*, of 'almost all the princes of Wales' whom, in true feudal fashion, he had 'summoned to him'.[60]

In view of the growing nucleation of political power in Wales, much of Anglo-Welsh politics resolved itself into relations between kings of England and princes of Gwynedd. By virtue of his marriage to the princess Joan and the carefully arranged marriages of his daughters with the leading barons of the March, and due in no small measure to the Crown's deliberate policy of assimilation, Llywelyn and his successors were drawn ever deeper into English society and its politics. Intended no doubt as a means of emasculating native ambitions, the princes were subsumed under a cloak of Englishness which, unfortunately for the Crown, backfired in as much as the Welsh rulers were able to take advantage of their position to involve themselves in English affairs more than was expected or desired. Hence Llywelyn's ready support of the baronial opposition to King John which sparked into open revolt in 1215. When the king was forced to concede Magna Carta at Runnymede, the terms of which contain three clauses which specifically provide for the interests of the Welsh princes, Llywelyn was there in league with his ally and son-in-law Reginald de Braose and the latter's brother Giles de Braose, bishop of Hereford. Where John had perfected the art of divide and rule in Wales, setting prince against prince, Llywelyn was himself proving equally adept at exploiting the fissures in English politics and taking advantage of the Crown's periodic weaknesses. So too his grand-son who took the barons' side in the armed conflict that ensued between rebel nobility and Crown during the 1250s and 1260s. Although short-lived, Llywelyn succeeded in overturning the terms of the charter of submission which he was forced to concede on being humiliated by John in the wake of the royal campaigns of 1211. The most significant clause therein concerned the fate of Llywelyn's territories should he die without heirs legitimately begotten of his wife Joan, for though he had a natural son, Gruffudd, of his mistress Tangwystl, English law did not provide for his succession, or at least John did not wish it so, which explains why Gruffudd was among the hostages taken by the Crown as a pledge of good behaviour. Therefore, Llywelyn was confronted with the very real prospect that his hard-fought for dominions would escheat to the Crown at his death.

That Llywelyn and the lesser princes were required equally to pay homage to John's successor, the boy-king Henry III, at Worcester in 1218 did not threaten his authority or diminish his power. On the contrary, the fact that the Crown requested him to use his influence to persuade 'all the magnates of the whole of Wales' to come to do hom-age at Worcester, a point noted by English rather than native chron-iclers, is indicative of his perceived authority within *pura Wallia* and the king's tacit recognition of it.[61] Nevertheless, it is important to remember that the Crown did not provide Llywelyn with any formal, much less constitutional, recognition of his authority beyond the confines of Gwyn-edd. For his part, Llywelyn's action at Worcester does not in itself suggest that he 'was not', according to A.J. Roderick, 'as yet claiming the fealty and homage of the other Welsh princes as his right', rather he was partly fulfilling and partly reinterpreting the terms of the 1201 treaty whereby their homage and fealty, whenever he managed to acquire it (along with that of his tenants-in-chief within his own kingdom) was, apparently, shared between himself and the king.[62] This would help explain his treatment of Gwenwynwyn who had become his vassal some time after 1201 but who was a vassal of the Crown also and had been for some time before he committed himself to Llywelyn. The strain on the likes of Gwenwynwyn must have been enormous, having to bow to two masters both of whom were equally determined to secure his compliance. In view of his ever increasing power and confidence, Llywelyn evidently thought that he had secured the principal native rulers within the ambit of his authority. It was as their military commander that Llywelyn 'made a solemn pact' with his fellow princes against King John in 1212, as their chief inspiration and organiser that he negotiated later that same year and 'with the common consent of all', a treaty with King Philip of France, and as their feudal overlord that he settled disputes and effected a redistribution of territories among the rival 'princelings' of Deheubarth at Aberdyfi in 1216.[63]

Towards a principality of Wales: Llywelyn ap Gruffudd and Henry III

The ambiguities in the nature of the feudal relationships between the princes and the king of England and between the princes themselves, were becoming more apparent in the thirteenth century, partly on account of the Crown's drive to identify and intensify its overlordship in Wales but more especially in light of the feudal practices being progressively established by the princes of Gwynedd within and without their kingdom. If Llywelyn ab Iorwerth did not aim to link Gwynedd and the rest of the native principalities together in a single polity – his dominion never amounted to anything more than a loose federation of territories – perhaps his grandson did. Llywelyn ap Gruffudd's primary objective was in making the 'princelings' and their respective nobility subject to a single ruling prince, a supreme overlord who alone would be expected to pay homage to the king of England. This he largely achieved in 1267 with the treaty of Montgomery the terms of which recognised him as prince of Wales, head of a developing nation-state to whom, in the words of the native chroniclers, 'the king granted that the prince should receive the homage of the barons of Wales, and that the barons should maintain themselves and their followers wholly under the prince'.[64] No longer princes but barons, their fealty and homage (with the notable exception of Maredudd ap Rhys Gryg of Dryslwyn) was reserved to the prince of Wales alone and not shared with or claimed by the Crown of England. Naturally there was a great deal of resistance not just from the Crown, save on the occasion of the framing of the treaty of Montgomery when it was weak and distracted, but from among the native rulers who saw in this plan their status and powers of lordship diminished. The feudal structure of native Wales, however, was never to become identical with that of England which had an altogether longer and more secure pedigree. Feudal obligations had yet to be fully defined, and though dependent tenure was widespread, based as much upon native as imported models, there is little to suggest that feudal incidents were generally accepted or enforced in Llywelyn's principality, certainly not in the manner characteristic of a later age. Consequently, the Welsh 'feudal' state, as established by the rulers of Gwynedd, was a pale reflection rather than a mirror image of the English state which, though itself continuing to evolve, was more fully formed and deeply rooted.

The fragility of the native 'nation-state' is most clearly revealed in the nature and swiftness of its destruction between 1276 and 1283. Following in the wake of his father and grandfather, Edward I determined initially on its complete subjection then, latterly, on its total destruction. His path had, to some extent, been cleared and clarified by his predecessors whose treatment of the native princes and, in particular, with the power of Gwynedd had set important precedents which he was to revive and enforce. The most forceful demonstration of the power of the Crown and *vis-à-vis* the impotence of the premier native ruler, is in the period between the death of Llywelyn ab Iorwerth and the succession of his grandson Llywelyn ap Gruffudd, i.e. *c.* 1240–55. In a series of treaties concluded in 1240, 1241 and 1247 the Crown sought to impose itself more rigorously than before. In 1240 Llywelyn's heir and successor, Dafydd, met the king and his council at Gloucester where he, in company with his fellow Welsh rulers, did homage. However, the native chroniclers were in no doubt that this homage was far from being the vague, open-ended and often misinterpreted oath of past treaties when they state that Dafydd attended the king in order that he might 'receive his territory legally from him'.[65] Clearly, the Crown sought a relationship in which the feudal dependence of the premier native ruler was to be expressed in patrimonial as well as in personal terms. This territorial basis of the relationship between king and prince was further solidified in the treaties of Gwerneigron and London when Dafydd agreed that should he breach his oath of fealty or should he die without direct heirs, Gwynedd would escheat to the Crown. The final humiliation was delivered in the terms of the treaty of Woodstock in 1247 when Henry III decreed that henceforth the ruling princes of Gwynedd – Owain and Llywelyn had succeeded their uncle Dafydd the year before – would hold their respective shares of the kingdom of the Crown in chief by military service. Never before had the native rulers of Gwynedd or any of the other principalities for that matter, been expected to perform military service which, in this instance, amounted to a specific quota of a thousand footmen and twenty-four well armed knights and who were to serve the king at the princes' expense. No longer were the princes of Gwynedd to be treated as sovereign rulers; they were reduced in status and forced to accept a position similar to that of the king's other tenants-in-chief whose authority derived entirely from the Crown. Gwynedd's overlordship of the nobles and barons of Wales was rendered null and void, their oaths of homage and fealty would be reserved for the king of England alone. Nor could Dafydd's successors ignore easily the terms of the treaty of Woodstock which were specifically and unambigiously spelt out in writing.

Henry III's achievement was outstanding. In a few short years he had succeeded not only in humbling the ruling house of Gwynedd but numbing the very nerve-centre of native aspirations for political and territorial aggrandisement. Though hard pressed, Dafydd did not cave in but continued to seek a means out of his predicament. Perhaps among the more innovative methods he adopted to wriggle his way out of his oath of homage to the king was in his attempt to surrender his kingdom to the Pope. In the words of a clearly unsympathetic English chronicler, Matthew Paris, Dafydd 'took flight to the wings of papal protection, pretending that he held part of Wales from the pope directly' and in seeking to place Gwynedd under papal overlordship he hoped 'to free his neck from the yoke of fealty to the king'.[66] Anticipating a possible rebuff he aimed to bolster his cause by more conventional means when he opened negotiations with the French in the hope of renewing the Franco-Welsh military alliances of his father and great-grandfather. Unfortunately for Dafydd it all came to nothing, for as Matthew Paris observed, 'Wales was brought to nought at this time', and early in 1246 Dafydd died. Perhaps intended as a calculated act of conciliation the king did not enforce the provisions of the treaty of London but allowed Dafydd's nephews to succeeded him, each being assigned a share of the patrimony. The price, as ever, was high: the Crown demanded their dependence and compliance.

Nevertheless, the Crown too had its problems and though not immediately apparent, by the mid-1250s Henry III had lost the political consensus that lay at the root of his success in Wales. Against a rising tide of disaffection, Henry III had no answer other than to turn the screw ever tighter on a hard-pressed baronage which served only to increase the tension that existed between them. By 1256, mutual distrust had turned into armed conflict which culminated in the Provisions of Oxford wherein the barons, led by Simon de Montfort, demanded reforms which, if implemented, would reduce the power and authority of the Crown. The contest between the king and his nobility dragged on for a further seven years during which time Gwynedd recovered and under the emerging leadership of Llywelyn ap Gruffudd challenged the diminishing power of the Crown. Having dispatched his brother and rival Owain to prison after the victory at Bryn Derwin in 1255, Llywelyn concentrated on rebuilding his power-base within Gwynedd by uniting the various territorial segments into which the kingdom had been purposely divided by the Crown. Within three years he had turned his attention to the rest of native Wales, and beyond, and after a sustained campaign in which he aimed to reclaim his grandfather's hegemony he surpassed his own expectations and emerged in 1258 stronger and more powerful than had any of his princely precedessors. As if to prove the point he assumed a title – prince of Wales – which was intended to advertise his success, elevate his status and enhance his dignity. Suitably overawed or sufficiently cowed into submission, the remaining native rulers, in the words of the *Brenhinedd*, 'on pain of excommunication, pledged their oath to Llywelyn'.[67] In short, and in a relatively short period, Llywelyn had restored the authority of the ruler of Gwynedd.

Hardly pausing for breath, the Welsh prince launched himself into the wider political arena, for in spite of his success in Wales he was astute enough to realise that it counted for little if the Crown refused to acknowledge, let alone recognise, his newly acquired status and authority. In a three-pronged strategy designed to pressurise the Crown into a formal settlement, Llywelyn resolved by diplomatic, military and financial means to 'encourage' the king to the negotiating table. In March 1258, Llywelyn's diplomatic machinations began to bear fruit when he concluded an alliance with a powerful faction of Scottish lords who were as equally determined to oppose the spread of royal influence north of the English border as the Welsh prince was west of it. This was followed in June 1258 by the conclusion of a truce, renewed no less than three times, between the Welsh prince and the English king which lasted the best part of four years. Although Llywelyn was able to use this period to strengthen his position in Wales, he was well aware that in political terms their relationship had reached stalemate. Nevertheless, he persisted in trying to break the deadlock by proposing solutions which Henry was equally insistent on rejecting. For example, as early as November 1259 Llywelyn had proposed that he should receive, without exception, the homage and service of his fellow Welsh rulers in return for which he would willingly give his homage to the king. To sweeten the pill, Llywelyn was prepared to offer Henry III a substantial sum of money – £16,000 – hoping that a temporarily financially embarrassed king might be tempted into a settlement. However, the king rejected this offer, as he had done previous ones – 1,500 marks (£1,000) in 1257 and 4,500 marks (£3,000) in 1258 – and by November 1262 Llywelyn had resorted to military action in order to impress on the king the seriousness of his intentions. It was a high-risk strategy but the prince had calculated wisely that in view of the ever increasing turbulence in English politics the king might be unable to meet the challenge. And so it transpired, having 'entered into the shifting pattern of alliances that constituted English politics',[68] Llywelyn allied himself with the baronial party under Simon de Montfort with the express aim of obtaining formal recognition of his paramount position in Wales. At Pipton in 1265 he achieved his objective; in return for '30,000 marks sterling in annul instalments for all his lands, liberties and possessions' the government conceded that Llywelyn 'holds the principality of Wales, and everything else he holds, of the king'.[69] Unfortunately for Llywelyn, de Montfort's government was close to collapse and within two months of sealing the agreement on behalf of the captive monarch Earl Simon was dead. The king and his resourceful son and heir Edward regained control of the government but their attempts to bring Llywelyn to submission foundered when a royal army under the command of Hamo Lestrange was soundly beaten and scattered.

Preoccupied with restoring order in England, and without the immediate prospect of military success in Wales, the king had little choice but to come to terms with Llywelyn, the result was the treaty of Montgomery.

The treaty of Montgomery, war and the struggle for independence 1267–83

'Agreed at Shrewsbury, 25 September 1267, and sealed and confirmed by the prince by homage and fealty', Montgomery witnessed Llywelyn's greatest triumph, in as much as the treaty stated that 'the king, with the consent of the Lord Edward, grants to Llywelyn and his successors the title of prince of Wales, and also the homage and fealty of all the Welsh barons of Wales'.[70] True, the treaty had not given him the wider territorial security he so craved, for though secure in Gwynedd there remained some doubt, at least in the minds of Marcher lords, as to the exact legal status of the outlying parts of his enlarged principality, former Marcher lordships like Brecon, Builth, Elfael and Gwrtheyrnion (he was forced to hand back Maelienydd to the Mortimers) captured during the 1260s. Nevertheless, despite the treaty's shortcomings, for 25,000 marks payable in instalments Llywelyn literally purchased the formal recognition of his status as the suzerain of all the native rulers in Wales. It was a heavy financial burden made worse by the fact that in meeting its repayments Llywelyn had little option but to make more rigorous and systematic the collection of his subjects' dues. This, coupled with the envy his success had roused in the ranks of his own vassals, the lesser native rulers, and the hostility directed towards him from dispossessed Marcher lords, added to his burden. Paradoxically, having achieved his primary objective, Llywelyn had unwittingly sown the seeds of his own destruction. Indeed, it might be true that 'once the intitial euphoria of his achievement had passed, Llywelyn can have known little peace of mind'.[71] Events, his brother and his own failing judgement conspired against him and in little more than a decade his reputation, status and princely authority were in tatters.

Although largely effected by military means, the devastating defeat inflicted on Llywelyn 'the Last' was accomplished as much by political as economic force. The Crown was always able to exploit the deep divisions in Welsh political life and make the most of family disunity particularly as it affected landed inheritance and the issue of succession. Thus were Llywelyn's vassal Gruffudd ap Gwenwynwyn of Powys (d. 1286) and brother Dafydd ap Gruffudd (d. 1283) courted and won over to the English cause. Nor were the other native rulers able to resist, periodically, the temptation of benefiting from the king's considerable wealth and bounty. The Pipe Rolls reveal that for nearly a decade between 1160 and 1169 the Crown subsidised, to the tune of more than £150, Owain Brogyntyn ap Madog, a natural son of Madog ap Maredudd the last ruler of a united Powys, and in so doing effectively detached him from the belligerent elements threatening the power of the king, Henry II. It was, in the words of Rees Davies, 'domination by munificence' which had been tried and tested in Ireland – 'spending much money in drawing into the king's peace divers petty kings'.[72] Llywelyn's coffers could not match those at the disposal of the king, even one who spent, as Edward I did, with almost reckless abandon in pursuit of his ambitions. It has been estimated that Edward expended a sum in excess of £100,000 financing his less-than-successful crusade to the Holy Land.

Economically Wales was almost entirely dependent on England, a fact noted by Gerald of Wales who advised any would-be conqueror of the Welsh that

> . . . he must make every effort to stop the Welsh buying the stocks of cloth, salt and corn which they usually import from England. Ships manned with picked troops must patrol the coast, to make sure that these goods are not brought by water across the Irish Sea or the Severn Sea . . .[73]

The principles of an economic blockade by land and sea, the latter being particularly effective against a nation that did not possess anything approaching a navy, were forcefully implemented by Edward as were the military lessons learnt from previous campaigns. Gerald too had some timely advice on how to proceed in a military conquest of the Welsh:

> Any prince who is really determined to conquer the Welsh and to govern them in peace . . . should first of all understand that for a whole year at least he must devote his every effort and give his undivided attention to the task which he has undertaken. He can never hope to conquer in one single battle a people which will never draw up its forces to engage an enemy in the field, and will never allow itself to be besieged inside fortified strong-points. He can beat them only by patient and unremitting pressure applied over a long period.[74]

Unencumbered by continental commitments and suffering from none of the distractions that hampered and weakened previous royal administrations and campaigns, Edward was able to fully focus on Wales and channel his considerable resources into its military subjection. He was helped in part by Llywelyn's intransigence, for in refusing six times to meet with and perform homage to the king since his coronation, a ceremony he was bound to attend but did not, and in withholding payment of the tribute agreed at Montgomery, Edward was enabled to punish his erstwhile vassal. For his part, Llywelyn did not trust the king or his motives, probably with good reason, especially as he was sheltering his enemies, most notably Dafydd and Gruffudd ap Gwenwynwyn who had sworn to kill him. Nevertheless, Llywelyn failed, or forgot, to appreciate the fact that his was the inferior position in the relationship and that, ironically perhaps, the ultimate guarantee of his continued survival lay with the Crown. To maintain his newly recognised status as prince of Wales, Llywelyn had to continue to play the dutiful vassal no matter what the provocation. Provocation there was, in abundance, not all of which was the fault of the king but perpetrated in his name by his officials. Evidence to this effect is furnished in a letter sent by Llywelyn to Edward in 1273 in which he complained at having been ordered not 'to construct a castle on his own land near Abermiwl, or to establish a town or market there'.[75] Whether the king was aware or indeed the instigator of the order or not, certainly Llywelyn preferred to toe the diplomatic line stating that he believed 'the said letter did not come forth with the king's knowledge'. Edward was left in no doubt as to the views of his Cymric vassal:

> For the king well knows that the rights of Llywelyn's principality are entirely separate from the rights of the king's realm although Llywelyn holds his principality under the king's power. And the king has heard and in part seen that Llywelyn's ancestors and himself had the power within their boundaries

to build and construct castles and fortresses and [set up] markets without prohibition by any one or any announcement of new work. Prays the king not to listen to the evil suggestions of those who would try to exasperate the king's mind against him.[76]

The terms of the treaty of Montgomery while clearly underlining his dependence on the Crown were also his defence, for therein lay the legal basis of his status and authority. Nevertheless, as this incident suggests, his interpretation of the terms of the treaty tended to differ from that of the Crown which apparently regarded his political independence as something less than sovereign.

When war came in 1276 the mechanisms designed to regulate and arbitrate the relationship between the king of England and prince of Wales had hardly been exhausted but both sides seem to have been overcome by a sense of the inevitability of the conflict. Declared a traitor on 12 November 1276, Llywelyn submitted to the king's exacting terms on 9 November 1277. In the space of a year he had been humbled militarily and humiliated politically, his lifetime's work lay in ruins, his principality having lasted barely ten years. The terms of the treaty of Aberconwy bear comparison with those drawn up by his father at Woodstock thirty years before in as much as the king intended that there would be no native principality of Wales. Llywelyn was allowed to retain the homage and service of five of the weakest native rulers and the use for life of the now-meaningless title 'prince of Wales' but little else. Henceforth his lordship was to extend over no more than a share of a truncated patrimony, he was forced to concede territory in Gwynedd Is Conwy to his brother, which was to be further reduced after his death with the surrender of Anglesey to the Crown. In fining the prince the almost impossible sum of £50,000 Edward intended that Llywelyn would never be free of the Crown. Llywelyn bore the humiliation with some dignity for five years, perhaps biding his time intending always to overturn his ill-fortune. He was never given the opportunity to 'bounce back' as many other native princes had done in the past. Impelled to arms by the reckless action of his brother Dafydd in attacking the royal fortress at Hawarden early in 1282, Llywelyn found himself at war once again. This time there was to be no settlement, the king determined on the death and destruction of both prince and principality. Llywelyn was killed in a skirmish in December 1282, and what remained of his princely authority tottered to its eventual downfall under the less than careful hands of his brother Dafydd.

By ties of fealty and homage, by dint of his own military efforts and by the sheer force of his personality did Llywelyn hope to maintain his hegemony in Wales. His undoing had as much to do with the weight of history and tradition as with bad luck and his own lack of judgement. In submitting to the will and authority of successive English kings, Llywelyn's ancestors had contributed to establishing a pattern of political dominance and dependence with which the Crown was well satisfied. Llywelyn's ambitions, however, challenged and threatened the pattern of this relationship, as did those of his grandfather Llywleyn the Great, which the Crown held to be unacceptable. The Crown, for its part, moulded and twisted history and tradition in its favour, and by the late thirteenth century the idea that Wales and its ruler(s) were in some way tied and beholden to the king, and had always been so, was accepted as fact. It was thought a pretext sufficient for Edward to declare war on Llywelyn that the latter had offended the king from whom he held his principality by gift. The thinking of Edward and his court can be gauged in a manifesto issued to justify his attack on Llywelyn:

> The ancestors of Llywelyn ap Gruffudd always held their lands of Wales of the kings of England in chief, doing homage and fealty and other services due, and doing and receiving right in the court of the kings of England.[77]

It was a blatant misrepresentation of the facts and a carefully planned manipulation of the truth, but it held sway simply because it was written by and eventually enshrined in the political code of the victors.

Notes

1. *BT. RBH*, 179.
2. *Guide to Welsh Lit.*, 116.
3. *Journey & Description*, 266. Gerald was quoting scripture: I Samuel 25.22 and I Kings 16.11.
4. R.R. Davies, *Wales*, 42. For a contrary opinion see D. Crouch, *The Reign of King Stephen 1135–1154* (London, 2000), 55.
5. *Journey & Description*, 266.
6. Ibid., 267; *Autobiog.*, 112.
7. *Journey & Description*, 266.
8. *BT. Pen.*, 17, 18; *BT. RBH*, 31; *B. Saes.*, 81, 83.
9. *BT. Pen.*, 51; *BT. RBH*, 113.
10. *Domesday Book: Herefordshire*, ed. F. Thorn and C. Thorn (Chichester, 1983), 179b. There is no evidence to show that Rhys ever paid the sum demanded. Not that this would have bothered William unduly, his aim had been achieved: to set in principle his right to make such demands; whether he wished to enforce them depended entirely on the political objectives of the day.
11. David Moore suggests that since Robert held his lands *de rege* or *ad firmam*, he was altogether more closely bound to the Crown. Idem, 'Gruffudd ap Cynan and the Medieval Welsh Polity', in *Gruffudd ap Cynan*, ed. K. Maund, 39.
12. *Anglo-Saxon Chronicle*, ed. and trans. M.J. Swanton (London, 1996), 220.

13. Ibid., 214.
14. Ibid.
15. *Mediaeval Prince*, 66.
16. *BT. Pen.*, 48. On the other hand, William of Malmesbury was firmly of the opinion that one of the king's own men was responsible for loosing the arrow.
17. *BT. RBH*, 107.
18. Ibid., 135.
19. *Gervase of Canterbury*, I, 165.
20. Walter Map, *De Nugis Curialium*, 465.
21. *Anglo-Saxon Chronicle*, 231, 233.
22. *BT. RBH*, 79. Also *BT. Pen.*, 37; *B. Saes.*, 121.
23. *Anglo-Saxon Chronicle*, 245.
24. *BT. Pen.*, 42.
25. Ibid., 35.
26. *Mediaeval Prince*, 79.
27. *BT. Pen.*, 26.
28. *Journey & Description*, 162–3.
29. *Gesta Stephani*, ed. and trans. K.R. Potter and R.H.C. Davis (2nd, edn, Oxford, 1976), 21.
30. Ibid., 18.
31. Lloyd, *Hist. Wales*, II, 462–86; J. Le Patourel, *The Norman Empire* (Oxford, 1976), 102.
32. P. Latimer, 'Henry II's Campaign against the Welsh in 1165', *WHR*, 14 (1989), 523–52.
33. *Journey & Description*, 197. Inexplicably, Gerald's account of Henry II's *three* expeditions to Wales omits any reference to the campaign directed against the Lord Rhys in the summer of 1158.
34. *BT. Pen.*, 25.
35. Ibid., 26.
36. Ibid., 39.
37. Ibid.
38. Ibid., 38.
39. Ibid.
40. *Chronicon Monasterii de Bello*, ed. J.S. Brewer (Anglia Christian Society, 1846), 164–5.
41. Ralph of Diceto, *Opera Historica*, I, 311.
42. W.L. Warren, *Henry II* (London, 1973), 163.
43. R.R. Davies, *Wales*, 52.
44. *BT. Pen.*, 60.
45. Ibid.
46. *B. Saes.*, 165.
47. H. Pryce, *WHR*, 19 (1998), 7 (in translation), 28 (in Latin).
48. Idem., *WHR*, 19 (1998), 19.
49. *The Letters of John of Salisbury*, ed. W.J. Millor, H.E. Butler and C.N.L. Brooke (2 vols, London, 1955–79), II, 606.
50. Ibid., II, 607.
51. Lloyd, *Hist. Wales.*, II, 542 n. 28.

52. *BT. Pen.*, 68. Deheubarth is here taken to mean native-held south Wales.
53. *BT. RBH*, 165.
54. *Gesta Henrici Secundi*, 159, 162; *Chronica Rogeri de Hovedone*, II, 133–4. The issue of whether Rhys and Dafydd actually swore oaths of liege homage, and we only have Roger of Howden's word for that, and if they did, whether this accorded them higher status than their princely contemporaries, has recently been questioned. J.B. Smith, 'Treftadaeth Deheubarth', in *Yr Arglwydd Rhys*, ed. Jones and Pryce, 18–52.
55. R.R. Davies, *Wales*, 291.
56. Idem, *Domination and Conquest* (Cambridge, 1990), 79.
57. *B.T. Pen.*, 83; *Foedera, Conventiones, Litterae, etc*, ed. T. Rymer (rev. edn, 4 vols in 7 parts, Record Comm., 1816–69), I, 101.
58. Lloyd, *Hist. Wales*, II, 617.
59. Annals of Barnwell priory in *Memoriale Walteri de Coventria*, ed. W. Stubbs (2 vols, Rolls Series, 1872–3), II, 203. Translation taken from R.R. Davies, *Domination and Conquest*, 82.
60. *BT. Pen.*, 92. The *BT. RBH* has 'called . . . to him', 209.
61. *Foedera*, I, 150. Translation taken from R.R. Davies, *Wales*, 243.
62. A.J. Roderick, 'The Feudal Relation between the English Crown and the Welsh Princes', *History*, XXXVII (1952), 207. See I.W. Rowlands, 'The 1201 Peace between King John and Llywelyn ap Iorwerth', *Studia Celtica*, XXXIV (2001), 149–66.
63. *BT. Pen.*, 86; T. Mathews, *Welsh Records in Paris* (Carmarthen, 1910), 57. See also R.F. Treharne, 'The Franco-Welsh Treaty of Alliance of 1212', *BBCS*, 18 (1958–9), 60–75.
64. *BT. Pen.*, 115.
65. *BT. RBH*, 237.
66. D.G. Walker, *Medieval Wales*, 106.
67. *B. Saes.*, 243.
68. D. Stephenson, *The Governance of Gwynedd* (Cardiff, 1984), xxvi.
69. *Royal and Other Historical Letters Illustrative of the Reign of Henry III from the Originals in the Public Record Office*, ed. W.W. Shirley (2 vols, London, 1862–6), II, 284–6. Translation taken from K. Maund, *Handlist of the Acts of Native Welsh Rulers 1132–1283* (Cardiff, 1996), 118, no. 396.
70. Ibid., 119, no. 398.
71. D. Stephenson, op. cit., xxvii.
72. R.R. Davies, *Domination and Conquest*, 54; *Calendar of Documents relating to Ireland 1171–1307*, ed. H.S. Sweetman (5 vols, London, 1875–86), I, 273–4.
73. *Journey & Description*, 267.
74. Ibid., 267.
75. *Cal. Anc. Corr.*, 86.
76. Ibid.
77. Ibid., 252.

chapter four

THE GOVERNANCE OF NATIVE WALES: THE PRINCES AS RULERS

M edieval government was not so much for the people or indeed by the people but essentially of the people by a privileged few. Neither the will nor the consent of the people was sought or demanded in the discharge of that government which aimed, above all, to control them. Yet if government is about controlling people it is also about controlling the land on which they live and from which they, the governed and the governing, derive their living. It follows that the power to govern is concentrated in the hands of those who own the one and command the other, and in medieval Wales this constituted the nobility. This was an economically differentiated group for whom ownership of land was one of the principal determinants of their status as freemen. However, ownership need not necessarily equate with rulership which is suggestive of something greater and more complex than the mere fact of private landholding. Indeed, for the native jurists there was more to a man's status or *braint* than his wealth: his birth and his 'office' were considered of equal importance; the one he enjoyed by accident the other by appointment. Those with the authority to appoint were those with the ultimate sanction to govern and they, of course, were the princes.

From warlords to landlords

Government, like 'office', is a term with lofty pretensions which almost presupposes the existence of a bureaucracy and a state, and though both the latter had developed sufficiently by the thirteenth century, in concept and design, to serve the needs of the princes of Gwynedd, they, like 'government', are terms hardly to be applied without qualification before that date especially when lordship and rulership will do. It is as lords of men that we first encounter the king-princes of Wales, and the chief attributes of lordship – leadership and dependence – manifest themselves most clearly in war. Kings in name but warlords by nature, the pre-Norman rulers of Wales roamed the land almost at will with their noble companions, plundering, 'ravaging' and causing mayhem as they went. They did this in the name of honour and in the cause of glory, and, as befitting a heroic society, in search of reputation. They were in essence conquerors of men not territory, which is why it was the wealth of a neighbour's territory rather than the territory itself that seems to have interested them. Laden with spoil, kings would reward their faithful followers and in so doing establish the means of controlling them. These dependants became the king's key supporters, a ruling elite bound to a common overlord by ties of service and comradeship in arms.

It was primarily by means of military lordship as distinct from purely landlordship and economic lordship that they ruled, so that terror more than territory formed the basis of their authority. This is not to underestimate the importance of the latter but it is probably true to say that the territorial kingdom, as opposed to the rule of peoples, was a relatively new concept; the administrative framework so familiar to us today of *gwlad*, *cantref* and *cwmwd*, may have been an innovation of a period no earlier than the eighth or ninth centuries. Until well into the twelfth century it is not unusual to come across a ruler identified in contemporary texts in the vaguest possible terms without either territorial designation or title. His subjects, essentially his nobility, fared no better, being oftentimes described simply as the 'men of the South' or, with a marginally greater degree of precision, the 'men of Ystrad Tywi'. Nevertheless, references such as these and others, for example to the 'men of Gwynedd', the 'men of Meirionydd' and the 'men of Arwystli', point to a greater correlation in the minds of contemporaries between people and territory, so that to conquer one was to be master of the other and thus a ruler of both. Therefore, gradually, over time, the king-princes of Wales evolved from being simply 'tribal' chiefs of men to becoming rulers of territorial states. In short, kingships evolved into kingdoms.

The territorial states or *gwledydd* that emerged in the period between the eighth and eleventh centuries varied not only in their size and strength but in their longevity also. The early kingdoms of Brycheiniog, Dyfed and Glywysing came and went but those of Gwynedd, Powys and Deheubarth not only survived but for short periods prospered. Unlike Morgannwg which fell in the initial Norman onslaught on south-east Wales, they, and Gwynedd especially, emerged much strengthened from the chaos of attempted conquest and dismemberment to stake their claim to a substantial tract of what was often referred to in Anglo-Norman texts as 'the land of Wales'. Of course, there was more to the 'land of Wales' than this disarmingly simple descriptive term might suggest; it was, according to one unnamed poet, more than a land of kingdoms but of many districts each shaped as much by politics and developments in administration as by 'geography, history, and sentiment'.[1] Writing in the first quarter of the twelfth century, the poet refers to more than thirty territorial divisions across Wales, ranging from kingdoms and former kingdoms (such as Powys and Brycheiniog), regional sub-divisions (such as Ystrad Tywi and Ceredigion), *cantrefi* (such as Ardudwy and Llŷn), to commotes or *cymydau* (like Edeirnion and Nantconwy).[2]

By the eleventh century the regional and local divisions of Wales had become more firmly fixed, with the *cantref*, but more usually and increasingly the commote, becoming the basic unit of lordship. However, we must not think of these territorial units, and especially not their boundaries, as immutable. The early *cantrefi* of Penychen in Morgannwg and Dunoding in Gwynedd had disappeared by the beginning of the twelfth century which, it has been suggested, may have been as a result of more intensive and regular lordship. Indeed, if the early princes did not govern in the bureaucratic sense of the word, they certainly ruled and they did so over a subject people of whom the majority served them less according to their 'office' and more on account of their class or status in society. In the traditional schema of the three orders, it was generally accepted that freemen fought, clerics taught but villeins wrought. Irrespective of their class or status, the focus for all was the royal court or *llys* which was established in every district and at which they rendered their submissions, paid their dues and performed their services. As befitting the personal nature of their rule, it was here that the princes might meet their subjects as they went on progress through their lands. The importance of this aspect of princely rule is underlined by the fact that having recovered Gwynedd from his enemies, Gruffudd ap Cynan's biographer reports that he was encouraged 'to go on circuit around his patrimony' so that he might 'subdue Anglesey and Arfon and Llŷn and the cantrefs bordering England' by taking 'homage (*gwrogaeth*) from their people' (*gwerin*).[3]

During the twelfth, and certainly by the beginning of the thirteenth century, there was a subtle but discernible shift in the attitude of the native *literati* towards their rulers, who came to be regarded not so much as all-conquering war-leaders, important though this remained, but as protectors, peace-makers and law-enforcers. Increasingly, native rulers were coming to be judged as politicians, diplomats, justices and administrators, hence the praise heaped on Gruffudd ap Cynan (d. 1137) by his biographer for having governed for many years successfully and powerfully with moderation and peace, and enjoyed neighbourly relations in accord with the kings nearest to him, namely Henry king of England, Murchadh king of Ireland, and the king of the Islands of Denmark.[4]

Gerald of Wales too was fulsome in his praise, stressing 'with what equity, prudence and princely moderation [the] three rulers have governed the three parts of Wales in our times'.[5] One of those to whom he was referring was the Lord Rhys who was singled out for praise on account of 'the nobleness of his mind', his wisdom, his reason and his generosity. Nevertheless, it must not be thought that by that taking on the mantle of civilian government in any way diminished their accustomed role as the military leaders of their people. The Lord Rhys may have been a 'protector of the vanquished', a 'counsellor . . . of his kinsmen' and a 'defender of his lands', he was also an 'inciter of armies', a 'powerful stormer of fortresses', and an 'assaulter of hostile troops'.[6]

Irrespective of the developing political and bureaucratic sophistication of the princes, the exercise of real power never moved far beyond their ability to field an effective fighting force and to fund the construction of castles. At the heart of this fighting force, the core element that made it effective and the hub around which Welsh military life revolved, was the *teulu*. A body of well-trained professional troops pledged to protect their prince, the royal retinue was ever present: a fact which served to remind the ruler that war was in large part his *raison d'être*. Yet if war enabled a prince to 'lord it' over his neighbours, demonstrate his military prowess and enhance his reputation, it contributed little to the effective government of his own realm. War was an expensive business, the spiralling costs of which threatened to outstrip the resources of the native princes. As the raids of the tenth and eleventh century gradually gave way to the campaigns of the later twelfth and thirteenth century, the princes had to find the means to raise, fund and equip an army rather than a retinue. A large army notwithstanding, it was in the competitive area of new technology linked to castle-building that the princes had to make their mark. The transition from wooden to stone castles is a tangible expression of the consolidation of a prince's power. For example, it is clear from contemporary evidence that possession of a castle in the vicinity of Aberystwyth also brought with it control of the lordship of Penweddig: 'Llywelyn . . . came to Aberystwyth and there built the castle again and gained for himself the cantref of Penweddig and held it'.[7] However, in seeking a permanent and visible symbol of his authority by means of a network of stone castles, the prince required not just new sources of continuing funding but also the administration to effect their construction, maintenance and garrison.

The evolution of princely governance: Deheubarth and Gwynedd

Deheubarth

The prince stood at the heart of developments in war, politics, government and their administration, each was conducted in his name and each was effected by means of his authority. The successful rulers were those able to convert this authority into power, and among the first of the princes to do this successfully, to any appreciable degree, was the twelfth-century prince of Deheubarth, the Lord Rhys ap Gruffudd (1155–97). Hitherto the increase of a ruler's power had seemed tied to the expansion of his authority, usually and primarily by military means, but expansion has its limits and can be dangerous if it outruns the means for control by contemporary techniques of administration. After spending some sixteen years in an almost unremitting struggle to define, defend and, ultimately, to consolidate the hard-won territories that made up his reconstituted domain, Rhys reached that limit in 1171. Having scored a diplomatic triumph in securing a lasting peace with his erstwhile foe King Henry II of England, Rhys turned to increasing the range and scope of his authority within his own domain. Although the way in which he achieved this is largely a matter of speculation, there is sufficient evidence to suggest that he did so by reconstructing the pattern of his authority within his dominions and by initiating a thorough reorganisation of his lands by means of a more systematic method of administration.

Whereas elsewhere in the late twelfth century the *cantref* was giving way to the commote as the chief unit of local government, in the Deheubarth of the Lord Rhys, the *cantref* was apparently revived to take its place at the apex of a threefold administrative division of territory consisting of the *cantref*, *cwmwd* or commote and *gwestfa* (in Ceredigion and Cantref Mawr) or *maenor* (in Cantref Bychan and Emlyn). The prince's authority was represented in the *cantref* by the castle and in the commote by the court or *llys*. Some six castles, all but one of which were most likely of stone, were either rebuilt or refurbished in each of the constituent lordships or *cantrefi* that made up the Lord Rhys' domain. Their purpose is clear: to promote and consolidate this internal reorganisation by acting as the focal point or *caput* of their respective lordships. They contributed to the maintenance of the prince's power, both real and symbolic, and provided the kingdom with the cohesion it had hitherto lacked. In the commote, the *llys* continued to function much as before with the chief royal officers in the locality, the *cynghellor* (chancellor) and *maer* (reeve), holding court and accounting for its revenue.

Assisted by locally appointed revenue collectors, like the 'dung maer' (*maer biswail*) who accounted for the bondsmen or villeins, and peace officers like the *rhingyll* (serjeants), the *maer-cynghellor* (the offices were sometimes combined in one man), was responsible also for supervising the general administration at this level.

Did the castles become centres of administration in the reorganised Deheubarth? There is no clear evidence to indicate that they did but neither is there any compelling reason for suggesting that they did not. Given the itinerant nature of princely rule, it is undoubtedly the case that when the prince was in residence these castles became, albeit temporarily, the administrative nerve centre of the kingdom. It may even be the case that the castle represented a means of streamlining the accustomed royal progress by enabling the prince to tour his dominions without necessarily attending each of the numerous *llysoedd*. In an enlarged Deheubarth this meant visiting anything between six castles and twenty-one *llysoedd*. Nor was he limited to visiting castles and *llysoedd*, since his patronage of the regular church ensured a ready welcome at each of the three monasteries (Strata Florida, Talley and Llanllyr) that lay within his domain. At least three of Rhys' six castles – Aberystwyth, Cardigan and Dinefwr – were located at the sites of ancient commotal *llysoedd* which suggests that they might have continued to function in the traditional way. The appointment of royal constables to all six castles, of whom we have but one named, Hengereint at Cardigan, may have provided an additional tier of officials to whom the local *rhaglawiaid* may have accounted. In the final analysis, all that can be said with confidence is that, given the disposition of Rhys' castles, there is a case for believing that as far as the purely military organisation of his principality was concerned the unit remained firmly fixed on the *cantref* or lordship.

Rhys' consolidation and defence of his authority in his dominions rested upon his mastery of the art of warfare and this in turn rested upon his ability to turn his capital resources into available wealth. His technique for enhancing his prosperity between 1171 and 1189 was not conquest and plunder but efficient management of his domain and in particular Ceredigion, which was the principal source of his wealth. Indeed, the fact that Rhys ap Gruffudd is acknowledged by historians to have been a builder and keeper of castles has not as yet drawn a considered response as to how he was able to resource and maintain them. G.R.J. Jones has identified a similar building policy in thirteenth-century Gwynedd and outlined the means by which the princes provided for the support of their stone castles.[8] Certainly, the very existence of such a castle-building and maintenance programme in twelfth-century

Deheubarth implies that it too possessed the resources, internal organisation and administrative capacity to cope. Such implications have been given a more concrete form as a result of the pioneering research published in 1959 by the late T. Jones Pierce who identified the way in which Rhys attempted to transform the social, economic and administrative organisation of his domain.[9]

Broadly speaking, Jones Pierce – with some qualification by R.A. Dodgshon (1994)[10] – has established that between c. 1165 and 1189, the commotes of Ceredigion and Cantref Mawr were neatly carved up and sub-divided into well organised geographical patterns of social and economic units called *gwestfau*.[11] The number of *gwestfau* per commote varied from four in Caerwedros to nine in Anhuniog and in total numbered some 56½ throughout the realm. A term once familiar to freemen throughout Wales, the *gwestfa* was originally a custom whereby the free community provided for their king his food or feast while on royal progress. Although the custom persisted, the universal use of the term did not, except in Deheubarth where it came to denote something more than simply a feast or food render but a unit from which such dues were collected. In effect, the custom had been institutionalised and territorialised which, if true, was a remarkable feat of administrative and governmental engineering. Naturally there are some, most notably R.A. Dodgshon, who have expressed reservations, but given this and in spite of being older in origin than its supposed twelfth-century application, there is no reason to dispute the central tenet of Jones Pierce's thesis that the Lord Rhys was responsible for creating a system of territorial order based on more modern and financially meaningful units called *gwestfau*. Their reform was, in essence, for fiscal purposes which enabled Rhys to convert the traditional food renders into cash payments. The law codes reflect this change from kind to cash stating that each *gwestfa* was to render a *twnc*-pound equivalent to 240*d*. To add further weight to the argument for reform is the fact that the *gwestfau* were themselves uniformly divided into smaller units called *rhandiroedd* (sharelands) which tends to support Jones Pierce's assertion that 'there was something very artificial about the look of the Cardiganshire *gwestfa*'.[12]

Cash payments aside, the prince's subjects were still expected to render dues and services that included time-honoured obligations by the freemen to provide accommodation for the king's officers when touring the *gwestfau*, and by the bondsmen to provide for the upkeep of their lord's warhorse. Perhaps these *gwestfa* units, either singly or collectively, were obliged also to maintain the lord's castle and/or *llys* located in their vicinity. Certainly, the law codes were amended to include a clause specifically tailored to the maintenance of the 'king's castles' which 'everyone is bound to do work on . . . when he [the king] wants it'.[13] Indeed, though the intention may have been for fiscal reform the structural and territorial changes inaugurated by the *gwestfau* and *rhandiroedd* must have impacted on the wider issue of local government and its administration. Where previously the princes' authority had been spasmodic in its impact and often nominal in character, the reorganisation provided them with the framework and the means to better and more effectively govern their domain. If, as is generally believed, the primary function of medieval government was the maintenance of order and the collection of revenue, then largely by virtue of his castles and *gwestfau* the Lord Rhys may be credited with fulfilling this.

Since the native princes did not mint coin the ultimate source of most of the money circulating in Wales must have been England. The gradual adoption of a moneyed economy in Deheubarth may have been facilitated in part, by Rhys' close relations with Henry II after 1171 and in consequence of his patronage of the Anglo-Norman boroughs of Cardigan and Llandovery. That he was able to establish anew the Cistercian monastery of Strata Florida (1184), found religious houses at Talley (*c.* 1184–9) and Llanllyr (*c.* 1180s) and patronise a further eight houses across south-west Wales presupposes the existence of surplus wealth. It is instructive that when 'his time to go from this world was approaching', it is in terms of coin rather than kind that Gruffudd ap Cynan 'divided all his wealth'.[14] According to his biographer, he willed between ten and twenty 'pieces of silver' (presumably silver pennies) to each of more than a dozen churches and monasteries in Wales, England and Ireland. 'What he gave to bishop and archdeacon, priests and those in orders and teachers, and to needy Christians' probably accounted for a great deal more.[15] Although princely incomes may still have been preponderantly in kind, there can be little doubt that by the mid-twelfth century elements of a money economy had penetrated deep into Welsh society.

The princes' growing dependence on cash revenues and monetary transactions is well illustrated by the growth of commutation in Gwynedd during the thirteenth century. Traditional renders, dues and services were systematically commuted into cash payments and its collection more tightly organised. It has been estimated that by the end of his principate in 1282 the annual cash revenues available to Llywelyn ap Gruffudd (1247–82) as a result of commutation was in excess of £650. Despite this considerable achievement it fell well short of meeting the spiralling costs of government, war and, in particular, the heavy demands of the treaty of Montgomery (1267) which required Llywelyn to pay King Henry IIII 25,000 marks (*c.* £16,600) in instalments. In an effort to put his principality on a more financially secure footing there was intensive exploitation of all the sources of income, both regular and casual, available in Gwynedd. Exploitation of the prince's demesne lands, which were to be found in every commote usually close to the *llys*, was systematised and regularised, commercial activity was encouraged, tolls and customs duties were levied and even a form of extraordinary taxation imposed. That he had managed to pay the king £10,000 within five years points to his success in this respect. Nevertheless, it is important to remember that Llywelyn's income probably pales in comparison with that enjoyed by the leading nobility in England, six of whom, all earls, received in excess of £3,000 a year in the 1290s. In fact, within two decades of Llywelyn's death the earls of Cornwall and Gloucester were receiving an annual income of £6,000 each while the Crown could count on an income, in peacetime, of at least £30,000 a year.[16]

Gwynedd

Economic lordship had implications for other aspects of lordship and, ironically, it was Llywelyn's success in financial affairs which ultimately contributed to his downfall in that his excessive demands had to be met from the limited resources of his patrimony which, despite the best efforts of himself and his grandfather Llywelyn ab Iorwerth (*c.* 1194–1240) at economic expansion, remained underdeveloped. Inevitably it was left to his subjects to foot the bill and, hard pressed and fearful of further exactions, it soured relations between them which led to his losing their trust and loyalty. Clearly, there were limits to how far a ruler could press his subjects particularly those on whom he relied to govern. If neither the will nor the consent of the people at large was considered a prerequisite for realising the potential of 'good lordship', it was essential that he have it of his 'leading men'. A descriptive term that recurs regularly in contemporary texts, the importance of these leading men is such that they probably had a significant impact on princely government and in the development of that government. These were the men with whom the princes hunted and generally consorted, in whom they trusted, of whom in war they boasted and on whom they relied for counsel. That their counsel was heeded is much in evidence in the native chronicles which offer tantalising glimpses of their work and worth. For example, it was only 'with the consent of the men of the land'[17] that in 1195 Maredudd and Rhys, sons of the Lord Rhys, were permitted to take possession of the castle of Cantref Bychan. Who these men were is not generally known other than they were often no whit less noble or powerful than the princes they served. Rarely are we permitted to put names to them much less tie them to a particular district or locality but one such glimpse is afforded by Gruffudd ap Cynan's biographer:

> Then Gruffudd sent messengers to the men of Anglesey and Arfon, and the three sons of Merwydd of Llyn, Asser, Meirion and Gwgon, and other leading men to ask them to come in haste to talk to him. And without delay they came and greeted him, and told him, 'your coming is welcome'. Then he besought them with all his might to help him to obtain his patrimony, beacuse he was their rightful lord.[18]

Having previously decided 'on his own' to carry on the war against 'the king of England', it was only 'after taking counsel of his leading men' that the Lord Rhys was induced to change his mind and he 'repaired to the king's court' to seek terms, 'and against his will he made peace with the king'.[19] Clearly, the leading men of Deheubarth could exert considerable pressure on their prince perhaps even to the point of compelling him to act contrary to his will. Nor was this unusual as Llywelyn ab Iorwerth found when, in 1211, 'by the counsel of his leading men' he too was advised 'to seek to make peace with the king on whatever terms he could'.[20] Unfortunately for them, one of the conditions imposed by King John was that Llywelyn give him 'hostages from amongst the leading men of the land'.[21] Nevertheless, it is equally clear that, ultimately, power rested in the prince and though his counsellors could advise, forcefully at times, they might not be permitted to decide or dictate policy. Evidence to this effect is furnished by Gerald of Wales who said of Owain Cyfeiliog of Powys (1160–97) that, 'he was well known for the sensible way in which he managed his lands' but that 'he had frequently opposed the plans of his own leaders'.[22]

At what point counsellors became councillors is not easy to determine, but that they did so is indicative of the gradual institutionalisation of significant aspects of princely government and administration. Although it is not until the early years of the thirteenth century that we have anything like a reliable reference to what appears to have been a properly constituted princely council, it is reasonable to assume that there had existed a council of sorts for some time before this. On a purely practical level the princes could hardly consult all their nobility on a regular basis, and for the sake of efficient government a core element, the so-called leading men, might be called upon to serve in council. This is hinted at in a communication of Llywelyn ab Iorwerth's to King Philip of France in 1212 where reference is made to a 'council of my chieftains' (*procerum meorum consilio*) when ratifying a treaty of alliance between them.[23] Thereafter, the councils of the princes of Gwynedd are much more in evidence and it is perhaps a measure of their importance that reference to them was usually in connection with great matters of state such as wars, treaties, alliances and settling disputes particularly between his 'leading men'. Indeed, it may be, as David Stephenson has indicated, 'a significant commentary upon the respect which Llywelyn [ap Gruffudd] might be expected to show for the men that composed his council [that] Archbishop Peckham, in his final attempt at mediation between the prince and King Edward, thought it politic to divide into two groups the peace proposals which he made . . . to the prince *coram consilio suo* [and] *in secreto*'.[24] On the other hand, it may be taken equally as evidence that it was the personality and will of the prince that dominated Gwynedd and that what mattered was not so much Llywelyn's 'right' or 'power' to act independently of his council and, in this instance, on proposals received *in secreto*, as the way in which he exercised those rights and effected his powers. In short, the sucessful prince was the one who tempered his masterfulness with concessions.

How far the council was a legislative much less an executive body, if such terms can be applied, cannot now be properly assessed since our knowledge of princely administration is incomplete. Nevertheless, it may not be too far short of the truth to suggest that though the council's primary duty was, and remained, to proffer advice and act as a sounding board, in some instances, such as in matters of jurisprudence, it did involve itself in what appears to have approximated a 'legislative' process. In a judicial inquiry convened by Edward I in 1281 to investigate the operation and jursidiction of Welsh law, depositions were taken from various witnesses, both English and Welsh, which sheds light not only on the role of the council in the making and amending of law but, more significantly, on that of the princes also. According to the evidence of a certain Ithel ap Philip,

> the prince can correct laws at his pleasure and reform them, giving as an example David ap Llywelyn, grandfather of the present prince, who abolished by himself and his council the 'galanas' throughout North Wales. It seemed to him and his council that a crime ought to bind its authors and not others who had not offended which used to be done otherwise in collecting 'galanas'.[25]

Apart from his mistake in identifying Dafydd (d. 1246) as the grandfather rather than the uncle of 'the present prince' Llywelyn (d. 1282), there is no reason to dispute the truth of his testimony or that of some others who gave evidence particularly those like Einion ap Dafydd or Gronw ap Philip who were said to be judges and thus seasoned practitioners in the law. Their evidence is crucial for they and their like (upwards of sixty-five Welshmen in Gwynedd Is Conwy alone were examined) leave us in no doubt that although the main body of native law was based on custom rather than on princely legislation, by the beginning of the thirteenth century, if not earlier, the princes had, for want of a better term, acquired the power not only to 'amend', 'correct', 'amplify' and 'abbreviate' the laws but to 'grant' and 'abolish' them also. Nor can we rule out entirely the possibility, as expressed by Huw Pryce, 'that custom had itself been shaped in part by princely legislation, which may also have left its mark on some of the legal rules'.[26] Even the surviving texts of the Welsh laws, written by lawyers for lawyers and without acknowledging the patronage of any one ruler, save Hywel Dda, betray their debt to the reforming zeal of princes like Bleddyn ap Cynfyn of Powys (d. 1075) and the Lord Rhys ap Gruffudd of Deheubarth (d. 1197), both of whom are credited with instituting changes in the laws.[27] Moreover, the fact that Llywelyn ab Iorwerth (d. 1240) and his grandson and namesake were thought by some deponents to have often disregarded native law in favour of English legal procedure suggests that the matter of the law, its administration and its development lay very much in the prince's will.

Their arrogation of legislative power in matters of law and justice notwithstanding, the princes may not have been entirely free to act, or thought it imprudent to do so, without consulting their nobility, particularly, but perhaps not exclusively, those in council. In a revealing statement to the king's commissioners, Gruffudd ap Tudur expressed his opinion that 'as to the correction of the laws' it is at the 'instance of the country and by their assent' that either king or prince 'may reform them for the better'.[28] Having the authority to 'reform' the law with the 'assent' of his nobility, it is perhaps only natural to find the prince working closely with them, particularly those sitting in council, in its administration and execution. Indeed, it is in terms of its judicial work that the council comes closest to fulfilling what might be called an executive role when it sat, along with the prince, in judgement of the latter's subjects. On one occasion in 1274, the council may even have acted alone in a preliminary stage of a judicial inquiry which, if so, suggests that by this date it had developed sufficiently institutionally to enable it to act in the prince's name. In short, it had become, if it ever had been, more than 'a mere cypher'.[29]

Clearly, the prince needed the advice and support of his nobility and, where applicable, he shared his lordship with them, but the successful prince was the one who managed at the same time to maintain his authority over them. The more astute and sensitive rulers realised that to behave with reckless abandon was to invite trouble and that it was in their interests to observe and respect the long-held customs of their subjects. Nevertheless, it was equally apparent that in order to meet the challenges of a changing world the princes had to adapt and adopt, and had often to test to the limit the tolerance of their subjects. The law, both native and borrowings from Angevin and later 'English' law, was taken in hand and fashioned to the needs of the princes thereby becoming an indispensable tool of government. Not that there was much to choose between them since, in truth, governing and law-keeping were not separate activities, which explains why the courts and councils of the princes, in common with those on the continent, had always exhibited a strong judicial aspect. By the making, amending and enforcing of law and the dispensing of justice, the princes were not only enhancing their status and prestige but adding materially to their wealth and power.

The profits of justice came to loom large in princely incomes: a fact which helps to explain the concomitant expansion of their judicial competence. No doubt as part of a deliberate policy to extend their authority the princes sought gradually to displace the communal and personal character of lawsuits in favour of one in which the state took the lead. Henceforward, crimes like homicide, which were once private matters to be decided between the kin groups of perpetrator and victim, were brought firmly into the public domain and deemed to be offences against the prince. Thus could the prince levy and collect fines from his subjects which not only augmented his revenue but reinforced his position as the fount of law and justice. If the evidence gathered from the *cantref* of Rhos between 1225 and 1254 be regarded as typical – imprecise and imperfect though it is – then the princes of Gwynedd could expect to supplement their regular income by as much as 15 or 20 per cent from the profits of justice.[30] Here the prince's officer, the *rhaglaw* or bailiff of Dinorben, accounted for fines in excess of £5 for crimes such as rape and certain unspecified thefts though the majority tended to be for much less, like the 25*s.* and £3 respectively exacted from sheep-stealers or the penalty of 30*s.* imposed on Einion Fychan 'lately detained' with 'two ells of stolen woolcloth' in his possession.[31] Of equal importance and as regular in occurrence, but almost impossible to quantify in cash terms, were the fines imposed and exacted in kind usually on culprits who had no means to pay other than to give up their goods and chattels. An example may be instanced from the records of the court of the *rhaglaw* of Denbigh *c.* 1240–5 when Gwilym ap Cadwgan was found guilty of stealing a cow and, as punishment, was forced to hand over his sole possessions of any value, his two oxen.[32] Women too are to be found among the lists of those punished for offences ranging from sheep-stealing, theft and fraud, but whereas their crimes were worthy of record their names, it seems, were not.

Gradually, but noticeably so, the agencies of princely authority, the commotal courts and royal officers, assumed a greater role in the dispensing of justice which in turn contributed to the growth of the concept of public order. Indeed, if the princes were guilty of judicial aggrandisement then their subjects too were culpable in so far as princely intervention, particularly in disputes over land, was often at the behest of the dissenting parties. Giving evidence at the judicial inquiry of Edward I in 1281, Tegwared ap John, a judge from Rhuddlan, offered information in three instances where parties in dispute over land appealed and 'gave £6 to the prince for having an inquisition'.[33] In seeking to invoke princely justice the parties' aim was to circumvent native law in favour of English common law, hence the desire for the case to be heard by inquisition, which strongly suggests that not only did they know this to be possible but that it was known that the prince had the power to so do. This is not to suggest that 'princely intervention' in cases of land disputes was an entirely new departure since there are references aplenty in the lawbooks, the contents of which have as much that is archaic as contemporary, i.e. thirteenth century, to the fee that might be claimed by the prince for settling the bounds of lands between dissenting claimants. What is significant here is the respect in which both the ruler and his law were held to the extent that his intervention in matters connected with land could take a more active form than merely that of an independent arbiter, as the men of Llangernyw found to their cost when they fell foul of the prince's prohibition on encroachment for which they were found guilty and fined £9.[34]

If these examples represent the typical, the routine of day-to-day judicial activity and scale of fines, then atypically, but becoming more common as the northern princes flexed their judicial muscle in the political arena within and beyond the borders of their native Gwynedd, was the fine of £100 imposed on Rhys ap Gruffudd ab Ednyfed Fychan in 1281.[35] His crime had been to behave in a contemptuous and disrespectful manner while attending Prince Llywelyn at his court at Aberffraw. The fact that he was a man of considerable standing and influence in his native Gwynedd underlines the power and omnicompetence of princely justice. Of greater significance is the appeal by Madog ap Gruffudd, who is alleged to have 'come to Prince Llywelyn and offered him 300 marks [£200] to enquire in his court regarding his right to the lands [of Cedewain in Powys] and to do him full justice therein'.[36] This shows the extent to which the law was being used at a higher political and constitutional level by the thirteenth-century princes of Gwynedd in their quest to establish a state or principate which extended far beyond the bounds of their patrimony to embrace the greater part of Wales. Not since the days of great kings of the calibre of Rhodri Mawr (d. 878), Hywel Dda (d. 949) and Gruffudd ap Llywelyn (d. 1063/4), had Wales been united and subject to the authority of a single ruler. Whereas their success in conquering and wielding power within an enlarged domain had been transitory, their would-be successors, the princes of Gwynedd, intended that theirs would not. In order to effect this the northern princes sought to use the law to create a legal basis for the principality and thereby establish firmer roots for their rulership.

Princely rule and the structure of governance in the thirteenth century

The foundations of a greater Venedotian state were laid by Llywelyn ab Iorwerth who, by 1216, had largely succeeded in binding the other lords and princes of Wales into ties of dependence which might have involved the swearing of oaths of homage and fealty. Llywelyn's achievement was lauded by the poet Dafydd Benfras (fl. 1220–60) who hailed his patron 'the great chieftain of fair Wales' and 'the ruler of rulers'.[37] Having obtained recognition of his superior status and claims to overlordship, Llywelyn turned to the task of ensuring that his achievements would endure by securing an undivided succession. This he did by ignoring the divisible, and ultimately divisive, element in the native laws on the inheritance of land between co-heirs, i.e. *cyfran*, and embracing instead English and continental legal custom, i.e. primogeniture. In addition, the prince issued a proclamation which effectively denied illegitimate sons the right to an equal share of an inheritance, landed or otherwise, with legitimate sons. To legitimise this significant change in the law, in 1222 Llywelyn sought and got the support of the king of England, Henry III (d. 1272), the archbishop of Canterbury, Stephen Langton (d. 1228) and the pope himself, Honorius III (d. 1227).[38]

Not content with vague notions of overlordship, Llywelyn ap Gruffudd, actively sought, partly by conquest but more by means of bilateral agreements and legal devices, to territorialise and make real his claims to lordship. This he did by attempting to institutionalise his position as prince of Wales, conceptualise the notion of the state and constitutionalise the relationship between himself and his vassals. With no legal or customary precedent to follow, Llywelyn had literally to create a native monarchy, forge anew the ties that bound the other lords and princes to him and regularise his relationship with them. 'There was therefore', according to A.D. Carr, 'a need to devise an entirely new body of law to govern the prince's relations with other rulers'.[39] It must not be forgotten that these 'other rulers' were themselves princes, or of princely descent, who, less than a century earlier would have considered themselves, and been seen by others, as the equal of Llywelyn but who were now reduced in status to becoming his barons or tenants-in-chief. That Madog ap Gruffudd, a scion of the royal family of Powys, albeit an illegitimate and minor one, had petitioned Llywelyn, as prince of Wales, to hear and determine his claim to the lordship of Cedewain and 'to do him full justice therein', points not only to the growing territorial jurisdiction of the Venedotian ruler, his court and his justice but also to the recognition by others of that fact. Although no native prince can lay claim to a Welsh version of the title accorded Edward I as 'The English Justinian' for 'the importance and permanence of his legislation and the dignity of his position in legal history',[40] they were, nonetheless, more than mere mechanics but engineers who sought not only to bend and shape the law to their own use but also, as per expectation of their subjects like Einion ap Madog, to 'change the laws into better'.[41]

If the twelfth century witnessed a great increase in the nature and scope of administrative acivity, it is in thirteenth that we encounter the trappings of bureaucratic government. True, there was little in the way of administrative specialisation, and institutions like that of the prince's council were not fully developed, but the fact that historians can speak in terms of a 'ministerial elite' serving the princes of Gwynedd, sporting such familiar titles as steward, chancellor, justiciar, chamberlain and treasurer, suggests that there were powerful forces at work making for change. The catalysts for change were the princes themselves since it was largely as a result of their ambition, drive and energy for power, wealth and territory which stimulated those around them to seek new ways to best serve them. Consciously, and sometimes unconsciously, the princes and their 'ministers' imitated, copied and borrowed from their neighbours, the Crown and the Anglo-Norman Marcher lords, so that theirs was a bureaucratic hybrid composed of several layers extending from the centre almost web-like into the localities. Of course, to contemporaries, government must have seemed almost entirely a local affair, and so it was and largely remained, but as in England so too in Wales there was a discernible shift towards concentrating the business of government in the hands of those at the centre. Where that centre was depended very much on the location of the prince around whom government was fashioned and in whom power was concentrated.

At the centre and the hub around which princely governance revolved was the court. Here would be found the prince's domestic servants, military retainers, courtiers and clerics, some of whom served as one of the twenty-four officers of the court. Largely domestic in origin and function, the elaborate hierarchy of court officials depicted in the lawbooks was seriously out of step with the reality of developments in the latter half of the twelfth and thirteenth centuries. By this time the more significant of the court officers (in Gwynedd certainly and possibly elsewhere), namely the steward (*distain*), chamberlain (*gwas ystafell*), possibly the court judge (*ynad llys*) and perhaps even the household priest (*offeiriad teulu*), had evolved sufficiently to take a more active role in government which had itself become a more complex administrative operation. At its heart was the council which, as we have seen, came to assume a more formal role under the auspices of the princes of Gwynedd and at its head was the steward (*senescallus*) who became the prince's chief governmental officer and principal adviser. Here, perhaps as elsewhere in Wales, such as in Deheubarth, northern and southern Powys where the stewardship was as familiar an office as in Gwynedd, the steward assumed powers very nearly approaching those of the prince himself. It is evident from the lawbooks and other contemporary sources that he had the authority to dispense justice, hence the frequency with which he is termed 'justiciar' (*justiciarius*), the power to act in the prince's absence – one of three officers so empowered – and the right to lead troops in war, hence the death in action of the last steward of Gwynedd, Goronwy ap Heilyn in 1283.[42] Moreover, the office appears to have become all but hereditary in that at least two, possibly three, sons of Ednyfed Fychan (d. 1246) – Gruffudd (*fl.* 1240–57), Goronwy (d. 1268) and Tudur (d. 1278) – followed their father as stewards of the princes of Gwynedd.[43] The same nepotistic tendencies were evident in southern Powys where father and son, most notably Gruffudd ap Gwen of Cyfeiliog, served as the justiciar of its last prince Gruffudd ap Gwenwynwyn (d. 1286) (*justiciarius . . . domini Griffini [filii Wenunwen]*).[44]

Despite the all-embracing power of the stewardship and the monopolistic tendencies of its familial incumbents, others managed to carve out a niche for themselves and their offices in the Venedotian administration. The office of chamberlain (*camerarius*), originally the keeper of the 'king's treasure', appears to have retained its role in financial affairs with one of its office-holders, Richard of Mold (*fl.* 1266–70) being described in some quarters as treasurer (*thesaurarius*) of Llywelyn ap Gruffudd.[45] This, and the fact that some years earlier the same Richard was described as vice-chamberlain (*vice-camerarius*), led the late T. Jones Pierce to declare that the volume of fiscal business was such as to warrant the setting up of 'a new department of the prince's government' with a new chief official at its head.[46] While there is no disputing the massive increase in the volume of financial business, current thinking suggests that it might be premature to argue for the creation of a separate department to deal with it. Indeed, much is made by historians, perhaps too much, of the fluidic nature of princely administration and the embryonic state of princely bureaucracy in the thirteenth century. True, there is much we do not know and in an effort to understand the nature of princely government historians have turned, rightly, to comparing the native model with that found in England but even this has its pitfalls. It assumes that the English model was anything but fluidic and embryonic when, in fact, it too was experiencing changes every bit as fundamental as those to be found in the courts of the Welsh princes. According to Marjorie Chibnall, part of the difficulty in describing the changes in the English administration 'arises from the lack of a technical vocabulary, inevitable in a time of growth and change, when new institutions were only half formed and imperfectly defined'.[47]

Yet, Rees Davies has affirmed his belief that 'None of the courts of the native Welsh rulers developed the specialisation of function which was coming to characterise the *curia regis* in England'.[48] But what was the *curia regis*? Walter Map (d. 1210), an intellectual and well-read contemporary, and a man long in the service of the Crown, did not know: 'in the court I exist and of the court I speak, and what the court is, God knows, I know not',[49] which suggests that we may be in danger of being too narrow and dogmatic, and perhaps too patronising in our appreciation of both the *curiae* of the rulers of Gwynedd and the level and sophistication of the administration operating within them. It may be, as David Stephenson believes, 'clear that the majority of the officials associated with the central *curia* were employed in any business for which their talents made them suitable, without any clear differentiation of function',[50] a fact evident in the *curia regis* of England also, but this does not in itself militate against the creation or evolution of specialised departments and functions. Certainly, the princes had a writing office, a 'great' and 'privy' or 'secret' seal to authenticate the ever increasing volume of charters and letters, the means to keep track of its records and a staff of clerks to see to its running. All this, added to the references in contemporary sources to the office of chancellor, even to that of a vice-chancellor (*vice-cancellarius*) in 1277, and one David *cancellarius* (*fl.* 1231–41) in particular, points to the existence of a chancery.[51] However, denied details of its nature and organisation, some historians are naturally shy of admitting to the existence of a properly constituted body, a 'department of state', and rightly so, for even in England 'there was no clearly organised chancery as an office of state, and chancery records did not begin until the end of the twelfth century'.[52]

Preferring to err on the side of caution, the general consensus of opinion favours the existence of a loosely organised secretariat staffed by a number of clerks any one of whom was capable of drawing up and issuing the prince's charters and letters. That said, it is likely that the chancellor alone of the secretariat had access to and possibly the keeping of the great seal, and it was to him that the prince's *diplomata* were brought for sealing. In one instance the absence of his chancellor may have caused Llywelyn ab Iorwerth some embarrassment in that he had to explain that he was 'sealing the letters with his secret seal, because he has not his great seal with him'.[53] Although the charters and writs that expressed the prince's will and pleasure must have originated in the *curia*, it has been suggested that much of the work of a 'chancery' may well have been done elsewhere, most probably in the religious houses dotted around Gwynedd but principally the Cistercian abbeys of Aberconwy and Cymer. Their skills in writing, copying and record-keeping in addition to the existence of fully functioning *scriptoria* (writing rooms) and *armaria* (book stores or libraries), made these houses ideally suited for the tasks required of a chancery. Moreover, their loyalty to the princes of Gwynedd was of long standing which earned for them the trust and patronage of their royal masters.

In fact it is to the church that we must turn if we are to identity these 'chancery' clerks, and others who served the princes, since they were, almost without exception, clerics. Even the post of chancellor is thought to have evolved from the household priest or *offeiriad teulu* which, if so, is in line with developments in England where the early to mid-twelfth-century royal secretariat or 'chancery' was often referred to as the chapel and its staff as *clerici*. According to the native laws, 'all the king's clerks' were to be lodged with the household priest who was evidently early acting as their head.[54] The household priest had the right to 4*d.* for every 'patent seal' issued by the prince but it was incumbent upon him to perform

> three kinds of service . . . in sessions: to delete from the roll every case which has been determined; second is to keep in writing up to judgement every case until it is determined; third is to be ready and unintoxicated at the king's need, to write letters and to read them.[55]

Princely patronage represented a significant element in the church. Much of its wealth in land and privileges in law were as a result of munificent endowments and generous exemptions by kings and princes. Its bishops and abbots, some of whom owed their clerical office to the patronage of princes, were among the wealthiest and most powerful men in the country and much the best educated. In return for their patronage the princes expected their leading clerics to serve them as advisers and administrators, ambassadors and mediators, and if the evidence from thirteenth-century Gwynedd is indicative of their participation in this respect, they did so willingly. Of the seventy-eight men known to have served the northern princes, twenty-seven of them were clerics, two-thirds of whom served as foreign envoys. In peace and war the princes' most enduring support was the church, which sustained the respective royal dynasties by forming lay opinion through sermons and ritual. Liturgical processions, coronation ceremonial and, ultimately, its sanction of the exercise of secular authority by men consecrated into their positions, all contributed to enhancing the prestige of princes. By publicly acknowledging them rulers *dei gratia*, by God's grace, the church also gave a focus to the participant aristocratic group whose own elite status was thus recognised and utilised. Increasingly the nobles were becoming more regularly employed alongside their clerical counterparts as agents and executants of the princely justice.

This is not to suggest that the relationship between prince and church was without problems since there were tensions and pressures here too. Second only to the princes in terms of its wealth and power, the church dominated much of the public life, politics and culture of Wales. Naturally, the princes sought to control the church and they attempted to do so through a combination of patronage and coercion depending on the pliancy of the personnel or institutions involved. In 1276, Llywelyn ap Gruffudd found to his cost that the two most senior clerics in his kingdom, the bishops of Bangor and St Asaph, Anian (d. 1305) and Anian II (d. 1293) respectively, were anything but compliant. They rejected his overlordship and resisted his attempts to impose his will on them which led to a conflict so bitter that they eventually abandoned their dioceses, fled to England and sought the protection of Edward I. In seeking to extend his authority over the church Llywelyn was doing no less and no more than his royal contemporaries across Europe, Edward I included, but it was his misfortune to be pitched against men of intemperate passion, particularly Anian II for whom obstinancy and a refusal to compromise with the prince was regarded as something of a virtue. Llywelyn too must bear his share of the burden of responsibility for the breakdown in relations, for in opting to coerce rather than to conciliate, he missed an opportunity to enlist their aid in governing the country.

In some respects, Llywelyn was the victim of his own success for the size of his dominions after 1263 required some form of delegation and where this did not arise or develop naturally it was imposed. For each of his provinces, methods of administration had to be developed which did not require the prince's presence, which means that the prince was obliged to rely, as never before, on the initiative, loyalty and ability of his officers. Llywelyn's officers in those territories that comprised his domain mainly within, but in some instances beyond the borders of Gwynedd, hitherto merely the agents of his will, came to be entrusted with powers more nearly approaching those of a viceroy. This is indicated by the development of the office of *rhaglaw* or bailiff, displacing that of the *cynghellor*, which led to the gradual restructuring of local administration. Like the *cynghellor*, the *maer* too quietly disappeared to be replaced by the *rhingyll* in an enhanced role, and a host of lesser officials each distinguished by their particular area of responsibility. Thus in the commotes of the Prefeddwlad or Gwynedd Is Conwy, it is not unusual to find the chief administrative officer, the *rhaglaw*, assisted by a local judicial officer, the *ynad* or judge, a *rhingyll* or chief sergeant and several *ceisiaid* (sergeants of the peace). Nor should we forget the constables of the prince's castles – Deganwy and Ewloe – who saw to the region's defence and whose general military needs impacted on the local administration. In addition, minor officials were appointed to collect revenues, some quite specialised such as the *amobrwr*, collector of the virginity-fines, while others saw to the woods and wastes.

These changes were not simply a result of confidence and convenience but of necessity and they may be seen as the culmination of a long process of development in the methods and structure of princely government. This is not to suggest that the system found in the Perfeddwlad was universally applied throughout Llywelyn's dominions: in some areas no doubt an older system still operated while in others, particularly those districts beyond the borders of Gwynedd where local custom and influence prevailed, different methods were adopted. For example, in his lordships of Maelienydd, Elfael, Gwrtheyrnion and Brecon princely authority was vested in bailiffs, but in Builth power was entrusted to the constable of the castle. Perhaps the most interesting of Llywelyn's attempts at restructuring his administration in those territories that lay beyond his patrimony is the appointment in 1276 of a *senescallus de Ultra Berrwyn*. Would that we had more information on the powers and duties of this stewardship for it suggests that Llywelyn was keen to establish an infrastructure of authority which might better promote the cohesion that his 'cobbled together' principality so seriously lacked. Certainly, there is evidence to suggest that he was attempting to establish a level of administration which answered directly to him and staff it with officials who were his appointees. In this way they might be removed and replaced without disturbing too much the administration of the locality. Of course, a system of 'removable' officials is very sophisticated and requires the necessary machinery for its supervision, but that there was such a system operating is suggested by a letter written sometime between 1267 and 1276 by Rhys ap Gruffudd, Llywelyn's bailiff of

Builth, in which he 'Acknowledges receipt of Llywelyn's mandate, addressed to him and the rest of Llywelyn's bailiffs, viz. the bailiffs of Brecon, Elfael and Gwrtheyrnion [and] asks Llywelyn for instructions for himself and Llywelyn's other bailiffs what they are to do'.[56]

This does not mean that the princes of Gwynedd had departed entirely from the system of administration that operated by delegating royal authority to prominent landholders in the localities in which they dwelt. It made sense to invest those who disposed of economic power, had jurisdiction over their vassals and tenants, and had great influence in the regions where they held their estates. However, these were men not easily removed from office and although it was hoped to bind them into a closer, and mutually beneficial, union, it was not always possible to trust them. Indeed, if the evidence from Gwynedd is typical then it seems the princes tended to rely on the service of a small group of powerful families, perhaps no more than half a dozen in north Wales, which suggests that there was little scope for reward or largesse for those outside this inner circle. This may have been due to a lack of material resources or else a deliberate policy for the better management of a restricted circle of servants. The greatest and most talented of these servants wielded substantial power, men like Ednyfed Fychan (d. 1246) who, as *distain* or seneschal of Gwynedd was, simultaneously, the prince's leading judge, chief financial agent and chief executive officer. The scope for further development in the government and administration of native Wales was ended with the death in 1282 of Llywelyn ap Gruffudd but that it had the potential to match that found elsewhere in continental Europe cannot be doubted.

A prince's greatest achievement was not that he might create a large dominion but that he should introduce to it the art of government. There can be no government without the control of men, and without a regular standing army, other than the *teulu*, that control came by means of the church and social bonds – kindred groups and local community chains of obligation. By overlaying these with a network of lordship and vassalage the prince was attempting to institutionalise his 'office' and thereby become the most important element in the government of the realm. Apart from the prince himself, there were two main foci of power: the administration, centring on the council, and the royal household or court. Both were gradually institutionalised and territorialised so that a prince's power and authority were widened and made real to those whom it employed and professed to govern. The reality of that rule is made manifest in a comment by Gerald of Wales that, 'rumour does in truth fly on wings to kings and princes, from whom scarce anything may be hid, notable events are ever quick to reach them'.[57]

Notes

1. R.R. Davies, *Wales*, 12.
2. J. Vendryes, 'Le poème du Livre Noir sur Hywel ap Gronw', *Etudes Celtiques*, iv (1948), 275–300.
3. *Mediaeval Prince*, 61; *Historia Gruffudd vab Kenan*, ed. D. Simon Evans (Cardiff, 1971), 8; *History of Gruffudd ap Cynan (1054–1137)*, ed. and trans. A. Jones (Manchester, 1910), 115.
4. *Mediaeval Prince*, 81.
5. *Journey & Description*, 203.
6. *BT. RBH*, 179.
7. *BT. Pen.*, 83; *BT. RBH*, 189; *B. Saes.*, 201.
8. G.R.J. Jones, 'The Defences of Gwynedd in the Thirteenth Century', *Transactions of the Caernarfonshire History Society*, 30 (1969), 29–43.
9. T. Jones Pierce, 'Medieval Cardiganshire – A Study in Social Origins', ch. IX in *Medieval Welsh Society*, 309–27.
10. R.A. Dodgshon, 'Early Society and Economy', in *The Cardiganshire County History*, ed. J.L. Davies and D.P. Kirby, (Cardiff, 1994), I, 344–56.
11. R.R. Davies, op. cit., pp. 257–8. For their location, see W. Rees, *South Wales and the Border in the Fourteenth Century* (Four Sheets, Ordnance Survey, 1932).
12. *Medieval Welsh Society*, 319.
13. *The Law of Hywel Dda*, ed. and trans. D. Jenkins (Llandusyl, 1990), 124.
14. *Mediaeval Prince*, 82–3.
15. Ibid.
16. For a full discussion of the income available to, and expenditure of, Llywelyn ap Gruffudd, see J.B. Smith, *Llywelyn ap Gruffudd*, 248–54.
17. *BT. Pen.*, 75.
18. *Mediaeval Prince*, 59.
19. *BT. Pen.*, 60.
20. Ibid., 85.
21. Ibid.
22. *Journey & Description*, 202.
23. D. Stephenson, *The Governance of Gwynedd*, 7.
24. Ibid., 8.
25. *Calendar of Various Chancery Rolls: Supplementary Close Rolls, Welsh Rolls, Scutage Rolls 1277–1326* (London, 1912), 199.
26. H. Pryce, *Native Law and the Church in Medieval Wales* (Oxford, 1993), 242.
27. *The Law of Hywel Dda*, 98, 164, 165.
28. *C. Chanc. R., Various*, 199–200.
29. D. Stephenson, *The Governance of Gwynedd*, 7.
30. Ibid., 85.
31. Ibid., 84–5.
32. Ibid., 84.
33. *C. Chanc. R., Various*, 200.
34. D. Stephenson, *The Governance of Gwynedd*, 85.
35. *Litt. Wallie*, 31.
36. *The Welsh Assize Roll 1277–84*, ed. J. Conway Davies (Cardiff, 1940), 254.

37. *Gwaith Dafydd Benfras ac Eraill o Feirdd hanner Cyntaf y Drydedd ganrif ar Ddeg*, ed. N.G. Costigan (Cardiff, 1995), 33.
38. H. Pryce, *Native Law and the Church*, 86.
39. A.D. Carr, *Medieval Wales*, 66.
40. M. Prestwich, *Edward I*, 267.
41. *C. Chanc. R., Various*, 203.
42. A.D. Carr, *Medieval Wales*, 68.
43. D. Stephenson, *The Governance of Gwynedd*, 213, 214–15, 218–21.
44. *Litt. Wallie*, 109–10.
45. D. Stephenson, *The Governance of Gwynedd*, 227.
46. *Medieval Welsh Society*, 33.
47. M. Chibnall, *Anglo-Norman England 1066–1166* (Oxford, 1986), 121.
48. R.R. Davies, *Wales*, 254.
49. Walter Map, *De Nugis Curialium*, 3.
50. D. Stephenson, *The Governance of Gwynedd*, 24.
51. Ibid., 223.
52. M. Chibnall, *Anglo-Norman England*, 133.
53. D.H. Williams, *Welsh History through Seals* (Cardiff, 1982), 19.
54. J.G. Edwards, 'The Royal Household and the Welsh Lawbooks', *TRHS*, 5th series, XIII (1963), 172.
55. *The Law of Hywel Dda*, 12.
56. *Cal. Anc. Corr.*, 53–4
57. *Autobiog.*, 57.

chapter five

CONQUEST AND CONSOLIDATION: THE PRINCES AS WARRIORS

Gruffudd, the foremost warrior, advanced to battle like a hero and a lion, without respite scattering his opponents with his gleaming sword.[1]

In a society where the warrior elite and the ethics of war were held in high regard, courage, military leadership and personal prowess in arms, such as displayed by Gruffudd ap Cynan (d. 1137), were attributes of kingship most commonly praised by contemporaries in chronicle, verse and song. The *Gogynfeirdd* regale us with tales of the Achillean exploits of their patrons, the king-princes of Wales, who are to be found, almost without exception, in the midst of battle leading their men by heroic example. Typical are the extracts from the poems of Cynddelw Brydydd Mawr (d.*c.* 1200) addressed to Owain Gwynedd (d. 1170):

> *I praise a patron high-hearted in strife,*
> *Wolf of warfare, challenging, charging . . .*
> *Sword-blade in hand and hand hewing heads*

and to Owain Fychan of Powys (d. 1187):

> *Leading his host mid the uproar of battle,*
> *A roar as of torrents falling into the full sea.*[2]

At their passing, be it in battle or bed, their greatness as kings or princes was oftentimes measured by their bravery and success in the field. Thus could the *Brut* exalt the Lord Rhys (d. 1197) in death for being in life 'warlike against the strong', an 'attacker in battles' and an 'overthrower of hosts', in fact, 'a second Achilles for the might of his breast bone'.[3]

The princes of Wales were first and foremost warriors. They stood at the apex of an aristocratic class whose shared culture was suffused with the values of a warrior elite. They were men for whom the call to arms and the blood and fury of battle was a way of life inculcated almost from birth. From an early age they were trained to master the skills of the sword, the bow and the lance, instructed in the principles of good horsemanship and taught the virtues of killing with their own hand their enemies in close combat. They were fed a diet of war stories, war poems and war songs, and, as befitting an heroic society, they were imbibed with the ethics of honourable war, the most famous expression of which is to be found in the stanzas of the poem *Y Gododdin*. Attributed to Aneirin, copied and preserved in a mid-thirteenth-century manuscript, the *Gododdin* has been described as a 'classic, and the only full length exposition of the ideals of the Heroic Age in Welsh Literature'.[4] It is indicative of an earlier tradition which dates in part from the ninth century though its theme is older still, since it celebrates the participation of warriors in the expedition to and subsequent battle at *Catraeth* (Catterick), thought to have been fought in the late sixth or early seventh century. The poem is full of heroic images and it exemplifies perfectly the ideals to which the warrior elite aspired. It was for fame and glory that Nai son of Nwython

> . . . *slew a great host to win reputation, the son of Nwython slew a hundred princes wearing gold torques so that he might be celebrated.*[5]

It was praise for his courage and fighting qualities that spurred Madog on.

> *Shattered was the front of his shield when he heard the battle-cry;*
> *He showed no mercy to those whom he pursued.*
> *He did not withdraw from the battle until blood flowed.*
> *Like rushes he cut men down. He did not flee.*[6]

It was for immortality that Tudfwlch gave his life on the field of battle.

> *His valour will live long*
> *And his memory among his handsome company.*[7]

Its antiquity notwithstanding, the themes expounded by the poet of personal valour and distinguished conduct in the face of the enemy was as real and as meaningful to the warrior-princes of the eleventh, twelfth and thirteenth centuries as it had been to their forebears. That honour and fame were regarded in tangible terms may be witnessed by the precepts of Welsh law which held that a man's honour had its price or *wynebwerth*.[8] It follows that in a society which laid stress on the ideals of heroism and courage, to deprive a man of his honour and fame was tantamount to destroying him since death was much preferred to suffering such ignomy. Nor can this be dismissed simply as literary convention on the part of the poets, some of whom, like Meilyr Brydydd (d.*c.* 1137) and Dafydd Benfras (k.*c.* 1258) were themselves warriors, the latter having been slain in battle.[9] With this in mind, we might better appreciate why much of the poetry written during this period was imbued with a distinctly militaristic spirit, and why it was the wont of all true warriors to die gloriously on the field of battle.

It is an image of the Welsh, as a war-hungry people, that impressed itself on other contemporary writers, most notably Gerald of Wales (d. 1223) who states quite emphatically that, 'In peace they dream of war and prepare themselves for battle . . . their only preoccupation is military training', indeed 'they esteem it a disgrace to die in bed, but an honour to be killed in battle'.[10] His opinion is shared by Walter Map (d.*c*. 1210) who speaks of 'my compatriots the Welsh' as 'warlike and skilled in arms'[11] but whose chief glory was in

> . . . plunder and theft, and they are so fond of both that it is a reproach to a son that his father should have died without a wound. For which reason few grow grey. There is a proverb there 'Dead youth or poor old man' meaning that everyone should brave death early rather than beg when he is old.[12]

Nor are these simply the biased opinions of men, though not wholly Welsh themselves, who were so well acquainted with the land and people of their birth as to lack the discrimination necessary to pass such judgements. English and French chroniclers from as far afield as St Albans in Hertfordshire and Mont Saint-Michel in Normandy (Mathew Paris and Robert of Torigny, respectively, to name but two) were equally awed, and at times disgusted, by the warlike character of the Welsh. Whether their impressions were formed by personal contact or word of mouth is immaterial, it is sufficiently noteworthy that news of the combative nature of the Welsh had been bruited abroad. Even the Byzantine emperor, Manuel Comnenus of Constantinople, had knowledge of the Welsh, courtesy of the Angevin king of England, Henry II (d. 1189), who shared his experience of fighting them in a letter sent east in *c*. 1176. In it he stated that

> In one part of the island [of Britain] there is a race of people called the Welsh who are so brave and untamed that, though unarmed themselves, they will do battle with fully armed opponents.[13]

It is impossible to assess the merits or otherwise of the fighting skills of individual princes since the evidence does not permit such detailed pictures to be drawn, but whether they were all as successful or as great as the native *literati* would have us believe is another matter. Certainly, Gruffudd (d. 1201), son and heir of the Lord Rhys of Deheubarth, seems hardly to have distinguished himself in battle, his solitary triumph the capture of Cilgerran castle in 1199, which may help to explain why no contemporary elegy to him survives. Moreover, he died relatively young, possibly early to mid-forties, and in bed 'without a wound' about his body. Even the Deheubarth-biased *Brut* could say of him only that he was a 'wise, prudent man', whereas his brother Maelgwn (d. 1231), though something of a hot-head, was praised for being 'in war a victor' and 'harsh towards his enemies' whom he pursued 'like a lion's whelp roaring'; unsurprisingly perhaps, 'all his neighbours dreaded him'.[14] Clearly, wisdom and prudence, though valued, were next to worthless without the martial characteristics of fearlessness and courage.

To measure a man's worth in this way must have put enormous pressure on those born to noble or royal households to live up to this glory-driven militaristic ideal. For some like Maredudd (d. 1227), son of the Lord Rhys, whose instincts were those of a cleric rather than those of a warrior, the life of a soldier held little appeal which, no doubt, impelled him towards a career in the church, and virtual oblivion. His modest share of the family patrimony and his death and burial alone were considered worthy of record.[15] However, for those princes who responded with enthusiasm to their militaristic upbringing, much was expected of them by men, the poets and annalists, the 'paparazzi' of their day, who analysed, quantified, eulogised or demonised their every action. Reputations could be made or lost, or never made at all, for there were princes whom the poets and annalists all but ignore. It is, moreover, an ignorance founded on more than simply 'lost' poems or annalistic bias towards a dynasty or individual. Cynwrig (d. 1237), son of the Lord Rhys, was a member of a dynasty well provided for in terms of contemporary annalistic and poetic journalism, but apart from the notice of his death and having served his brother in a military capacity, his literate countrymen are all but silent on the details of his long life.[16] Yet Cynwrig was sufficiently charismatic to attract the attention of Gerald of Wales who met him out hunting while he journeyed around Wales in 1188. Gerald was impressed by his 'natural dignity' and thought him a young 'man adorned with nature', which suggests he possessed a physique fitted for the rigours of war.[17] Here was a young man thought most likely to succeed; that he did not, at least to the satisfaction of his critics, suggests that either he had failed to distinguish himself in battle or he may simply have lacked the ambition or the independence of mind and deed to command the attention of his countrymen. Clearly, contemporaries were concerned only with winners, princes who fitted their ideal of the consummate warrior, and for them the eulogists would ensure a fitting and lasting memorial.

True to the eulogistic tradition of contemporary native prose, the poets and chroniclers magnified and exaggerated their patrons' personal contribution to the success of battles. The battle of Coed Ysbwys in 1094 may be instanced as an example:

and then the French [Normans] led hosts into Gwynedd; and Cadwgan ap Bleddyn met them and attacked and defeated them, and drove them to flight and slew them, and overthrew and subdued them with great slaughter.[18]

The chronicler hardly admits to the existence of the corps of noble warriors that must have assisted in Cadwgan's military triumph. Such is the contemporary *littérateur's* preoccupation with all things royal, that rarely are we permitted the privilege of putting names to the 'faceless military force'[19] which, by the equal skill and dedication of its members to the profession of arms, enabled the likes of Prince Cadwgan (d. 1111) to claim outstanding victories. On the other hand, to impugn the integrity of the chronicler in this respect, and quite possibly in this instance, might be to misinterpret the thrust of his message which was also to highlight the superior generalship of Cadwgan. Much as we today associate military successes with the names of, and the tactics employed by, the commanding generals, so too did the medieval poets and annalists attribute victory to the princely generals of their day. This serves to illustrate the crucial role played by the princes as commanders and strategists rather than simply as participating soldiers. They were keenly aware that their power, perhaps their very survival, relied on military might which, in turn, depended as much on their own personal courage and prowess as a warrior as on their abilities to inspire and command others. The princes were war-leaders, and as such, their acknowledged generalship notwithstanding, they were expected to be 'the foremost warriors' leading their troops from the front rather than urging them on from the back. It is this authority to lead and power to command which in part separates them from the nobility.

Reward, profit and plunder

If the chroniclers and poets were a little slow to recognise and reward the heroic deeds of others, not so the princes. This can clearly be evidenced in the compositions of the poet-princes Hywel ab Owain Gwynedd (d. 1170) and Owain Cyfeiliog of Powys (d. 1197), both of whom, but especially the latter, praise their noble comrades in arms. *Hirlas Owain*, translated as *Owain's Long Blue Drinking Horn*, is a model of contemporary war poetry much influenced by the *Gododdin* with stock epithets aplenty.[20] But the essence of its composition is more than merely conventional praise rhetoric, it is suggestive of a deeper motive, of a prince's tribute to and acknowledgement of the fighting skills of his warrior nobility, without whose courage and loyalty his rulership would be less than it is. By virtue of their noble blood these 'fellows in feast and fight',[21] differed hardly at all from their royal masters in terms of their upbringing, lifestyle, culture and delight in martial pursuits. Although this was a source of social cohesion, the exclusivity of an elite, it could also be a force for disruption. These were men upon whom the princes relied to fight for them, but they were equally capable of fighting against them, and frequently did. The successful princes were those able to harness this restless and aggressive energy and turn it to their advantage, but for this they required a compelling motive and a diverting purpose.

Praise was one thing, reward another, and if war was the source of honour and glory it was also the source of plunder and profit. Thus in 1056 could the *Brut* equate Gruffudd ap Llywelyn's (k. 1063/4) success in taking 'vast spoil' from his enemies with returning 'home eminently worthy'.[22] What could not be taken or carried was usually damaged or destroyed, and the devastation wrought in an opponent's territory could be considerable. In some instances the reason for such raids was quite simply revenge, a fact which explains why, in 1110, Owain and Madog, sons of Cadwgan ap Bleddyn, reacted so savagely to an unprovoked attack by the men of Meirionydd that they 'ravaged the land, burnt the houses and the corn and killed the stock, as much as they found', but significantly, 'without taking aught with them'.[23] However, this was the exception rather than the rule; the success of princes was measured as much by the glory attached to the expedition as by the spoil they had amassed and distributed.

The native lawbooks make clear what constituted the spoils of war and what the prince and his warriors could expect by way of recompence for their efforts in the field. As one might expect of an agriculturally based society whose economic well-being was largely dependent on pastoral farming, plundered livestock constituted by far the most important part of the spoil. After taking his customary third-share of the plunder – the rest was divided among his surviving warriors – the prince was obliged to reward his senior court officials; the *distain* or steward and chief justice received a bullock each, while the *pencerdd* could expect either a cow or an ox.[24] Until the gradual adoption of a moneyed economy, livestock was useful as a means of defining currency. It was in terms of cattle that the anonymous biographer of Gruffudd ap Cynan judged the success or failure of William Rufus's campaign in north Wales in 1095: 'He [King William] did not obtain any kind of profit or gain, except for one cow'.[25] In 1121, ten thousand head of cattle was the tribute exacted by King Henry I from the ruler of Powys, Maredudd ap Bleddyn (d. 1132), as the price of peace.[26] The delivery of two thousand head of cattle was the ransom agreed between Cadwaladr, a prince of Gwynedd, and his Irish captors in 1144. A century later the Welsh economy had changed to the extent that King Henry III could demand of his Welsh vassals tribute or fines in either cash or kind. Hence it was in terms of cattle, horses and money in equal parts, that in 1241 Senana intended to pay the king for the release of her imprisoned husband Gruffudd ap Llywelyn (d. 1244).[27]

Not only cattle, but horses too were highly prized, and in one raid across the border in 1102 the Welsh took both in equal measure.[28] In common with the wider community of European nobility, the Welsh equated horseback travel with status, and the possession of a warhorse or *destrier* as being an especial privilege. Warhorses were specially bred and trained and, consequently, were very expensive. When the Crown required its officers to supply the royal army with horses for the expedition to Ireland in 1171 they were instructed to pay the going rate of 40s. (£2) per steed.[29] Inevitably, the value and quality of each warhorse could vary considerably, but it seems that the demand for them was such that men like the abbot of Jumièges in Normandy had little difficulty in finding some prepared to pay anything between ten and fifteen times what the English Crown was willing to pay.[30] Clearly, purchasers and plunderers alike needed to use their discretion when selecting their mounts which may explain why, after netting a considerable number of horses from their successful campaign in Norman-held Ceredigion in 1136, Owain and Cadwaladr, sons of the Gruffudd ap Cynan, ruler of Gwynedd, chose to 'ham-string' (*trychu*) some while 'others were carried off into captivity'.[31] Doubtless, some of these horses were added to their father's already impressive stud, the existence of which is evinced in the poetry of Meilyr Brydydd. According to the poet, Gruffudd was the proud owner of 'a glorious line of horses' and his bounty was such that Meilyr was permitted the privilege of having his 'choice from among the war-horses of the yard of his court'.[32] Indeed, Meilyr may not have been far short of the truth when he sang of his royal master defending 'his right with one thousand horsemen'.[33] Whereas generally the wealth and status of a man was determined by the number of cattle in his possession, his honour was increasingly measured more in terms of the number and quality of the horses he owned.

If the theft of horses was becoming ever more popular, so too was the acquisition of armour and other 'warlike apparel'. The Welsh had the Normans to thank for this alternative source of plunder since it was the Norman knights with their hauberks of mail, helmets, kite shields and other forms of body armour together with their well-fashioned weaponry, that so impressed the native nobility. Initially lacking the technological skill to match the Normans in the quality of either weapons or 'warlike apparel', the Welsh found plunder a less expensive if not more convenient means of acquiring the latest military hardware. As is generally recognised, the cost of equipping a man 'from head to foot' for war was quite considerable.[34] It has been estimated that the time taken for an experienced metalsmith to make a hauberk ('not one of the finest quality but with rings merely butted as opposed to rivetted') and sword, perhaps two of the most expensive items of hardware, was in the region of 140 and 200 hours of work, respectively.[35] Add to this the cost of obtaining and maintaining a warhorse and it becomes clear that the business of war was beyond the means of all but the very rich. Little wonder that Owain and Cadwaladr returned from their successful expedition to Ceredigion 'happily rejoicing', being heavily laden with 'costly rainment and armour'.[36] Nor was this plunder entirely the result of sacking strongholds for, as the chronicler makes plain, much of the arms and armour taken north by the sons of Gruffudd ap Cynan came from the reported three thousand Anglo-Norman and Fleming dead that littered the battlefield at Crug Mawr and in the two-mile stretch of open country between it and the perceived safety, from the point of view of the routed Normans, of the town of Cardigan. To veterans of medieval warfare, stripping the dead was not scorned or considered particularly ghoulish, nor was it a peculiarly Welsh trait (despite what some fifteenth-century English chroniclers would have us believe), as the Bayeux Tapestry well illustrates.

The Bayeux Tapestry's graphic depiction of the stripping of the dead, even before the battle was won, was very much the routine of war and an indication of the fact that to the victor the spoils, whenever and wherever they might be found. To Owain and Cadwaladr, this included the living as well as the plunder of the dead, and their triumphal return to the court of their aged-father, possibly at Aberffraw, has a Roman quality about it, accompanied as they were by 'an exceeding great number of captives',[37] the best of whom may have been publicly paraded to magnify the heroic exploits of their conquerors. The taking of captives had been long-practised by the Welsh in their quest for prestige and additional sources of income, and the profits raised from the captives' ransom would no doubt have been used partly to offset the costs of the campaign and to fund future sorties. So profitable was it (for example, in 1229 William de Braose is alleged to have paid his captor, Llywelyn ab Iorwerth of Gwynedd, the sum of £2,000 for his realease) that soon noblemen other than princes were indulging in the practice of what was becoming little more than kidnapping. There was no glory or heroism involved in Hywel ab Adda's raid on Neath in 1220 (a man otherwise unknown to the eulogy-prone poets) in which several people returning from the town's fair were captured and sent to his brother 'in Wales' (presumably *pura Wallia*) to be ransomed.[38]

On the other hand, hostage-taking for political rather than purely financial purposes was very much a matter for kings and princes. It was a practice well used by English kings to extract from their Celtic adversaries, be they Welsh, Irish or Scottish, promises (at the very least) of good behaviour or, depending on the ambition of the individual monarch, oaths of allegiance. Henry II (d. 1189) was particularly active in this respect, forcing both Rhys ap Gruffudd, prince of Deheubarth (d. 1197) and his counterpart from the north, Owain Gwynedd (d. 1170), to part with their sons. Although the princes had reason to feel aggrieved at the treatment their hostage-sons received at the hands of a notoriously bad-tempered king, three of the five princelings held were blinded in 1165, they had little cause to complain of a practice in which they were active participants. In 1171, Rhys ap Gruffudd defeated his neighbour Owain Cyfeiliog then 'forced him to submit to him, and took seven hostages from him'.[39] Nor was the policy of hostage-taking a respector of family ties: Owain was Rhys's son-in-law, a fact which seemed to make not the slightest difference. Hostages were the currency of diplomacy and their taking, in large part, was intended to ensure a measure of political compliance. In the event of promises being broken the life of each hostage lay very much at the mercy of those to whom they had been entrusted.

War and politics

The taking of hostages as opposed to captives for ransom marked but one aspect of a general shift towards a more sophisticated method of waging war. War was becoming more a matter of politics in conjunction with, rather than, economics or indeed ethics. The princes came to realise that war for plunder, in effect asset stripping, was transient, whereas war for territory, the taking over of assets in situ, was more enduring. Both brought profit in their wake but the latter was more substantial and in the long term would augment the victor with greater wealth, power and prestige. The evidence from the chroniclers leaves us in little doubt that in the three centuries after the coming of the Normans, the king-princes of Wales gradually abandoned war primarily as a means of plunder and destruction in favour of combat for the acquisition and consolidation of territory. It is an evolutionary feature echoed in later redactions of the Welsh laws which stated emphatically that 'chattels are perishable [but] land is eternal'.[40] This is not to say that destructive raids ceased or that war was any less glorious in the thirteenth century than it had been in the eleventh; on the contrary, the bards were as fulsome in their praise as ever but they sang of captured castles and annexed lordships as opposed simply to cattle, horses and armour. Hence when Dafydd ab Owain Gwynedd (d. 1203) 'ravaged Tegeingl' in 1165 and 'removed the people and their cattle with him into Dyffryn Clwyd', it was not simply an old-style raid for plunder but, significantly, a prelude to his annexing the district.[41] Once occupation had been effected, assisted perhaps by means of a castle or two, the victorious ruler set about exploiting his new territory by exacting tribute in kind and cash. The more secure the conquest, the more generous and enlightened the conqueror even to the extent of recruiting members of the defeated ruler's *teulu* or elite household troop and adding them to his own.

This gradual change in the purpose of if not the motive for war may be gauged by comparing the methods adopted by successive princes of Gwynedd towards their foes, in this instance the rulers of Arwystli, Cyfeiliog and Powys, the territories of whom bordered their own. Determined to avenge himself on Trahearn ap Caradog (k. 1081) of Arwystli and Meilyr ap Rhiwallon (k. 1081) of Powys for opposing him at the battle of Mynydd Carn in 1081, Gruffudd ap Cynan (d. 1137),

> marched towards Arwystli and destroyed and killed its people; he burned its houses, and took its women and maidens captive. Thus did he pay like for like to Trahearn. Then he proceeded to Powys, where he straightway displayed his cruelty to his adversaries according to the manner of a victor; and he spared not even the churches. After he had thus killed his enemies and destroyed their land completely, he returned to his own proper possession and patrimony to rule.[42]

When faced by a similar threat to his authority from the ruler of Cyfeiliog in 1167, Gruffudd ap Cynan's son, Owain Gwynedd (d. 1170), took a very different approach. He, together with his ally the prince of Deheubarth, the Lord Rhys ap Gruffudd (d. 1197), invaded the lordship but stopped well short of its destruction. After ejecting its ruler Owain Cyfeiliog,

> they took Caereinion from him and gave it to Owain Fychan ap Madog ap Maredudd. After that they took Tafolwern, and that was given to the Lord Rhys . . .[43]

Clearly, occupation rather than destruction was the preferred policy. It provided Owain Gwynedd with the means of distributing the 'spoil', albeit on a more massive scale than had hitherto been usual, and, more importantly, the opportunity to openly display and formally exercise his superiority over his allies, themselves princley rulers of substantial territories. It was a lesson ably learnt by the Lord Rhys for whom, in the first sixteen years of his rulership of Deheubarth (1155–71), the chief instruments of political pressure and military mastery had been raids of devastation and plunder. After 1171, construction rather than destruction characterised his military policy – the castle – while treaties, accords and promises of fidelity, backed up by taking the odd hostage or two, marked his political dealings with Norman and native alike. Increasingly, the cut-and-thrust of debate was taking its place next to that of the sword, and although diplomatic pressure could not replace the actuality of war, it added a new dimension to the military dynamic that characterised the war policies of the warrior princes. It was by means of coercive diplomacy rather than military conquest that, in 1263, Llywelyn ap Gruffudd (k. 1282) of Gwynedd came to control southern Powys by forcing its ruler, Gruffudd ap Gwenwynwyn (d. 1286), to acknowledge his overlordship. When, eleven years later in 1274, Gruffudd attempted to cast off his allegiance to Llywelyn, only then did the latter resort to arms to expel his erstwhile vassal and effect the formal conquest of his territory. This illustrates perfectly well that the princes of the late twelfth and thirteenth century may have been more statesmanlike in their demeanour but at heart they were still warriors prepared to field and lead an army if all else failed.

Military organisation

If plunder, profit, conquest, territorial acquisition and glory were the driving forces for war, the army was its engine. The medieval army existed on many levels, and its composition and purpose varied across both time and place and, of course, between rulers depending on the military resources available to them. At its core, however, the hub around which Welsh military life revolved, was the *teulu*. A term that defies simple definition, the *teulu* (literally, family) has been variously described as a royal bodyguard or household troop, even 'a *comitatus*-like band of warrior-retainers',[44] but the most favoured and oft-quoted translation is that of the war-band. The fact that none is entirely satisfactory in defining the *teulu* has led historians into comparisons with the military households or *familia* of Anglo-Norman lords and kings.

At their simplest, the words *teulu* and *familia* bear comparison on a linguistic level and there is much to commend the institutions in terms of their noble composition, military organisation and *raison d'être*. It is known that the household troop or *familia regis* of Henry I (1100–35) was composed mainly of well-trained and well-equipped mounted mercenaries who might be deployed anywhere within the Anglo-Norman *regnum*. Henry's household knights were of noble origin, often the youthful, landless younger sons of established landholding families, many of whom were themselves vassals of the Anglo-Norman kings and who were bound to serve their royal masters in the general feudal levy. In addition to these 'regular' household troops drawn mainly from territories under his rulership and from families who owed him allegiance, Henry I also employed mercenaries, both cavalry and footsoldiers, from elsewhere, usually Brittany and Flanders, who were hired for limited periods and for specific campaigns. This is not to suggest that the twelfth-century *familia regis* was made up entirely of mercenaries to the exclusion of the king's vassals who served out of feudal duty rather than for wages.[45] This is indicated by Henry II's willingness to swell the size of his *familia* with an almost equal number of vassals as mercenaries in his campaign against the Welsh princes in 1165.[46] To accommodate and pay for his *familia*, Henry II billeted them in his castles so that they earned their keep even in times of peace by garrison or 'castle guard' duties, and he frequently adjusted their number to suit the prevailing political and military situation.

Apart from the *familia regis*, aspiring knights might find employment in the households of the aristocracy which varied in size and composition according to the status, wealth and influence of the individual lords concerned. To distinguish the military arm of the households or *familia* of these Anglo-Norman lords, contemporaries employed a variety of descriptive terms such as *comitivae* or *mesnie*, even occasionally *milites strenui*, which also serve as an additional distinction between baronial and royal households during this period. When called upon to serve his king in war, the Anglo-Norman baron would be accompanied by his *mesnie* or, occasionally, they might go in his place. When peace prevailed, the baronial *mesnie* would be scaled down to reduce cost though sufficient numbers of knights would be retained to enforce lordship and maintain public dignity. No such luxury was afforded those barons who owned land in Wales where the hard-bitten professional knights of the *mesnie* were on a constant war-footing, ready at a moment's notice to defend the life of their lord and his land and, no doubt, their own.

Every prince had his *teulu* or *familia principis* which in Welsh law was regarded as one of the three indispensable necessities of royal status (the others being his priest and court justice).[47] The primary function of the *teulu* was the protection of its royal master, about whom it was to be found at all times and without whom it would cease to exist. It was a permanent military retinue which was, according to David Crouch, 'all that stood between a Welsh prince and death and defiance, and all too frequently failed to prevent both'.[48] The truth of this statement is plainly illustrated by the cruel fate that befell Rhys ab Owain of Deheubarth who, after the destruction of his *teulu* in the battle of Pwllgwdig in 1078, was hunted 'like a wounded frightened stag' before being killed.[49] However, the *teulu* was more than simply a royal bodyguard, it was an elite fighting force of professional soldiers who, from the twelfth century, were every bit as well trained and well equipped as their Anglo-Norman counterparts. As early as 1136 the native chroniclers are able to speak in terms of mailed or armoured horsemen serving the princes of Deheubarth and Gwynedd which strongly suggests that the *teulu* consisted, for the most part, of mounted troops which could be deployed anywhere within or without the *principatum*, and frequently was.[50] Gerald of Wales admits as much when he stressed that 'their leaders ride into battle on swift mettlesome horses which are bred locally'.[51] It was this mobility which, in the space of a few months in 1153, enabled the Lord Rhys and his 'great host of horsemen', to 'subdue' their northern compatriots in Penweddig, later ejecting them from Ceredigion, move south to 'breach' the Fleming-held castle of Tenby in Pembrokeshire, turn east against the Anglo-Normans of Ystrad Cyngen or St Clear's (all this before the end of April), thereafter to make for the native-held castle of Aberafan which was destroyed, and finally 'after killing many and burning houses' and carrying off 'vast booty', they wheeled north to defeat in battle the Welshmen of Cyfeiliog thence to 'ravage' the lordship.[52]

If contemporary estimates are to be relied on, and in the absence of other evidence we are in no position to dispute them, the twelfth-century princes had at their command a *teulu* of around 120 or 140 men.[53] However, in view of the fact that these men were a permanent force which had to be accommodated on the prince's demesne, and supplied and paid for out of the prince's personal resources, in some cases it is probably an overestimate of what many rulers could afford to maintain. Indeed, it is not known whether this represents the strength of a prince's military household during peace and war or merely when on a war-footing. Certainly, only the princely households of Deheubarth and Gwynedd, and before its partition in 1160, Powys, could reasonably be expected to maintain such a force, and in times of crisis probably more, but their lesser brethren, the princelings of the upland regions of Gwent and Glamorgan and those settled precariously in the Middle March, could not. By the thirteenth century this figure should perhaps be regarded as a median rather than as an absolute since it is fair to say that as the resources available to the princes of Gwynedd increased so did the size of their *teulu*. Of course, the households of Welsh princes, even those as powerful as the princes of thirteenth-century Gwynedd, could never hope to match the *familia regis* of English kings, which during the reign of Edward I (d. 1307) numbered over eight hundred.[54]

On the other hand, the fact that the more powerful Anglo-Norman Marcher barons were able to command a *familia* or *comitivae* of at best thirty or forty men, suggests that individually, they were no match for the native princes who opposed them.[55]

The *teuluoedd* of the ruling princes may have provided the main focus for military service but theirs were not the only households to recruit warriors eager for action. The *teuluoedd* of lesser members of a ruling dynasty, the sons and nephews of princes, were also a fertile recruiting ground, as were the households of those whom the native laws refer to as the territorial lords, i.e. the nobility or *uchelwyr*. The chroniclers furnish us with but one example of the existence of a nobleman's war-band when, in 1176, it makes mention of the *teulu* of the otherwise unknown Cedifor ap Dinawol.[56] Unfortunately, and unlike their Anglo-Norman neighbours, the Welsh had no terms, other than the all-embracing *teulu*, to distinguish the households of lesser lords from those of the ruling princes. Nor are we in a position to assess the relative size or strength of these lesser *teuluoedd* though it is probably safe to say that in the majority of cases they were smaller and less well resourced. This is suggested by the decision taken in 1193 by an overstretched Hywel Sais, a younger son of the Lord Rhys, 'after he had seen that all his castles could not be held unless one of them was demolished', to invite his older brother Maelgwn and his 'host to destroy the castle of Llawhaden'.[57] Clearly, Hywel's resources in men and materials was insufficient either to hold or demolish the three, possibly four, castles he had taken, more 'by treachery' than by assault, in a very successful campaign. In stark contrast, Maelgwn had the means not only to take castles by direct assault, 'with slings and catapults', repair and hold them, he could afford also to trade them for hostages.[58] Evidently, Maelgwn's *teulu* was altogether of a more substantial and sophisticated nature, having at its disposal the very latest military technology. At the other end of the scale, two of Maelgwn's youngest brothers, Rhys Gryg and Maredudd, apparently had at their command but one *teulu* between them.

Almost from the time they were old enough to cut free from the restraining bonds of their father, the sons of the Lord Rhys had gathered about them a force of young warriors who owed allegiance to none but their respective princelings. Thus, during the 1190s, the ruling house of Deheubarth was able to field an elite force consisting of the combined *teuluoedd* of eight members of the dynasty. Whence many of these warriors came or were recruited is a mystery, for it seems unlikely that Deheubarth alone could furnish let alone sustain such numbers of professionally trained noble youth. Unfortunately for the ruling prince, the Lord Rhys, his was the only *teulu* that could be relied on for consistent support in the cause of Deheubarth's independence. All too frequently, competition between princely brothers would spill over into open warfare involving their respective *teuluoedd* which had the effect of widening the scale and scope of conflict. In truth, little is known of the nature of the relationship that existed between the *teuluoedd* of members of the same dynastic family and the command structure that may or may not have operated during times of war. Certainly, the unruly conduct of the *teuluoedd* of the Lord Rhys' sons Maelgwn and Gruffudd at the siege of Swansea castle in 1192 suggest that although their father, together with his host and household troop, was nominally in charge of the operation they retained command of their respective war-bands. Needless to say the ten-week siege ended in ignominious defeat and retreat for Rhys when his sons opted to fight each other instead of the enemy. It was this internecine warfare that tore apart the ruling dynasties of Deheubarth and Powys and which bedevilled the house of Gwynedd for long periods during the twelfth and thirteenth centuries.

According to the laws, all freemen from the age of 14 were eligible for military service and it was the duty of the prince or the territorial lord to train them in arms. Once trained, the newly qualified warriors need not take up arms professionally but the best of those that did were most likely to be found among the ranks of the princely *teuluoedd*. Therefore, the men, and boys, that served in the *teulu* were almost without exception drawn from the class of freemen who, by virtue of their noble status, were entitled to earn their living by fighting. T.P. Ellis captures the prevailing attitude of the native nobility to war when he stated that 'the privilege of fighting was a privilege, and not a burden, and was claimed and exercised by freemen as their birthright, incidental to their freedom'.[59] Therefore, to suggest that 'the *teulu* had little aristocratic cachet' and that 'it was very much a mixed bag' is to oversimplify a more complex issue.[60] True the *teulu* cited to support this statement, that of Gruffudd ap Cynan (d. 1137), was indeed composed of Irish mercenaries and landless, and lordless, Welshmen, but this was not a normal state of affairs and was due to Gruffudd's having lived in exile in Ireland for some years. In exile Gruffydd was denied the normal channels of recruitment open to a territorial lord who sought to make use of the traditional regional and personal bonds which governed the relationship between a lord and his men. In returning to his patrimony and attempting to recover his rulership, which had for some time been in the hands of the conquering royals of Powys led by Cadwgan ap Bleddyn (d. 1111), Gruffudd had to re-establish, and in some cases forge anew, his links with the native nobility of Gwynedd on whom, in happier times, he might expect to follow him willingly to war.

Gruffudd ap Cynan was not the only Welsh ruler to face the task of restructuring the nature and composition of his *teulu*, the same problem confronted his similarly dispossessed son-in-law Gruffudd ap Rhys ap Tewdwr (d. 1137) who twice attempted to recover control of the family patrimony of Deheubarth. Forced out by the all-conquering Anglo-Normans, Gruffudd, like his namesake from Gwynedd, had spent several years, perhaps as many as twenty, in exile in Ireland, and on returning in 1113 he took fully two years to establish himself and to gather about him a band of warriors drawn from the nobility of the former constituent parts of the now defunct kingdom of Deheubarth. Except for those committed to his cause on account of either a revived sense of regional loyalty to the son of the late king or on a more personal, even familial level, and more narrowly defined, as the territorial lord of Ystrad Tywi, Gruffudd relied heavily on military success for recruitment. It follows that the size and composition of his *teulu* may have varied according to success and failure in the field rather than to any deep sense of allegiance and obligation. Indeed, it has been convincingly argued that the warriors who flocked to Gruffudd's side after his intial successes against the Normans were men formerly in the service of other less resistant native lords.[61] In abandoning the *teuluoedd* of other lords, much to the chagrin of the native chroniclers who term them *ynfydion*, or imbeciles, as a result, these warriors were breaking the traditional bonds and obligations within native aristocratic society, so for them the term 'mercenary' is probably apt.

This restructuring of the traditional bonds of native society was in large part due to the pressure brought to bear by the invading Normans whose piecemeal conquest of Wales was responsible for creating new relationships and new patterns of authority. This is evident in south-east Wales where the ancient kingdoms of Gwent and Glamorgan were all but extinguished within half a century of the arrival of the Normans in 1067. The conquest, partition and settlement of large tracts of territory altered radically the vertical bonds of obligation that bound the native nobility to their royal superiors especially where the latter had been forcibly ejected or eliminated. The native freemen who remained and had once looked to the royal houses for leadership had to confront a new reality in the shape of the Anglo-Norman Marcher lord. Armed with the former dynasty's regalian rights and supported by a fully equipped military retinue of professional soldiers, the native freemen were either forced or persuaded, depending on their local status and influence, to serve their new masters. Thus, in the aftermath of the destruction and partition of Deheubarth after the death of its last king Rhys ap Tewdwr in 1093, we find the likes of Maredudd ap Rhydderch ap Caradog, a nobleman from Cantref Bychan, and his *teulu*, serving the Norman Richard fitzPons in defending his newly conquered territory against the claim of the late king's heir, Gruffudd ap Rhys ap Tewdwr. Having disavowed his claim to the throne of Deheubarth, even the late king's brother Rhydderch ap Tewdwr agreed to serve castle-guard duty at the royal castle of Carmarthen, the capital of Anglo-Norman south-west Wales under King Henry I (d. 1135).[62] Of course, such fundamental changes or restructuring as occurred in native society was as much the result of the processes of natural evolution and development within that society as of the impact on it of outside influence such as the Norman 'conquest' and settlement of Wales, an 'event' once thought by historians to be so cataclysmic in its consequence.

In more settled times, men of the royal blood line, such as Rhydderch ap Tewdwr, could expect to serve in a senior capacity within the military household. The office of *penteulu*, the chief or captain of the royal retinue, was a prestigious position of high status, second only to the ruler himself, which carried with it a great deal of power and influence. As one of the chief ministers of the prince, the *penteulu* had the authority (and the military muscle) to act in his master's place should he absent himself from the court. That the *penteulu* was reserved for close members of the royal family is emphasised by the Welsh laws.

> It is right for the captain of the household to be the King's son or nephew, or a man so high that he can be made captain of the household. It is not right that an *uchelwr* should be captain of the household; the reason it is not right is, that the captain's status depends on the King, and that no *uchelwr*'s does so.[63]

The inference is clear, *uchelwyr* were born but *penteulu* were made. What is made can also be unmade and it was this fact coupled with ties of kinship which bound the *pentuelu* even closer to the ruler whom he had sworn to protect. In the ruthless and brutal world of Welsh dynastic politics where princely brothers, uncles and nephews can frequently be found killing or mutilating each other, there is no recorded instance of a *penteulu* betraying his royal master. The same cannot be said for members of the *teulu* of whom some were as capable of cowardly acts as they were of performing feats of heroism. In the absence of the Lord Rhys at the court of King Henry II in 1163, his young nephew and *penteulu* Einion ab Anarawd 'was slain in his sleep by Gwallter ap Llywarch, his own man'.[64] The reference here to Einion's 'own man' is intriguing for it suggests that although he was the *penteulu* of his uncle, he too had a personal retinue of warriors (his *mesnie*) who are to be distinguished from the troops he commanded on behalf of the prince (the *teulu*). This may help explain how, in 1158, Einion was able to mount an attack against Humphrey's Castle, located just over the frontier in the neighbouring Norman lordship of Ceredigion, apparently without the knowledge or consent of his uncle.

> Then Einion ab Anarawd, nephew, son of his brother, to the Lord Rhys, young in age but manly in strength, made an attack, because he saw that Rhys, his uncle, was freed from the pact and from every oath he had given to the king, and because he himself grieved at the oppression of his own folk through the treachery of their enemies.[65]

It is only some time after this successful raid, during which Einion 'slew the bravest knights and the garrison of the castle outright' enabling him to carry away 'the spoil of the castle and all its booty and all the horses and armour',[66] that the Lord Rhys himself mounts and leads an attack in Ceredigion. The chronicler of the *Brut* seems to emphasise the fact that whereas Einion had sufficient troops only to attack a single stronghold in Ceredigion, the force at the disposal of the Lord Rhys was able to take and burn a number of castles, perhaps as many as half a dozen, scattered over a wider area throughout the lordship. This leads us to consider other factors such as the extent to which the *penteulu* was free to act independently of his royal master. Did Einion's attack on Humphrey's Castle include some or all of the prince's *teulu* or did his force consist entirely of his own troop of warriors? Were any of Einion's warriors, like Gwallter (or Walter) ap Llywarch, also members of the prince's *teulu* or were they entirely separate? Would that we had the evidence to answer such questions.

The fighting qualities of the warriors that served in the princely *teuluoedd* was recognised and admired even by their enemies the Anglo-Normans. It was not long before they were recruited to serve as mercenaries in and alongside the Anglo-Norman baronial *mesnies* and they may be found in large numbers at the battle of Lincoln in 1141.[67] However, depending on which of the English chroniclers is consulted, the Welsh contribution to the battle was either to swing the balance of victory in favour of their employers, the earls of Gloucester and Chester, or to be humiliatingly driven from the field.[68] Whatever the truth of their conduct on the battlefield that day the most important fact is that they were there at all. Welshmen, we are informed by Gerald of Wales, do 'not shine in open combat and in fixed formations', but prefer instead to 'harass the enemy by their ambushes and night attacks'.[69] From this it has been deduced that their tactics and temperament were more suited to guerrilla warfare as it seems, were their arms. 'They make use of light arms', says Gerald, 'which do not impede their agility, small coats of mail, bundles of arrows, and long lances, helmets and round shields, and more rarely greaves plated with iron.'[70] In view of the fact that Wales was, according to Gerald, 'the worst corner of Britain . . . full of woods, mountains and bogs',[71] it is unsurprising to find the natives making good use of terrain well suited to the skirmish, the ambush and the raid.

Nevertheless, to suggest that the Welsh were little more than guerrilla fighters, who 'cannot meet the enemy on equal terms', and that 'in a single battle they are easily beaten',[72] would be to do them a disservice. Contemporary writers other than Gerald amply testify to the willingness of the Welsh to participate in open combat when it served their purpose. Outstanding victories over the technologically advanced and tactically proficient Anglo-Normans at the battles of Coedysbwys (1094), Loughor (1136), Cardigan (1136), Radnor (1196), Cymerau (1257) and Llandeilo (1282) serve to modify Gerald's opinion. Neither, it seems, were the Welsh dissuaded from confronting royal armies such as those led by Stephen at Lincoln (1141), Henry II at Coleshill (1157) and Henry III at Evesham (1265). There were battles too between princes, at least thirty-eight are listed by the *Brut* between 682 and 1100, but apart from the odd few such as Mynydd Carn in 1081, they are hardly to be compared with the larger set-piece affairs of the twelfth and thirteenth centuries. In truth, to speak of armies, battles and counter-offensives at this early stage, pre-eleventh century, would be to ascribe the native rulers motives which can hardly be matched by the military means at their disposal. It was the era of the raid as opposed to the campaign, of the war-band as opposed to the army, and of the petty warlord as opposed to the statesmanlike prince.

Yet times were changing, and during the twelfth century the princes can be seen to be adapting to the new conditions. Those with vision enough to want to establish a state needed the support of a force more substantial than a war-band: they needed an army, commensurate with the ambitions of their statecraft. The Welsh laws make clear that the military forces available to the king-princes were made up of more than just the warrior nobility: they consisted of the king's subjects entire. This was the general military levy, the army, which the native chroniclers tend normally refer to as the host or *llu* as opposed to the *teulu* or war-band. For much of the medieval period the *llu* catered only for those freemen, the majority, who did not serve as part of the *teulu*. Trained though they were in arms, their entitlement to land enabled them to take up its cultivation and management so that they 'passed into the general body of tribesmen',[73] who could be called on to serve their princes in war only according to fixed rules. Within the bounds of his kingdom the prince could call on all freemen to serve him at will, and should any not be capable of bearing arms the onus was on the incapacitated to provide able-bodied men in their stead. In stark contrast, the prince's right to raise troops for service beyond those territories that constituted his domain was limited to but once a year and for a period not exceeding six weeks. This system is entirely in keeping with that found in England and the continent where the obligation of military service was limited to forty days.

If, as has been claimed, the stringency of the law in this respect made continued offensive warfare beyond the border almost impossible for the princes of the eleventh and twelfth centuries, it appears not to have hindered unduly the last prince of Wales, Llywelyn ap Gruffudd (k. 1282). In one twelve-month period alone (November 1256 to September 1257), Llywelyn led his troops on no less than six separate campaigns, all but two of which took him beyond the boundaries of his native Gwynedd.[74] It can be estimated that at least one of these 'foreign' expeditions, which took him to southern Powys, Ystrad Tywi, Gower, Carnwyllion and Cydweli, may have lasted up to twelve weeks from early January to Easter week or mid-April 1257. Unless the forces led by Llywelyn were made up entirely of his *teulu*, and there is evidence to suggest that his permanent troop of household knights was quite substantial, then it is reasonable to assume that the militia at his disposal was raised by means of the general military levy. In an effort to be militarily flexible, it is possible that Llywelyn may have been operating a system whereby he could purchase the services of those troops who ordinarily would have returned home after having discharged their contractual obligation. This is suggested by the fourteenth-century cadastral survey of Caernarfonshire and Anglesey, the so-called *Record of Caernarvon 1352*, which states that the men of the free-township of Cororion in Arllechwedd-Uchaf were liable for service as cavalry at the prince's cost beyond the traditional six-week period.[75] This is entirely in keeping with development in the rest of western Europe where the commutation of military service for money payment, called *scutage* in England, enabled continental rulers to hire mercenaries for longer campaigns thus freeing them from having to rely solely on the forty days' service of feudal forces.

According to the laws, military service was a privilege in which the bondsmen or unfree peasants were not permitted to share, their contribution being limited to non-military duties such as transport and general supply work. However, this is contradicted by Gerald of Wales who suggests that they were no whit less militaristic than their noble comrades.

They are . . . totally dedicated to the practice of arms. Not only the leaders but the entire nation are trained in war. Sound the trumpet for battle and the peasant will rush from his plough to pick up his weapons as quickly as the courtier from the court.[76]

If evidence dating from soon after the conquest of Wales in 1282–3 can be relied on and applied retrospectively, then it seems that in Gwynedd at least some, though apparently not all, of its bondsmen or villeins had indeed become liable for military service.[77] Subject to the same rules of service as their noble comrades in arms, it is of them, 'the common people', that Gerald speaks, who 'prefer to fight on foot, in view of the marshy and uneven terrain'.[78] By the second half of the thirteenth century it is likely that few freemen fought on foot, so that the social distinction between those who served in the cavalry and those in the infantry was brought more sharply into focus.

It is not unreasonable to suggest that the bondsmen would have been far more susceptible than the freemen to the temptation of serving for pay after their six-week contract was up. Attracted by the additional means to make their fortune in plunder and booty, they would have formed a willing contingent of volunteers when called upon to serve in different theatres of war. This might go some way to explaining how the Lord Rhys of Deheubarth was capable of raising a substantial force numbering well in excess of a thousand men for service on behalf of his overlord King Henry II in 1174.[79] Encamped with his men around Tutbury castle in Stafforshire, the siege is estimated to have lasted from mid-April or early May until the last week in July, a period of service far in excess of the mandatory six weeks. Once the siege had concluded, Rhys is said by an English chronicler, Ralph of Diceto, to have transferred to the immediate service of the king a force thought to be in the region of a thousand men who crossed to the continent with him in August.[80] There they fought against the armies of the French king and may not have returned home until the king himself did so in May 1175. To raise, organise and supply, let alone later to transfer, such a large force of men, suggests a certain degree of sophistication in the system of administration employed by the prince of Deheubarth. Inevitably perhaps, success in war had become dependent as much upon military might as on its conduct, organisation and resourcing and, as if by way of tribute to his talent in this respect, at his death the *Brut* hails Rhys as an 'arrayer and ruler of armies',[81] the only Welsh prince to be so honoured.

Yet it was a talent for military organisation that was evidently shared by others of his class. According to the Welsh chroniclers, the two sons of Gruffudd ap Cynan, prince of Gwynedd, Owain and Cadwaladr, were able to raise a force of some six thousand infantry and two thousand cavalry for a campaign against the Anglo-Normans in Ceredigion in 1136.[82] If the figures quoted are accurate, then the pool of men available to the Welsh princes for war service in the twelfth century, and doubtless in the thirteenth, was quite considerable and almost certainly more than could be supplied from the class of noble freemen alone. As the twin demands of war and defence allied to ever greater political ambition impacted on the princes, they were forced to widen their recruitment base which in turn enabled them to field larger and more professionally organised armies. Inevitably, this impacted also on tactics and the methods employed in meeting the enemy in the field, particularly in open combat. In August 1198, at a battle fought near Painscastle, Gwenwynwyn ab Owain Cyfeiliog of Powys (d. 1216) is said to have arrayed his considerable force into three divisions: one of infantry, one of cavalry and one mixed. In the event his tactical plan failed and the Welsh suffered a crushing defeat, sustaining something approaching three thousand casualties according to one contemporary estimate.[83] Increasingly, it was the size of the princely *llu* or host rather than the *teulu* which came to reflect the princes' growing power, importance and ambition. This is confirmed to some extent by the chronicles which, significantly, make no mention of the *teulu* of any prince after 1215. This is not to say that the *teulu* as a military institution disappeared or even declined in importance but merely to suggest that its role may have changed from being the principal offensive weapon of the princes into a body more concerned with his defence and personal protection. Clearly, the thirteenth-century princes needed more than the war-bands of their eleventh-century predecessors, many of whom were concerned only with honour and plunder achieved by means of the destructive raid. Increasingly, success in war became less the magnification of reputation, important though it remained, and more the augmentation of power. That power was dependent on more than accumulated wealth from a neighbouring territory and more the acquisition of the territory itself. To achieve this, the ambitious, would-be conqueror required something more substantial than the *teulu* – he required an army and the means to sustain it in the field.

Castles

If the war-band or *teulu* in particular, and the army or *llu* in general, was primarily the instrument of conquest then the castle may be regarded as the primary instrument of consolidation. That the intrusion of the Normans contributed much to the rapid evolution in the art and

science of war in Wales is nowhere better illustrated than by the introduction of the castle. At their most basic the strongholds erected by the
earliest Norman invaders consisted of little more than earthworks and
timber. The most common type of *castellum* was the *motte* or earthen
mound surmounted by a timber watchtower which made up the majority of the three hundred or so surviving earthwork castles in Wales. A
fair proportion were built with an attached bailey or outer courtyard
within which timber buildings such as the hall block, kitchen, chapel,
stables and military, sometimes civilian, accommodation would be located.
Less common was the ringwork which was, in effect, a large bailey without a motte, surrounded by a ditch and defended by a wooden pallisade
and gatehouse.

Although simple in concept and design, these early earth-and-timber
strongholds were more than a match for the Welsh who, initially at least,
had no answer to them. They could be constructed quickly and cheaply,
with readily available materials, and without the necessity of a skilled
labour force. Moreover, they could be erected to support continuing
offensive operations thereby serving as a secure base from which the
garrison could dominate or devastate, almost at will, the surrounding
hinterland. Military lordship was most clearly represented by the castle,
a fact which manifests itself in the, ultimately abortive, Anglo-Norman
conquest and settlement of Ceredigion *c.* 1094–1136. Here the invaders
attempted to establish a castle in each commote, around ten in all, and,
wherever possible, located as close to the existing commotal centres or
llysoedd as was practicable.[84] The pattern of control was such as to be
effective only so long as the invaders held the initiative in terms of
supply and resourcing and so long as the natives remained in awe of
their fortress-like structures. Thus, by the early twelfth century the castle
had become, and would henceforth continue to be for a few centuries,
the predominant instrument of conquest, consolidation and defence. As
a result of its evolution and refinement the principles of military success,
political survival and secure hegemony were the harsh lessons taught the
princes by their would-be conquerors, the Anglo-Norman lords of the
March.

That the Welsh had experience of attacking well-defended sites with
walled enclosures is suggested by the *Brut*, which recounts with glee
Gruffudd ap Llywelyn's victory over the Saxons in battle in 1056 after
which he 'pursued them to within the walls of Hereford, and there he
massacred them and destroyed the walls and burned the town'.[85]
Archaeological evidence suggests that the *llysoedd* or provincial court
palaces of the princes were sometimes defended by earthen banks and
wooden pallisades or occasionally by stone walls. Nevertheless, the castle

offered the Welsh a greater challenge and it took time before they were to become proficient at its destruction. This they achieved with clinical efficiency in 1094 when the men of Gwynedd 'threw off the rule of the French, and . . . destroyed their castles', to be followed 'at the close of that year' by the men of Deheubarth who 'razed to the ground' all but two strongholds.[86] Having mastered the art of destruction it took the Welsh a further two decades before contemplating the task of construction. In 1111, Cadwgan ap Bleddyn 'came to Welshpool and there he thought to stay and build a castle',[87] but his death soon after robbed him of the opportunity to be among the first of the Welsh princes in this field. That distinction goes to Uchdryd ab Edwin whose newly built castle at Cymer near Dolgellau did not stand long ere it was attacked, taken and burnt by his fellow countrymen in 1116.[88]

The castle symbolised lordship just as it consolidated lordship and it was in full recognition of these principles that, within half a century of the destruction of Uchdryd ab Edwin's stronghold, the Welsh princes were either building castles of their own or refurbishing those captured from their Anglo-Norman adversaries. Although no more than a dozen earth-and-timber castles can positively be identified from contemporary sources as foundations of the Welsh princes, it is highly likely that this represents but a fraction of the true figure.[89] The problem lies in the fact that it is almost impossible to distinguish native from Norman-built castles since the one has copied the other and in the absence of a discernible, let alone classic, Welsh design, historians are forced to consider alternative methods of identifying additional princely strongholds. This they have done either by relying on the all too rare opportunities afforded by archaeological excavation, or by considering carefully the geographical, topographical and historical evidence associated with the location and possible function of many undocumented castles the earthen mounds of which are all that remain to remind us of their existence. As a result, it has been possible to decipher an identifiable overall pattern in the way in which these and other such castles were used during the second half of the twelfth century by at least one of the Welsh princes, namely the Lord Rhys ap Gruffudd of Deheubarth.[90]

Though not the first to erect native castles, the Lord Rhys was foremost among the more powerful princes to grasp the wider strategic significance of castle-building, in pursuit of political as well as military objectives, as opposed to its narrower tactical advantages. Rhys was concerned with maintaining the integrity of his borders and it is in terms of frontier defence and clarification that he built his first castle, Aberdyfi in 1156. Erected within a year of becoming prince, the isolated motte was located on the frontier between Deheubarth and Gwynedd and was intended, according to the chroniclers, to forestall an invasion by his uncle Owain Gwynedd.[91] Having secured his northern border, Rhys turned his attention to the frontiers in the south and west which, on account of the conquests of the Anglo-Normans, were new, unstable and far from clarified. A region devoid of naturally defensible frontiers, Rhys sought to compensate for nature's deficiencies by means of strategically located earth-and-timber castles which had the additional function of clearly delineating the limits of his rulership. It has been suggested that sometime between 1162 and 1170, five, possibly more, castles – Cilgerran, Llandovery, Pencader, Llanegwad and Ammanford – were used in this way, of which three had been captured from his Anglo-Norman adversaries and refurbished for the task.

The princes of Gwynedd evidently shared Rhys' concern, for they too can be seen erecting castles on the borders of their domain. Between 1147 and 1149, the princely brothers of Gwynedd, Cadwaladr and Owain, were responsible for building on the southern boundary Cynfael near Tywyn and on the eastern rim, Tomen y Rhodwydd near Llandegla.[92] Like Rhys they too seem to have adopted a flexible castle strategy which enabled them to re-site their strongholds, either by erecting new or refurbishing old fortifications, whenever the frontiers moved. The castle ringwork of Llanrhustyd, the only one of its kind built by the Welsh, marked the limit of Cadwaladr's territorial acquisition in Ceredigion in 1149. Similarly, in 1167, the Lord Rhys pushed his northern frontier beyond the river Dyfi to include the lordship of Cyfeiliog which he annexed and hoped to defend by occupying the castle of Tafolwern. That he intended to remain is indicated by his apparent willingness to abandon the original border fortress of Aberdyfi. However, within a year he was driven out of Cyfeiliog and the frontier assumed its traditional, and pre-1167, line along the Dyfi, at which point, Rhys, unsurprisingly, opted to restore his former border stronghold.[93]

The princes also showed that they were no less concerned than their Anglo-Norman lords to erect castles with the express purpose of controlling land either for strategic or for administrative/political reasons. Again the Lord Rhys figures prominently, being in the vanguard of developments in this field. His contemporary, King Henry II of England (d. 1189), had long practised the principles of an established castle strategy which involved 'a systematic programme for strengthening and rebuilding his own castles and for neutralising the dangerous strongholds of his barons if he could not acquire them by war or other means than war'.[94] This was essential for any ruler who claimed to rule, as Henry did, over a vast territorial entity which embraced the greater part of France and the British Isles. Although the domain over which the

Lord Rhys claimed suzerainty amounted to but a small part of this so-called Angevin empire, his castles functioned in much the same way serving, initially, to define and defend the territorial limits of his rulership before evolving into more sophisticated stone structures that were used as a means of consolidation and, quite possibly, a focus for administration.

Having secured his borders by agreement with King Henry II in 1171, Rhys abandoned his earth-and-timber frontier strongholds and turned instead to consolidating his power from within by building a series of stone castles in each of the constituent lordships or *cantrefi* that made up his domain of Deheubarth. The chroniclers make much of the fact that in the summer of 1171 Rhys 'built with stone and mortar the castle of Cardigan',[95] a stronghold which, thereafter, became his chief royal residence. There are good grounds for believing that sometime between 1172 and 1194 he was responsible for the construction of a further six stone castles – Cilgerran, Dinefwr, Llandovery, Nevern, Rhayader and Ystradmeurig – all of which formed part of a broader pattern of land control. Rhayader (built 1177), and Nevern (built c. 1191–4) illustrate well the castle in an offensive role being sited beyond the traditional and the agreed frontiers, respectively, of twelfth-century Deheubarth (see map 5, p. xxiv). Irrespective of their size and structural sophistication, stone castles may be regarded as major fortresses that could do more than define a frontier or oppose a neighbour's aggression: they could provide defence in depth or even influence campaigns. They were, in short, castles that might repay the increasing financial cost of construction. Accordingly, Henry II 'put up the cost of defiance' and only the mightiest of his vassals could afford to sustain a network of fortifications. The Lord Rhys was among them.[96]

Increasingly in the twelfth century (especially after the 1170s) it is the equation between disposable income and masonry construction and military/political imperatives that is critical. In order to survive, the princes had to compete, which required them to bend their resources towards masonry construction on a massive scale using the latest technology. Following the dismemberment of Powys after the death of Madog ap Maredudd in 1160 and the fragmentation of Deheubarth after the death of the Lord Rhys in 1197, Gwynedd and its princes alone had the necessary resources to initiate such a programme. As early as 1188 Gerald of Wales noted on his tour of Gwynedd that 'two stone castles have been built there recently' – Aber Ia near Porthmadog and Carn Fadryn in the Llŷn peninsula – which may suggest a conscious imitation on the part of the northern princes of the systematic building programme and strategic policies followed by the Lord Rhys in the south.[97]

Although these two early stone castles appear to have been simply built of unmortared masonry they were but the first of some fifteen stone castles, of ever increasing size and sophistication both in terms of the quality of the materials used and the methods of construction adopted, erected by the princes of Gwynedd in the century between 1180 and 1280.

The prince thought to be responsible for erecting all but five of these fifteen fortresses was Llywelyn ab Iorwerth (d. 1240).[98] It has been demonstrated by Glanville Jones that by taking account of the location and structural sophistication of Llywelyn's castles, it is possible to reconstruct a coherent picture of the purely military aspect of his state-building activities in the first half of the thirteenth century.[99] The disposition of Llywelyn's castles suggest that they were sited with deliberation perhaps partly, as Glanville Jones argues, 'to establish control over a barrier zone to the south and east so as to protect the Venedotian heartland in Arfon, Llŷn and Anglesey', but certainly, as A.D. Carr suggests, 'to cover internal lines of communication and as a defence against an external enemy'.[100] Unlike in Deheubarth under the Lord Rhys, Llywelyn did not establish a stone castle in each of the thirteen lordships or *cantrefi* that made up his domain; his castles were built purely for military and strategic reasons with no apparent thought to supplanting the old commotal *llys* as an administrative centre. Indeed, a number of the more impressive commotal *llysoedd* continued to function, no doubt fortified for the purpose, alongside the castles as occasional residences for the itinerant royal family, Aberffraw and Aber near Bangor prominent among them. The efficacy of Llywelyn's castle-building programme and its strategic importance for Gwynedd are testified by the fact that his successors, his son Dafydd (d. 1246) and more particularly his grandson Llywelyn ap Gruffudd (k. 1282), sought only to strengthen, rather than to supplement or replace, the existing strongholds. The castles of Cricieth, Carndochan, Deganwy, Dolbadarn, Dolwyddelan, Ewloe and Y Bere exhibit signs of having been refurbished, some to a considerable degree. Clearly, these castles had become pivotal points in the defence of Gwynedd and in the maintenance of order within the principality.

The two castles built entirely by Llywelyn ap Gruffudd – Dolforwyn and the 'new castle beyond Brecon' which is believed to be Sennybridge – reflect the geographical extent of his interests and authority as prince of Wales rather than simply as prince of Gwynedd.[101] Their location in territories conquered by Llywelyn, far beyond the borders of his native Gwynedd, reveal how the castle had become essential to the efficient conduct of warfare. They were also a powerful demonstration of his power for those Welsh lords over whom he claimed overlordship. Therefore, we should not discount the importance of symbolism as a factor in their construction and certainly not regard the castle as an 'optional extra'. In fact, the castle was quickly absorbed into the militaristic culture of the Welsh warrior elite, so much so that a new clause was added to the native lawbooks specifying that everyone, with few exceptions, was required to undertake castle-building duties for the ruler. There were other changes also, not least in the methods of warfare, for the natives had to adapt to new technology not only in terms of castle construction but also of castle destruction, and new techniques of siege warfare. This called for a radical rethink on the part of the Welsh, but they were not found wanting, and as early as the second half of the twelfth century the native rulers had in their service men with specialist expertise in the area of siege warfare. For example, in 1165–6 the Lord Rhys had cause to be grateful to a nobleman of his called Cedifor ap Dinawol who engineered the capture of Cardigan and Cilgerran castles 'not through strength but by means of contrivances devised by the man and his own war-band, . . . namely, hooked ladders which grasped the walls where they were placed'.[102] By the 1190s Rhys had acquired more sophisticated siege equipment with which to take castles such as the 'slings and catapults' (presumably trebuchets and balista) deployed to take the castle of Ystradmeurig.[103]

Failure and defeat

No matter how courageous, adaptable or resourceful the numerically inferior Welsh proved to be, they would for ever be at a disadvantage when confronting their enemies from across the border. No Welsh prince, not even one as powerful as Llywelyn ap Gruffudd, could hope to match the military might of an English king, nor could he begin to rival the economic resources at his enemy's disposal. By the 1270s and 1280s King Edward I was able to put into the field an army more than five times the size of what Llywelyn could hope to muster, he could deploy a fleet where Llywelyn had none, and he could expend a sum well in excess of £100,000 while Llywelyn could raise but a fraction of this. Nevertheless, the Welsh might, and they did, continue to enjoy some military successes, but in a war of attrition that encompassed both the political and economic realities of warfare as waged in the thirteenth century, defeat was, perhaps, inevitable. Indeed, when the end came, it came swiftly, by means of two relatively short campaigns, each lasting less than a year, that reduced the once impressive native principality to ruins. Military alliance, born of political expediency, with dissident elements within the English aristocracy had come to Llywelyn's aid in the 1260s, to the extent that he was confident enough to face a royal army in open combat at Evesham, but there was to be no such alliance either military or political during the 1270s and 1280s so that Llywelyn had to confront Edward I alone. If anyone, it was Llywelyn who faced the distraction of tension and political vicissitudes within his own kingdom, a debilitation that had once plauged, and temporarily weakened, his foes.

Llywelyn's martial prowess is not in doubt; this 'brave battle-lion', 'worthy, fierce and bold like a blazing fire', 'armed and wreaking destruction in battle', according to the poet Llygad Gwr, was every bit as courageous, resourceful and daring as had been his forebears.[104] However, the world had moved on and success required a thinker as much as a fighter and although Llywelyn had proved himself adept at both, the conflict had cruelly exposed the military ineffectiveness of a prince who was forced to fight a largely defensive campaign. Unable to use to best effect the strengths of the Welsh military – highly mobile, lightly armed infantry whose favoured tactics were ambushes and guerrilla strikes – Llywelyn lost the twin advantages of surprise and speed. Nor, it seems, could he depend either on his castles to slow the English advance – they, despite heavy investment, being unequal to the task of resisting Edward's siege armies – or deploy his troops swiftly enough so as to concentrate what limited resources he had at the point of greatest need. This was due in large part to the sheer scale of the triple-pronged thrust of Edward's attack on the native principality from bases at Chester, Shrewsbury and Carmarthen. They had the effect of cutting in three Llywelyn's principality, isolating him and his princely vassals and detaching them, both physically and emotionally, from their allegiance. This highlighted and exacerbated the weakeness of Llywelyn's military organisation, the apparent lack of coordination in the raising and deploying of forces for the defence of the principality as a whole. He was unable to support them, and they him, since each had to see to their own fronts thus narrowing their theatre of operations. When, in the second war of 1282, he did attempt a new strategy by breaking out of Gwynedd and moving south to aid his allies in the Middle March, he came unstuck near Builth where he was killed in a skirmish. The defeat of Llywelyn in 1282, the most powerful of the princes of Wales, was not so much due to the failure of his military strategy or organisation as to the material wealth, organisational sophistication, deft planning and grim determination of the enemy. Indeed, it has been remarked that 'Welsh independence did not as much perish in a clash of arms as suffocate in a welter of parchment'.[105] It was the patient amassing of men and material and the orders issued by Edward via his efficient bureaucracy, which bound all together, that eventually ground down Welsh resistance.

Although personal bravery on the battlefield continued to find favour with the *literati*, songsters and poets, and no doubt did no small service in greatly augmenting the prestige of a prince, it was to be his skill as a strategist and tactician, as a besieger of castles and commander of armies in the field that would ultimately contribute to his political success, which, by itself, had probably become the only sure means of safeguarding a Welsh ruler's survival and the continuation of his kingdom. In the final analysis, it was not for any lack of bravery or martial skill, or the quality of his generalship that led to the defeat and death of Llywelyn ap Gruffudd in 1282, but his failure to grasp securely the political and administrative nettle.

Notes

1. A. Jones, *History of Gruffydd ap Cynan*, 129.
2. G. Jones, *The Oxford Book of Welsh Verse in English* (Oxford, 1977), 25, 26; Lloyd, *Hist. Wales*, II, 533.
3. *BT. RBH*, 179.
4. A.O.H. Jarman, 'Aneirin – The Gododdin', in *Guide to Welsh Lit.*, I, 70.
5. Quoted in Wendy Davies, *Wales in the Early Middle Ages* (Leicester, 1982), 69.
6. *Guide to Welsh Lit.*, I, 74.
7. Ibid., I, 77.
8. *The Latin Text of Welsh Laws*, ed. H.D. Emanuel (Cardiff, 1967), 94.
9. *DWB*, 99, 625; J.E.C. Williams, *The Poets of the Princes* (Cardiff, 1978), 32.
10. *Journey & Description*, 233–4.
11. Walter Map, *De Nugis Curialium*, 183.
12. Ibid., 197.
13. *Journey & Description*, 234–5.
14. *BT. Pen.*, 73, 81. We must be alive to the strong possibility that the chroniclers were biased in Maelgwn's favour.
15. *CW*, 15; *BT. RBH*, 227; *BT. Pen.*, 101; *B. Saes.*, 227.
16. *CW*, 15; *BT. RBH*, 235; *BT. Pen.*, 104; *B. Saes.*, 233.
17. *Journey & Description*, 178–79.
18. *BT. RBH*, 35.
19. R.S. Babcock, 'Imbeciles and Normans: The *Ynfydion* of Gruffudd ap Rhys Reconsidered', *The Haskins Society Journal*, 4 (1992), 2.
20. T. Gwynn Jones, 'Catraeth, and Hirlas Owain', *Y Cymmrodor*, XXXII (1922), 1–57.
21. Ibid., 49.
22. *BT. Pen.*, 14.
23. *BT. RBH*, 69.
24. *The Law of Hywel Dda*, 41.
25. *Mediaeval Prince*, 75.
26. *BT. Pen.*, 48.

27. R.R. Davies, *Wales*, 156.
28. R.H.C. Davis, *The Medieval Warhorse* (London, 1989), 80.
29. R.A. Brown, 'The Status of the Norman Knight', in *Anglo-Norman Warfare*, ed. M. Strickland (Woodbridge, 1992), 138.
30. R.H.C. Davis, *The Medieval Warhorse*, 81.
31. *BT. RBH*, 114, 115.
32. J.E.C. Williams, 'Meilyr Brydydd and Gruffudd ap Cynan', in *Gruffudd ap Cynan*, ed. K.L. Maund, 184–5.
33. A. French, 'Meilyr's Elegy for Gruffudd ap Cynan', *Etudes Celtiques*, xvi (1979), 268. J.E.C. Williams has 'a thousand knights'.
34. M. Bloch, *La Société Féodale (Feudal Society)*, trans. L.A. Manyon (London, 1961), 152.
35. R.A. Brown, op. cit., 138.
36. *BT. RBH*, 115.
37. Ibid.
38. *Rolls of the Justices in Eyre being the Rolls of Pleas and Assizes for Gloucestershire, Warwickshire and Staffordshire, 1221–2*, ed. D.M. Stenton, Selden Society, lix (1940), 567, no. 1346. Quoted in F.C. Suppe, *Military Institutions on the Welsh Marches: Shropshire 1066–1300* (Woodbridge, 1994), 12.
39. *BT. Pen.*, 66.
40. *Ancient Laws and Institutes of Wales*, ed. and trans. A. Owen (London, 1841), II, 381.
41. *BT. RBH*, 145.
42. *Mediaeval Prince*, 69.
43. *BT. RBH*, 149.
44. F. Suppe, *Mil. Inst. Welsh Marches*, 11.
45. C. Warren Hollister, *The Military Organisation of Norman England* (Oxford, 1965), 167–90.
46. *Pipe Roll*, 11 Henry II, 14, 95–6; P. Latimer, *WHR*, 14 (1989), 523–52.
47. *The Law of Hywel Dda*, 39.
48. D. Crouch, *Image of Aristocracy*, 160.
49. *BT. Pen.*, 17.
50. Ibid., 51.
51. *Journey & Description*, 234.
52. *BT. Pen.*, 58; *B. Saes.*, 157.
53. *BT. Pen.*, 14. Around seven score men of Llywelyn ap Gruffudd war-band were slain.
54. J.O. Prestwich, 'The Military Household of the Norman Kings', in *Anglo-Norman Warfare*, ed. M. Strickland, 94.
55. D. Crouch has conservatively estimated William Marshal's *familia* or *mesnie* to have been around eighteen knights in the first decade of the thirteenth century. Idem, *William Marshal: Court, Career and Chivalry in the Angevin Empire 1147–1219* (London, 1990), 137–8. A.J. Otway-Ruthven indicates that in 1169 Robert fitzStephen, late constable of Cardigan castle, could call on thirty knights to serve him in war. Idem, *A History of Medieval Ireland* (2nd edn, Dublin, 1980), 43.
56. *BT. Pen.*, 71.

57. Ibid., 75.
58. Ibid.
59. T.P. Ellis, *Welsh Tribal Law and Custom in the Middle Ages* (Oxford, 1926), 336.
60. D. Crouch, *Image of Aristocracy*, 158.
61. R.S. Babcock, *The Haskins Society Journal*, 4 (1992), 1–9.
62. *BT. RBH*, 89.
63. *The Law of Hywel Dda*, 8.
64. *BT. RBH*, 143, 'his own man'; *BT. Pen.*, 62, 'a man of his own'; *B. Saes.*, 165, 'a man of his'.
65. *BT. RBH*, 139.
66. D. Crouch, 'The March and the Welsh Kings', in *The Anarchy of Stephen's Reign*, ed. E. King (Oxford, 1994), 277.
67. Ibid., 277 n.54.
68. *Journey & Description*, 260.
69. Ibid.
70. Ibid., 234.
71. *Journey & Description*, 224.
72. Ibid., 260.
73. T.P. Ellis, *Welsh Tribal Law*, 337.
74. *BT. RBH*, 247–50; *BT. Pen.*, 110–11; *Ann. Camb.*, 91–5.
75. *The Record of Caernarvon*, ed. H. Ellis (Record Commission, 1838), 12.
76. *Journey & Description*, 233.
77. D. Stephenson, *The Governance of Gwynedd*, 93.
78. *Journey & Description*, 234.
79. Ralph of Diceto, *Opera Historica*, I, 384; *Pipe Roll*, 20 Henry II, 21, 77, 121.
80. *Gesta Regis Henrici Secundi*, I, 74.
81. *BT. RBH*, 179.
82. *BT. Pen.*, 51.
83. *Autobiog.*, 125.
84. J.G. Edwards, 'The Normans and the Welsh March', *PBA*, 42 (1956), 155–77.
85. *BT. Pen.*, 14, *BT. RBH*, 25 and *B. Saes.*, 71 use the term 'fortress' (Welsh *gaer*) and close reading of the text suggests that this may refer to a stronghold within and in addition to the walled town.
86. *BT. Pen.*, 19.
87. Ibid., 35.
88. Ibid., 46.
89. R. Avent, 'Castles of the Welsh Princes', *Chateau Gaillard*, xvi (1992), 11–17.
90. For much of what is to follow, see R.K. Turvey, 'The Defences of Twelfth-century Deheubarth and the Castle Strategy of the Lord Rhys', *Archaeologia Cambrensis.*, CXLIV (1998), 103–32.
91. *BT. Pen.*, 59.
92. Ibid., 56–7.
93. *Ann. Camb.*, 52.
94. W.L. Warren, *Henry II*, 234.
95. *BT. RBH*, 155.

96. W.L. Warren, op. cit., 234.
97. *Journey & Description*, 183.
98. G.R.J. Jones, *TCHS*, 30 (1969), 29–43.
99. R. Avent, *Chateau Gaillard*, xvi (1992), 11–17.
100. G.R.J. Jones, *TCHS*, 30 (1969), 34; A.D. Carr, *Medieval Wales*, 69.
101. D.J.C. King, 'Camlais and Sennybridge castles', *Brycheiniog*, 21 (1984–5), 9–11.
102. *BT. Pen.*, 71.
103. Ibid., 73. For the use of such weapons at this time, see J. Bradbury, *The Medieval Siege* (Woodbridge, 1992), 241–95.
104. J.B. Smith, *Llywelyn ap Gruffudd*, 336.
105. I.W. Rowlands, 'The Edwardian Conquest and its Military Consolidation', in *Edward I and Wales*, ed. T. Herbert and G.E. Jones (Cardiff, 1988), 48.

chapter six

CULTURE AND RELIGION: THE PRINCES AS PATRONS

P atronage was a public demonstration of power by the powerful, and those in whose hands was concentrated the greatest power in medieval Wales were the princes. As patrons, the princes had an influence on many aspects of life in Wales. By dispensing their largesse to institutions and individuals they sought to dominate government and control political life, shape economic fortunes and affect religious, cultural and social developments. As princes, they did this as a matter of duty, tradition and by weight of public expectation. Patronage was also a personal expression of taste and interest, like and dislike and in large measure may be taken as a true reflection of the private individual. Yet it is almost impossible to separate the individual from the institution, the person from the prince, and although in the sphere of cultural and religious patronage the princes were given some scope to behave as individuals, the issue of power and control was never far from the forefront of their minds.

The bardic tradition

One of the principal social and cultural functions of the leaders of native society, be they princely or lordly in origin, was the patronage and sustenance of the bardic tradition. Drawn almost exclusively from among the class of native freemen – 'I am of noble habits,' declared Gwalchmai ap Meilyr Brydydd (d.*c.* 1180)[1] – the bards occupied a central position in the cultural life of Wales. They regarded themselves, with some justification, as a cultural and cultured elite, a band of well-educated and professionally trained poets and songsters and the guardians of a literary tradition that stretched back to the sixth century. Nor was this self-esteem and self-worth misplaced for they were highly regarded by their contemporaries, both high and low born, and sometimes treated with a reverence usually reserved for the clergy. This was certainly so in the case of those bards, the minority of so-called inspired poets or seers (*awenyddion*), who claimed to have the gift of prophecy.[2] Although Gerald of Wales was rather disdainful of these 'Welsh soothsayers, who behave as if they are possessed', he was more complimentary of those bards or *beirdd* who 'in their narrative poems and their declamations . . . are so inventive and ingenious that, when using their native tongue, they produce works of art'.[3] The more 'artistically' gifted among them found fame, reward and, if they were fortunate, regular employment in the courts of the princes.

It is in their patronage of this select band of bards or court poets, the so-called *Beirdd y Tywysogion* (literally, poets of the princes), that the native rulers took a direct hand in the support and encouragement of Welsh culture. Few of them were found wanting in this respect and the royal courts of Wales, those of Aberffraw, Dinefwr and Mathrafal among the more prominent, became cherished venues for much music-making. There the bards entertained and delighted their royal and noble audiences with their 'inventive and ingenious' poetic verse which was almost exclusively sung or chanted to musical accompaniment, primarily the harp. As befitting the age, the warrior audience and the prevailing 'fashion' in poetic composition, much of the verse was panegyric and elegiac in content and style. Poetic renditions of heroic deeds and glorious battles, fine deaths and honourable victories were popular and very much in demand. Nor is this surprising when one comes to consider that many of the finest bards were themselves warriors, blooded in the field of battle and thus in a position to root their compositions in the reality of experience. One such warrior-poet was Gwalchmai ap Meilyr Brydydd from Anglesey who saw active service in the *teulu* of Owain Gwynedd (d. 1170). Vividly recalled by Sir J.E. Lloyd as a man capable of 'handling the sword with the same impetuous passion as the harp',[4] he sang proudly,

> *Gwalchmai am I called, a foe to the English.*
> *Bloody is my sword and fierce in battle*
> *In the tumult of the host I am a killer*
> *Multitudes praise me that have not seen me.*[5]

With death an ever present spectre on the horizon, the bards did not neglect the church and its personnel, temporal or otherwise, in their poetic encomiums. Saints Cadfan, David and Tysilio were eulogised as was God, Christ and the Virgin Mary. Heaven too figures prominently, but also the terrifying prospect of the torments of Hell; indeed, in many instances bardic verse was as much a sermon as might be preached from the pulpit by the very best fire-and-brimstone preacher. Sin, the Last

Judgement and the brevity and fragility of life are recurring themes in works designed to remind their composers as much as to warn their listeners of their conduct here on earth. The death-bed song or *marwysgafn* was a device whereby the bard looked over his life enabling him to make a full and frank confession of his sins thereby hoping to secure his place among the blessed in heaven. Praise poetry in honour of the princes, God and the saints, was thus the order of the day, not that there was much to choose between them since the princes were often eulogised to the point of appearing almost god-like in terms of their virtues and qualities. This concern for things spritual underlines the fact that the royal courts were far from being the only centres of cultural life and literary patronage in Wales: the church too played its part particularly in the developing field of vernacular and Latin literature. The monasteries were particularly active in encouraging the development of native scholarship, chief among them the ancient *clas* church at Llanbadarn Fawr which was one of the major seats of learning in eleventh- and early-twelfth-century Wales. Some clerics too became poets, like Madog ap Gwallter, a Franciscan friar thought to hail from Llanfihangel Glyn Myfyr, who is believed to have composed his affecting religious poetry sometime during the second half of the thirteenth century.

Despite the formal and stylised nature of the poetry (to us at any rate) there is no reason to dispute its ability to entertain the princes whose love for and patronage of the art was as much a product of habit as of conviction. Not content simply to be among the entertained, a minority of princes took up the art and proved themselves to be every bit as worthy of bardic honours as the fully trained professionals they patronised. Two of the most prolific composers were Hywel ab Owain Gwynedd (d. 1170) and Owain Cyfeiliog of Powys (d. 1197); that there may have been others is suggested by Gerald of Wales and the bardic master Cynddelw Brydydd Mawr (*fl.* 1155–1200) who speak of the Lord Rhys (d. 1197) as a man given to singing the poetic compositions of others though 'a hidden poet himself'.[6] Freed somewhat from the stylistic and thematic restrictions imposed on his bardic contemporaries, Hywel ab Owain Gwynedd deserves especial attention for his poetry which gives vent to his personal feelings and is perhaps the closest one might get to uncovering a princely personality. Here was a prince who loved to love and be loved, and his love poetry is unashamedly romantic with no less than eight named and a dozen more unnamed women, not all of whom were unattached, attracting his amatory muse.

> *I am involved in the strife that has come to me*
> *and longing, alas, is natural,*

for pretty Nest, like apple blossom,
my golden passion, heart of my sin.[7]

Hywel also had a soft spot 'For the virgin Generys who does not relieve my passion;/may she not insist on chastity'.[8] Women aside, Hywel was wont to praise the natural beauty of his native land, expressing his deeply affective love for

> .... *its strand and its mountains,*
> *its castle near the woods and its fine lands,*
> *its water meadows and its valleys*
> .... *its fields under the little clover*
> *its wide waste lands and its wealth.*[9]

Yet though he took delight in 'the nightingale in the wild woods' and 'lovely women', war, honour and glory were never far from his mind. With hardly a pause for breath he was extolling his love of Gwynedd's 'soldiers, its trained stallions, [and] its brave men' while revelling in his own contribution in war, 'With the thrust of a spear I did splendid work'. If Gweirfyl or Lleucu cannot be his then he desires that he 'May have, before my grave, a new conquest, the land of Tegeingl, fairest in the world', and this because 'I love today what the English hate, the open land of the north'.[10] Clearly, Hywel was a man of many parts, but it is his passions, desires and sensitivity which flesh him out as an individual of note.

It is perhaps on account of his princely status that Hywel was able to express himself with a freedom denied his bardic contemporaries for whom the rigours and complexities of their craft served to maintain their rank and dignity and acted as protection against interlopers. The bards were self-consciously elitist and they maintained their caste-like exclusivity by vigorous examination, stiff competition and by dint of princely patronage. The princes had within their gift two of the most coveted positions within the bardic order, that of the *pencerdd* or chief of song and the *bardd teulu*, poet of the king's retinue or war-band. The fiercest competition was reserved for the office of *pencerdd* which was by far the most exalted of the two. Few attained this rank and they did so only after proving their worth in contest before their princely patrons from whom the winners would be awarded a chair as a mark of their pre-eminence and invested with the rights and privileges commensurate with their newly acquired status. These included automatic right of access to the prince and his court, the opportunity to regularly address in song both God and the prince and the privilege of sitting next to the *edling* or heir-apparent in formal feasts and festivals held in the royal hall.

The *pencerdd* could also expect to be rewarded with grants of land or gifts of horses and cattle, all of which added greatly to his prosperity and prestige. Such was the fame and accumulation of wealth of some that they were able to establish bardic dynasties blessed with the talent and an almost God-given hereditary right to practise the art over a number of generations. One such bardic master was Meilyr Brydydd (d.*c.* 1137/8), who gave rise to two, possibly three, generations of poets and whose own son and heir, Gwalchmai ap Meilyr (d.*c.* 1180), followed in his footsteps to become *pencerdd* to the princes of Gwynedd. If the bards' own musings on the subject are to be believed, it was not for the sake of riches and reputation that they strove to attain the position of *pencerdd* but on account of the opportunities it afforded them to influence the current and shape the future development of the craft. In this they were assisted by the prince who saw to it that none but his *pencerdd* had the right to apprentice and teach students and to issue other, lesser bards licence to practise their craft within the limits of his kingdom. According to the law codes, 'no bard can solicit for anything within his *pencerdd* area, without his permission, unless he is a bard from a strange country'.[11] Indeed, despite his lofty position and apparent freedom to practise his art, the *pencerdd* was very much tied to the prince and kingdom which had bestowed his title. This is not to say that the *pencerdd* of one kingdom was prevented from singing the praises of rulers from another if he were not native to that territory: quite the contrary – as the law codes make clear, if the 'chaired bard' has nothing to sing of him to whom the court belongs, 'let him sing of another king'.[12] That said, the *pencerdd* was always careful to cultivate the goodwill of his patron, aware that to offend might lead to loss of privileges and even exile. That such strife happened between a prince and his *pencerdd* may be instanced from the experiences of Gwalchmai ap Meylir who, for reasons unknown, fell out with Owain Gwynedd never to be reconciled. His poet-son too suffered at the hands of an ungrateful patron, declaring, 'Weary am I of the service of rulers, blessed are they, monks in churches'.[13]

This highlights the weakness of the position of the *pencerdd*, for although he exercised considerable authority within the kingdom at large, he was never made an officer of either the prince or his court, and although he retained his chair and bardic dignity for life, it seems that upon the death of his princely patron his unique status might be terminated also. In short, the *pencerdd* of a deceased prince might become one rather than *the* chief of song to his successor. It might have been the death in 1160 of his patron, Madog ap Maredudd, that convinced Cynddelw Brydydd Mawr (d.*c.* 1200) to transfer his allegiance from the court of Powys to that of Gwynedd where, for possibly the next ten years, he sang in praise of Owain Gwynedd (d. 1170) and his son, the poet-prince Hywel. With their deaths he switched again, this time to the court of Dinefwr where he eulogised the Lord Rhys whom he subsequently offended and, despite his best poetic efforts, failed, as far as we know, to achieve a reconciliation. With that he returned to his native Powys where he found favour with the family of his former patron, namely the poet-prince Owain Cyfeiliog, his son Gwenwynwyn (d. 1216) and their cousin Owain Fychan ap Madog ap Maredudd (d. 1187).

Second only in rank to the *pencerdd*, the *bardd teulu* was, in some respects, more secure than his superior for he at least had the satisfaction of knowing that only the destruction of the entire household guard could terminate his appointment. Although not unknown, fortunately for the *bardd teulu* such calamities were rare. As one of twenty-four officers of the court, the *bardd teulu* was in regular attendance of the royal family, and being ranked eighth (or eleventh in the courts of the southern princes) in importance, he was entitled to claim from the prince 'his land free', clothes and a horse.[14] His seat in the hall was reserved next to that of the captain of the household guard, the *penteulu*, to whom he looked for protection in times of war. Besides lauding the bloody exploits of the prince's warriors he was also required to sing for the prince's wife, 'and that quietly, so that the hall is not disturbed by him'.[15] That he too, like the *pencerdd*, was free to leave the court to practise his craft is suggested by the law codes which state that 'when he travels with other bards, he is entitled to two men's share'.[16] Precisely what this 'share' entailed is never made clear though it is known that he was entitled to a cow or an ox from the booty taken in war by the *teulu* 'in a strange country'. Although by the thirteenth century the distinction between the *pencerdd* and the *bardd teulu* was breaking down – it is not unusual to find one man serving in both capacities – the importance of the role of these bardic masters to the cultural life of the court and kingdom was as vital as ever.

It was for these positions that the talented and ambitious would compete, often engendering bitter dispute, in public contests held in the royal court. It is a measure of the importance attached to these appointments that these bardic contests were initiated and presided over by the princes themselves, keen to secure the services of the most gifted, and those more able to do them good. It is a fact that the princes regarded their bards as more than mere entertainers and at the very least their employment contributed to what one might term the trappings of royalty, as vital to upholding the image and authority of the ruler as his court, his officers and his *teulu*. In return for his patronage the prince had certain expectations of his bard: his bard might serve him additionally as a soldier or courtier, perhaps even as an adviser, but his true worth was as publicist and propagandist; the one giving shape and form to his rulership, the other magnifying and popularising his achievements. 'You without me have no voice; I without you have nothing to say',[17] so stated Cynddelw Brydydd Mawr in an address to the Lord Rhys which sums up perfectly the interdependent relationship between the prince and his poet which is as complex as it is mysterious. The bard more than the priest was the conscience of the prince, reminding him of his duties and responsibilities, of his oaths and obligations, and although he was disposed to eulogise so also might he satirise and even chastise his royal master. In a sharp reminder to his patron Rhys Ieuanc (d. 1222), Phylip Brydydd (*fl.*1210–30) proudly declared 'I made fame for thee'.[18] In similar vein a boastful Cynddelw declaimed: 'In the vale of Llangwm I contemplated our leader, and what I sang will be contemplated'.[19] Few among either the bards or princes would have found cause to disagree with the Irish poet who confidently asserted that 'No man can be famous without an *ollam*' (court poet).[20]

Doubtless there existed more than the currently known list of the thirty or so court poets or *Beirdd y Tywysogion* and it may be surmised that in its totality the bardic order, which enjoyed clearly, and legally, defined privileges, encompassed many times more poets than those represented at the royal courts. Certainly, references in an elegy to Gruffudd ap Cynan (d. 1137), composed by one of the most gifted bards of his day, Meilyr Brydydd (d.*c.* 1137/8), to 'minor bards' (*man feirdd*) and 'pompous wandering bards' (*cychwilfeirdd cyhuseidiawg*), serves to confirm their existence though we know next to nothing about them.[21] It is reasonable to assume that they plied their trade in the halls of the aristocracy, 'wandering' from one noble household to another or were perhaps retained by one or more patrons with the resources to maintain them. It is possible also that some of them had the means to sustain themselves: being free-born members of the social elite they were entitled to hold land or at the very least had landed expectations. The laws make clear that the three arts that a villein's (*aillt*) son was not entitled to learn without his lord's leave were clerkship, smithcraft and bardism. Thus, for a peasant to be trained up in the bardic craft required not only an exceptional talent but an enlightened master and a tolerant teacher; the one to provide the necessary instruction (an apprenticeship which might take anything up to seven years), and the other to furnish the qualification fee, if successful, of twenty-four pence and, no doubt, of other expenses incurred during training. Regardless of the strictures of the laws in this respect it is likely that some were invested with the freedom of status that membership of the bardic order implied. Certainly the leading exponents of this exclusive of cultured trade were keenly aware of each other's social status and they took every opportunity to deride their less exalted brethren and, at times, each other. Phylip Brydydd was particularly vociferous in his condemnation of the 'vain bards' and 'unskilled dabblers' against whom he was forced to compete for the attention of the princelings of Deheubarth, Rhys Gryg (d. 1233) and Rhys Ieuanc, sons of the Lord Rhys.[22] When two of the leading poets of their day, Cynddelw Brydydd Mawr (d.*c.* 1200) and Seisyll Bryffwrch (*fl.* 1155–75), competed for the post of *pencerdd* to Madog ap Maredudd, prince of Powys, the latter taunted his rival by claiming that 'from your stock no bards have sprung'.[23]

If the bardic order distinguished its membership by rank or grade it did so also in terms of artistic talent, for although poetry, and strict metre poetic composition at that (*cynghanedd*), was its mainstay, the bardic craft embraced musicianship, story-telling and more sedentary pursuits as history and genealogy. In this hierarchical structure, the bards with a singular faculty for and primary interest in music playing (*cerddorion*) or story-telling (*cyfarwyddwyr*) were of lesser stature than those talented few who reached the top of their profession by mastering all.[24] Not that this deterred the princes from supporting these lesser lights, and such may have been the otherwise unknown Gellan, 'harpist and chief of song' to Gruffudd ap Cynan, killed in his master's service in 1094, and the unnamed son of Eilon the *crythor*, court musician to the Lord Rhys and winner of the music chair at the eisteddfodic-like festival held at Cardigan castle in 1176.[25] Certain it is that the princes' cultural interests extended beyond the bardic boundary and that they were prepared to support those not of the bardic order but with skill enough to merit royal patronage. Gerald of Wales clearly distinguishes between the 'bards, singers and jongleurs' whom he found at the courts of the Lord Rhys and Dafydd ab Owain Gwynedd (d. 1203) in the late 1180s.[26] According to him, the courts of the princes rang to the sound of music played on instruments like the pipe, the crwth and the harp.

> When they play their instruments they charm and delight the ear with the sweetness of their music. They play so quickly and in subtle harmony. Their fingering is so rapid that they produce this harmony out of discord.[27]

So taken were the Welsh with their music that, according to Gerald, 'in every house there are young women just waiting to play for you', and in a land in which 'there is certainly no lack of harps', guests (whether they wished it or not) are 'entertained until nightfall by girls who play to them on their harps'.[28] As much as they enjoyed music, poetry, story-telling and genealogical recitation, the princes liked to laugh, and in one court at least a fool or jester was employed. Would that we knew more of the likes of John Spang, court-fool to the Lord Rhys of Deheubarth and described by Gerald of Wales as 'a jester who by his pretended folly and his witty tongue was wont to give the court much entertainment'.[29] It is likely that other courts too were enthralled by similar tomfoolery causing their princes also to give 'way to merry speech and jocularity'.[30] The Lord Rhys was a man who wore his cultural heart on his sleeve and it is no coincidence that the means through which he chose to publicly proclaim his pre-eminence as the premier prince of Wales was by virtue of a festival of the arts and music held during the Christmas of 1176 in his recently constructed stone castle at Cardigan. Here was a man who relished playing the role of a culture-prince, and though we have no way of knowing the extent to which his patronage formed a conspicuous part of his consumption, Gerald of Wales, a man with a wealth of experience at the courts of the kings of England and France, was sufficiently impressed by his cousin's munificence as to praise him for his 'liberality'.[31]

Wales and the twelfth-century renaissance

Clearly, the courts of the princes of Wales were important cultural centres where bards, musicians, minstrels and the *literati* generally would receive a warm welcome. Nor is this surprising or unusual since this was the age of what has often been called the 'twelfth-century renaissance', a period and a process, considerably more than a century in time and influence, which witnessed an appreciable increase in intellectual activity that embraced learning and, in its broadest sense, artistic creativity. Accordingly, so it has been claimed, 'Everywhere in so-called western Europe during the twelfth century, in France, Germany, England, Italy and Spain, men's hearts and minds were waking to a new appreciation of the world, its colour, its vastness, its perils and its beauty. There was curiosity about the world in all its aspects, the world of men, the world of the spirit, the world of the cosmos and the world of nature'.[32] Nor were Wales and its princes immune to this influence. Far from being a cultural backwater, Wales was very much a part of this general European 'humanist' movement which extolled the virtues of studying Latin and vernacular literature, art and architecture, politics and theology, and which promoted interest in the human condition.

In spite of being an Europe-wide movement, the cultural and intellectual heart of the renaissance during the twelfth and thirteenth centuries was Paris. Site of the most celebrated centre of learning, the city's university attracted scholars and students from across Europe, and although few, if any, were Welsh, its influence nonetheless managed to penetrate the remotest corner of Cambria. Gerald of Wales claims to have met two youths from the diocese of St David's studying at schools in France, and although they were as likely to be Anglo-Normans as Welsh, this points to the possibility of wider cultural exchange between west Wales and the continent.[33] North Wales too may have furnished continental academies with a student or two; certainly there is good evidence to suggest that Owain Gwynedd had access to the services of skilled letter secretaries who show evidence of having been trained in the French schools and who were, it seems, equally well versed in Welsh traditions of Latin prose composition. Contact between the courts of the Welsh princes and those of continental Europe was made and maintained through trade, visitation, the exchange of letters and upon the conclusion of treaties. As early as 1164/5, Owain Gwynedd had dispatched an embassy to the court of the French king, Louis VII (d. 1180) to be followed, less than half a century later, by his grandson Llywelyn ab Iorwerth (d. 1240) who concluded a treaty in 1212 with Louis' successor Philip Augustus (d. 1223). It was by such means as this and via the courts of the kings of England and through the church that the Welsh were subjected to the influences of the continent.

The works of scholars of the calibre of the Frenchman Hugh of St Victor (d. 1141), the Breton Peter Abelard (d. 1142), the Italians, Peter the Lombard (d. 1160) and Thomas Aquinas (d. 1274) and the German Albert of Cologne (d. 1280), all of whom were collectively responsible for some of the most outstanding theological, philosophical and legal texts of the period, were surely not unknown to the princes. Closer to home, Paris-educated Englishmen, John of Salisbury (d. 1180) and Stephen Langton (d. 1228), archbishop of Canterbury, were perhaps among the leading representatives of this 'humanist' trend in England. From Wales, though hardly Welsh, Walter Map (d.c. 1210) and Gerald Cambrensis (d. 1223), had ventured to Paris as students whence they returned imbued with the teachings of the renaissance and which they used to great effect in their writings on things Welsh. The celebrated, if somewhat shadowy, Franciscan friar and writer John of Wales (Johannes Wallensis) was a teacher and doctor of theology in Paris where he died (c. 1285) and is buried. These were intellectuals well known to the princes and with whom it is likely they had chanced to engage in discussions other than politics and war.

It was a period which witnessed a veritable explosion in literary output much of which was devoted to the writing of history and biography. The chronicles of Roger of Howden, Ralph of Diceto and Mathew Paris (d. 1259) rank high among the histories of the period as, in their field, do the biographies of Thomas Becket, particularly those by Edward Grim and William fitzStephens, St Hugh of Lincoln by Adam of Eynsham, and of Henry II, the *Gesta Henrici Secundi*, penned possibly by Roger of Howden. Equally important is the early-thirteenth-century *Histoire de Guillaume le Marechal* by virtue of its being the first (as far as is known) medieval biography of a layman who was not of royal blood. The Welsh-born son of Breton parents, Geoffrey of Monmouth (d. 1155) brought his scholarship to bear on the history of Wales and in 1136 appeared his *Historia Regum Britanniae* (*History of the Kings of Britain*) which purported to give a true account of the Britons from the coming of Brutus to the arrival of the Saxons. In dedicating his work, in its various editions, to the likes of Robert, earl of Gloucester (d. 1147), King Stephen (d. 1154) and to Robert (d. 1168) and Waleran (d. 1166) de Beaumont, earl of Leicester and count of Meulan, respectively, Geoffrey betrays the possible source of his patronage and his Anglo-Norman inclinations. Nevertheless, his work, especially his *Vita Merlini* or *Life of Merlin* (*c.* 1150), popularised the legends of Merlin and King Arthur and it did much to promote wider interest in the culture and heritage of Wales. By the beginning of the thirteenth century, Geoffrey's *Historia* had been translated from Latin into Welsh after which, if not before, it might have found its way into the courts of the princes as did other works of literary merit. It is known that the more popular continental prose tales such as the *Chanson de Roland* and the epic poems collectively known as the *Chanson de geste*, as well as the works of Chrétien de Troyes (d. 1183), were known to the princes and their courtiers, some having been translated into Welsh as early as the beginning of the thirteenth century.

The Welsh were no less productive in the literary field than their continental counterparts, being responsible for the collection of tales known as *The Four Branches of the Mabinogi* (*Pedair Cainc Y Mabinogi*) which, together with *Culhwch* and *Olwen*, are among the finest examples of medieval prose literature in Welsh. If the findings of a controversial new study by Dr Andrew Breeze on the *Mabinogi* are to be believed, then we need look no further than to one among the princely families for their authorship namely, Gwenllian (d. 1136), the daughter of Gruffudd ap Cynan of Gwynedd and the wife and mother of Gruffudd ap Rhys (d. 1137) and the Lord Rhys (d. 1197) of Deheubarth respectively.[34] Whether or not we accept Gwenllian as the author is not at issue, the importance of Dr Breeze's research is in the fact that there is sufficient evidence to conclude that literacy was a skill common to many who moved in royal circles and that even as early as the first half of the twelfth century, a period which witnessed a quickening of the transition from an essentially oral to a written cultural tradition, native literature in its many forms played an essential part in court life. It is evident, for example, that the bards known to Gerald of Wales (d. 1223) had in their possession 'old manuscripts', containing genealogical data which may have been committed to writing as early as the late ninth or early tenth century.[35] It is entirely possible that by the twelfth century the princes too possessed books and manuscripts and may even have been proud owners of a library or two. Therefore, far from being the exception, the poet-princes Hywel ab Owain Gwynedd and Owain Cyfeiliog may well have represented the norm: noblemen and noblewomen for whom being well versed in the arts was an integral part of who and what they were.

Although the princes seem not to have been directly involved in commissioning works, poetic, prose or otherwise, they nevertheless provided a focus for the ambitious *littérateur* hoping to attract their attention, support and sponsorship. In this way verse, prose and song would be dedicated to and woven around would-be patrons and sponsors whether they wished it or not.

The fact that such tales as the *Mabinogi*, together with a near contemporary biography of Gruffudd ap Cynan, were written originally in the twelfth century, suggests that the Welsh were early exploring alternative literary forms to poetic, annalistic and hagiographical works, the last two for which they were justly famed. The various editions of the *Brut y Tywysogion* (*Chronicle of the Princes*) and the surviving lives of the saints, among them Rhigyfarch's (d. 1099) celebrated *Life of St David*, are models of native scholarship, and what the Welsh did not write themselves they borrowed or translated from others.[36] This may help explain how some Welsh tales like *Geraint ac Enid* and *Owain* (*Iarlles y Ffynnon*) bear more than a passing resemblance to the French romances of Chrétien de Troyes, *Erec et Enide* and *Yvain* (*Le Chevalier au Lion*).[37] It is likely that portions of Welsh literature were themselves 'borrowed' by continental writers, some of whom may have travelled to Wales via Norman-conquered England or else having met a wandering story-teller in the ducal and royal courts of Europe. Such was the enigmatic *Bleheris*, of whom little is known other than what we are told by the anonymous author of the *Conte del Graal* that he 'was born and bred in Wales'.[38] The same author tells us that his story of the adventures of the Arthurian knight Gawain enthralled, among others, William X, duke of Aquitaine (d. 1137) 'who loved it and held it more than any other firmly in his memory'.[39] He was known to that cousin, friend and acquaintance of Welsh princes, Gerald of Wales (b. 1146), who refers to him as *Bledhericus* (or in Welsh *Bledri*), 'the well-known story-teller, who lived a little before our time'.[40]

There are grounds for believing that, in origin, even that most Welsh of cultural insitutions, the *Eisteddfod*, was itself borrowed from the French, an adapatation no less of the twelfth-century festivities or *Puys*.[41] In view of the close connections established between the Lord Rhys and his erstwhile foes the Anglo-Norman settlers of Cardigan and Llandovery, and the time spent by his son Hywel Sais in Normandy in 1174, the means of cultural transmission were present. All that was required was a man as confident and forward-looking as Rhys to adopt and fashion to his own use cultural features hitherto peculiar to others. It is perhaps ironic that it is to Gruffudd ap Cynan, a prince not noted in contemporary texts for his cultural patronage, rather than to the Lord Rhys, that tradition assigns a central role in enacting a 'statute' for reforming the practice of the arts in music and poetry. The so-called Statute of Gruffudd ap Cynan can be dated no earlier than the sixteenth century but the fact that it was thought important to attach the name of a twelfth-century prince to the regulations drawn up to govern the conduct of the Caerwys Eisteddfod of 1523 is not without significance.[42] More plausible is the tradition that Gruffudd ap Cynan brought with him from exile in Ireland musicians and poets who may have had some influence on the development of the arts in Wales.[43] By the same token there is no reason to dismiss the possibility that the Welsh may have 'borrowed' equally from their Celtic cousins, with whom they enjoyed close relations in the three centuries before 1200, as they did from the Anglo-Normans.

If not the harbinger of the cultural renaissance, the Lord Rhys ap Gruffudd can at least lay claim to being among its most active proponents particularly in the field of native law. More a matter of tradition than fact, the so-called Laws of Hywel Dda probably have little to do with the king that bears their name and much to do with his descendant Rhys. He is thought to be the prince most likely responsible for imitating the current European fashion for codification of law and adapting it to the texts of the native law. By turning them into the book form we know today he was doing no less than his contemporary, King Henry II (d. 1189), was attempting to do in England. His transformation of the practice of English law gave rise to an early attempt at a systematic treatise on the subject, commonly called *Glanvill* after the king's justiciar Ranulf de Glanvill (d. 1190), who is thought either to be its author or patron.[44] As was the case with the so-called Statute of Gruffudd ap Cynan, so too with the Laws of Hywel Dda which may be put down to the affectation of a twelfth-century prince wishing to cloak his reforms in the guise of conservatism and tradition. Fact or fiction in either case, it matters not, what is important is that it points to the princes as a group willing and capable of taking the lead in cultural affairs.

It was an age of improvement that went beyond the literary and artistic. According to Gruffudd ap Cynan's anonymous biographer, under his enlightened rule,

> every kind of good increased in Gwynedd and the people began to build churches in every part therein, sow woods and plant them, cultivate orchards and gardens, and surround them with fences and ditches, construct walled buildings, and live on the fruits of the earth after the fashion of the men of Rome.[45]

Gruffudd himself contributed directly to this upsurge in building by erecting 'large churches in his own major courts' with the result that 'Gwynedd glittered then with lime-washed churches, like the firmament with stars'.[46] Although not unknown before the twelfth-century, the adoption of stone for building became considerably more widespread so that by the beginning of the thirteenth century Wales glittered also with lime-washed castles, monasteries and, to a lesser extent, secular-domestic buildings such as the halls and palaces of nobility and royalty. This led to a corresponding upsurge in interest in 'the mother of the arts', namely architecture, which, together with the creative application of sculptural decoration, earned for the Welsh builders of the period a distinctive style known today as Celtic Romanesque. The most striking example of this decorative style is to be found at the monastery of Strata Florida where the archway of the great west door survives, 'symbolising its [Strata Florida] position at the summit of native church architecture and its prestige as an important medieval centre of Welsh culture and learning'.[47] To what extent the architectural styles and sculptural embellishments employed by native craftsmen in the twelfth and thirteenth centuries reflected the views, tastes and interests of the princes will never be certainly known. It is reasonable to assume that, as patrons, they may have exercised some influence and even if they were not directly involved in the creative process, they at least provided a focus for inspiration. This can be seen in the finely carved stone head found at the castle of Deganwy which is thought to represent Llywelyn ab Iorwerth and which may have been but one of many similar carvings that existed across Wales adorning a castle here or a *llys* there, representing other equally distinguished princes.

The greatest architectural heritage of Wales is its masonry castles and it is in the design and construction of them, apart from the *llysoedd* of which little remains above ground, that the influence of the princes was most keenly felt. Although they account for only a fraction of the stone castles built in Wales, the princes invested a great deal of time, effort and expense in those fortresses that served them as bases for residential use, defence and administration. Apart from the apsidal or D-shaped towers and keeps, native-built castles do not exhibit architectural features peculiar to the Welsh. In fact, they adopted, adapted and borrowed heavily from their Anglo-Norman neighbours, so much so that in some instances where the written records fail us, it is impossible to tell a Welsh from an English castle, as at Castell Morgraig. Erected sometime in the thirteenth century halfway between Caerphilly and Cardiff, Morgraig is unique in having a polygonal plan consisting of four irregularly shaped round towers linked by a curtain wall to a square keep.[48] Its surviving architectural features are a bizarre mixture of archaic and modern which display a blend of native and English buildings styles. Once thought to be Welsh, the current consensus of opinion is that it is an English castle for which the use of carved stones as dressings for doorways and windows, and which was only available from quarries in the English-held Glamorgan lowlands, is cited as evidence. However, as the carved stone head from Deganwy castle illustrates, native craftsmen were no whit less skilled than their English counterparts in this respect and if this is insufficient to make a case on their behalf one need look no further than the early-thirteenth-century Castell-y-Bere which boasts finely carved stonework in 'the latest international style'.[49] That historians are able to point to similarities in the design and construction of a number of castles attributable to both Llywelyn ab Iorwerth and his grandson Llywelyn ap Gruffudd (k. 1282), suggests that the princes may well have drawn on the expertise of a small pool of master-craftsmen, men of ability like the Savoyard Master James of St George, Edward I's chief architect and builder of his now-famous Welsh castles, who were less employed than patronised by their royal masters.

If, as has been suggested, this use of finely sculpted decorated stonework in at least two of the castles attributed to Llywelyn ab Iorwerth is tantamount to demonstrating his 'concern with a conspicuous display of status',[50] then it suggests that beyond their domestic and military use, these castles had a higher purpose as symbols of the princes' authority designed as much to overawe their own subjects as to impress their visitors, hostile or otherwise. The symbolism of power was important to the princes, who appear intent on rooting some of their most strategically valuable fortresses in the culture and mythology of their Celtic past. Built away from traditional sites, commotal *llysoedd* or places of especial cultural significance, these castles were erected for their strategic importance alone. It has been demonstrated that of the castles built in Gwynedd by the princes Llywelyn, only one, Deganwy, a traditional site dating back to the post-Roman period, was located at the commotal *llys*.[51] In a number of cases the castles utilised by the princes, particularly those in south Wales, were originally Anglo-Norman foundations, a factor which may have prompted some to invest in a little myth-making and cultural manipulation.

There is a strong case for believing that the Lord Rhys was responsible for cultivating the Arthurian tradition and associated stories which came to be closely identified with his castle of Cardigan. Scene of his greatest triumph in 1165, his destruction of the castle and capture of the borough and Benedictine priory enabled him not only to rid Ceredigion of the last vestiges of nigh on seventy years of Anglo-Norman rule, but also to accomplish the task of reassembling much of the old kingdom of Deheubarth. In a display calculated to impress both friends and foe alike, he rebuilt the castle in stone (1171), moved his court there (*c.* 1172) and celebrated his achievements by holding an eisteddfodic-like festival of the arts within the castle precincts (1176). Moreover, it is at Cardigan that he chose to entertain eminent dignitaries like Baldwin, archbishop of Canterbury (1188) and possibly Peter de Leia, bishop of St David's (1197), and it is from here that he issued one of his two surviving charters. Clearly, Cardigan was intended to be something more than just another fortress garrisoned and maintained at the prince's expense, and though in an era of itinerant kingship we may hesitate to call it his capital, there is no doubt that it became a favoured royal residence and important focus for his rule.

However, having been for so long a bastion of Anglo-Norman power in west Wales, since at least 1093, and certainly for most contemporaries beyond living memory, Cardigan may have been stigmatised by its close association with alien influence. Yet rather then eradicate all traces of Anglo-Norman settlement by the traditional native method of wanton destruction, Rhys opted instead to extend his protection and patronage to the borough and priory thereby encouraging its burgesses and clerics to remain and continue as before. If examples of the literature of the period may be taken to reflect the views of contemporaries, there is every reason to suspect that Rhys' policy with respect to Cardigan and, indeed, generally, may not have found favour with those of his nobility who did not share his cosmopolitan outlook. According to D.M. Lloyd, even his own *pencerdd* Gwynfardd Brycheiniog may have been expressing his unease through his poetic compositions by deliberately 'seeking deep roots in Welsh tradition for the Lord Rhys's policy'.[52] Perhaps in an attempt to assuage the concerns of the more conservative elements in his court and in an effort to magnify his own achievements, Rhys may have set about making capital of his gains by fashioning native myth, history and tradition to underpin his conquest. In this way Cardigan could be represented as more than just a victory of native over Norman but as a rediscovery of an ancient tradition and recovery of an equally ancient burial site.

According to tradition, the earliest reference to which occurs in the late-eleventh-century *Life of St Teilo*, the body of a West Country king with Arthurian connections called Gerennius or Geraint was transported by sea from Cornwall for burial in west Wales. Thought by contemporaries to be at or near the ancient burial site on the river Teifi, the same possibly as that referred to by the *Brut* in 1110 as *Dingereint* (Geraint's Fort), Cardigan castle soon came to be associated in the minds of 'patriotic Welsh chroniclers . . . with a venerable spot in Arthurian tradition'.[53] It is likely that some story-teller or other, perhaps even Gerald's *Bledhericus*, a man who 'knew the acts and tales of all the kings, of all the counts who have been in Britain' and, who, coincidentally, seems to have had some knowledge of coracle fishing on the Teifi, was responsible for embellishing the tradition.[54] Whether there is any truth in the story mattered not at all to the likes of Prince Rhys who seized any and every opportunity to manipulate and distort, minimise or mangify, embrace or discard aspects of native and non-native history, tradition and culture in order to publicise and propagandise their regimes.

Religious patronage

If the castle represented the chief monumental prop to the military and political power of the princes then the church lagged not far behind. The princes were as active founding and constructing ecclesiastical structures as they were building castles. The one they built out of necessity – they had no choice because their very survival depended upon it – the other they built out of piety in the desperate hope that their charity might secure for them a place in the afterlife. Piety and necessity aside, the act and fact of building were as important as the structures themselves, for in erecting churches, monasteries, palaces and castles, the princes were underlining their hegemony, both real and symbolic, and thereby considerably enhancing their prestige. In all, it has been calculated that of the 427 extant castles in Wales, both timber and stone, only 36 or some 8.5 per cent of the total, can positively be identified as Welsh foundations. Of course, this takes no account of the fact that the date and foundation of more than half the castles in Wales are unknown, and of these it is reasonable to suppose that some were Welsh. Also it is important to remember that the Welsh were responsible for capturing, utilising and refurbishing more castles, which often involved considerable rebuilding or repair work, than they are credited with establishing.[55] Of the 49 religious houses established in Wales between *c.* 1071 and 1271, some 14, or 28.5 per cent of the total, may be attributed to the patronage of native princes. That this did not represent the sum total of their ecclesiastical building is certain: the anonymous biographer of Gruffudd ap Cynan states clearly that the prince, and 'the people', presumably intended to denote the nobility, erected an untold number of large, lime-washed churches in Gwynedd. Whether these churches were 'monastic' or 'secular' in character is not made clear, neither is there any hint as to their structural sophistication, which might have provided evidence of their importance and the level of investment committed to their building. All that can be said with confidence is that, structurally at least, the monasteries alone stand today as a tangible testament to the religious beneficence of the princes.

The princes may be described, in a phrase so beloved of historians, as conventionally pious. If this is taken to mean that they were no better or worse than the majority of their contemporaries, then it is apt. Unlike Louis VII (d. 1180) of France, no contemporary ruling prince of Wales could be described as being so pious that 'you would think he was not a king but a man of religion'.[56] Nor could any Welsh prince rival the extravagant claim made on Louis' behalf by contemporary French chroniclers of his being 'the most christian of all princes'.[57] On the other hand, unlike King John (d. 1216), the princes were never charged with irreligion nor did any earn the epithet ascribed Henry II by Gerald of Wales as 'the hammer of the church'.[58] Those best placed by their contemporaneity and best qualified by their clerical office to pass such judgements on the princes, the native chroniclers, and monks all, are rarely to be drawn on the issue of princely piety and grace. Apart from Bleddyn ap Cynfyn (d. 1075), praised for being 'merciful towards pilgrims' and for defending 'the honour of churches', Gruffudd ap Cynan, who 'after building many churches and consecrating them to God and the saints' is said to have made 'a good end in his perfect old age', and Madog ap Gruffudd Maelor (d. 1236), 'who surpassed all for [his] generosity and piety: for he was an outstanding founder of monasteries', the princes seem not to have impressed unduly their clerical critics.[59] True, there are frequent references to them receiving 'extreme unction' or 'taking penance and communion and confession' and thereby 'making a good end', and to a number who even went so far as to 'becoming a monk', like Gruffudd ap Cynan or Owain Cyfeiliog who, 'after he had assumed the habit of the Order at Strata Marcella', was buried within the walls of his own foundation in 1197.[60] However, these may be taken as examples of custom and regarded as expressions of conventional piety and, consequently, are not in themselves suggestive of sincere devotion.

That the Welsh were capable of 'sincere devotion' is attested by Gerald of Wales who was deeply impressed by their reverential conduct in church which, he believed, was 'the reason why the churches in Wales are more quiet and tranquil than those elsewhere'.[61] Gerald's opinions cannot easily be dismissed, for as he himself stated, 'I can bear witness' to the fact that 'they pay greater respect than any other people to their churches, to men in orders, the relics of the saints, bishops' crooks, bells, holy books and the Cross itself, for which they show great reverence'.[62] Indeed, so much in awe was the Lord Rhys of these relics, particularly the fabled torque of St Cynog, that he stole it from a church in Breconshire and brought it back to his castle at Dinefwr. 'For this act alone', mused Gerald, 'he deserved to be captured and locked up, as an example of the judgement of God'.[63] On reading Gerald one wonders whether he ever intended that his general picture of the devoutly religious Welsh should include the princes whom he frequently castigates for their wrongdoing, as if he were an Old Testament prophet, with hardly a hint of their good deeds. He relates with almost undisguised glee the ill-fortune that befell Gwenwynwyn ab Owain Cyfeiliog when the prince, motivated it seems by jealousy and avarice, refused to support the archdeacon's bid to become bishop of St David's:

> Wherefore the vengeance of heaven soon after followed; for he received such a hurt owing to his horse trampling on his foot, that he suffered from grievous lameness and weakness almost past cure.[64]

The tale may well be apocryphal but it nonetheless conveys the sense of responsibility Gerald, and presumably others of his clerical contemporaries, believed was attendant on those with the power to decide or the authority to influence outcomes. It was for those nobles and princes who either refused to take the cross or opted out of their vows to venture to the Holy Land on crusade that Gerald reserved his most vitriolic diatribes. He invested a great deal of his time and energy in ensuring the success of Archbishop Baldwin's mission to Wales early in 1188. Owain Cyfeiliog was among the first to fall foul of this religious zeal which admitted of no greater sin than to refuse service on behalf of the Christian Church. He was promptly excommunicated 'because he alone of the Welsh princes had made no move to come with his people to meet the Archbishop'.[65] Gerald relates with relish, and not a little pride and conceit, the fact that the great and the good, and the not so good in some instances – 'To the great astonishment of everyone present . . . some of the most notorious criminals of those parts were among those converted, robbers, highwaymen and murderers'[66] – queued up in numbers to meet the archbishop and pledge themselves to crusade. However, the truth is rather less sanguine than Gerald would have us believe since few, if any, of those who promised to serve, as did Einion ab Einion Clud of Elfael in order 'to avenge the injury to God the Father Almighty',[67] actually accompanied the expedition which left England in the autumn of 1189.

Clearly, the gulf in the relationship between faith and deed could, and frequently did, become a chasm. It is a paradox which manifests itself at every turn and it is not unusual to find outwardly devout men behaving in a manner more akin to evil than good. Within two years of castrating and blinding his nephew Llywelyn ab Owain, Maredudd (d. 1132), son of 'the merciful' Bleddyn ap Cynfyn, died and was honourably buried 'after having done penance on his soul and body and worthily receiving the Body of Christ'.[68] Nor must it be assumed that the Normans were immune to wrongdoing and the committing of sinful acts: lamenting their brutal treatment of the Welsh, Orderic Vitalis opined that, 'It is not right that Christians should so oppress their brothers, who have been reborn in the faith of Christ by holy baptism'.[69] His explanation for this is disarmingly simple: 'Pride and greed which have a hold on the hearts of men everywhere, were the incentives that drove [them] to unrestrained plunder and slaughter'.[70] These were men for whom the sacking of a monastery, the killing of a priest or the mutilation, even murder, of their close kin were regrettable but sometimes unavoidable by-products of violent times. It did not necessarily mean they were irreligious, only that within every individual there might coexist 'a very worldly and often frivolous temperament coupled with a devotional spirit which one shrinks from stigmatising as hypocrisy. It has rather to be regarded as a kind of reconciliation, hardly conceivable to the modern mind, between two extremes'.[71]

Inevitably perhaps, the higher up the social scale one travels the greater the incredulity borne of life's experiences, clerical corruption and political expediency to mention but a few of the more common frailties of earthly existence. To a lesser extent than elsewhere it seems, the Welsh laity were confronted by secular images in what, ostensibly, was intended or taken to be religious institutions. Ever to the fore with his percipient observations and moralising tales, Gerald relates the story of a well-travelled knight from Brittany who, on coming by chance to the church of Llanbadarn Fawr, wished to observe the natives at prayer. Accordingly,

> when the clergy and the parishoners were awaiting the coming of their abbot, so that Mass could be celebrated, this knight was there to witness the abbot's arrival, in the midst of a crowd of other people. What he actually saw was a band of about twenty young men, all armed and equipped according to the local custom. He asked which was the abbot. They pointed out to him a man with a long spear in his hand, who was walking in front of the others. The knight gazed at him with amazement. 'Has the abbot no other vestments?'

he asked. 'Has he no other staff to use, instead of the spear which he is carrying?' 'No,' they said. 'Upon my soul!' answered the knight. 'What I have seen really is a novelty! I have never heard of anything so odd!' Without more ado he gave up travelling . . . and went straight back home.[72]

Nor was this merely for effect, as the *Brut* makes clear in respect of its generous reference to Morfran's stout defence of Cynfael castle in 1147. Abbot of the *clas* church of St Cadfan in Tywyn, Morfran was eulogised in the poetry of his onetime guest Llywelyn Fardd (fl.*c.* 1140–80) as the very model of Christian humility and piety, under whom the monastic community had become a seat of 'faith, religion, trust, and communion', located as it was in 'a valley without tension, without false religion, where the Cross and the offerings and the trees are well kept'.[73] Paradoxically perhaps, Morfran was also constable of the local fortress which he refused to surrender when called upon by the victorious nephews, Hywel and Cynan ab Owain Gwynedd, of his defeated master Cadwaladr. Preferring instead 'to die honourably rather than to lead a life of shame through treachery to his lord', it was with great difficulty that he 'escaped through friends' when the stronghold was stormed but not before 'some of his men had been slain and others had been wounded'.[74] Clearly, these were men for whom the lance, sword and shield were as necessary as their clerical vestments, with dichotomic attitudes to match.

The faith that caused pilgrims from Wales to journey to Jerusalem in 1144 – a fateful decision as it transpired since they all met with an accident at sea and drowned – was shared evidently by Cadell ap Gruffudd (d. 1175), ruler of Deheubarth, who made a pilgrimage to Rome in 1153. His motive may well have had something to do with the fact that some two years before he had been set upon by 'some men from Tenby . . . as he was hunting, and they did him some injury' which, in the vividly brutal words of the *Brut* 'left him half-alive for dead'.[75] His pilgrimage suggests that Cadell may have survived his injuries but not the experience, and although 'he entrusted all his authority to Maredudd and Rhys, his brothers, until he should come back', he was to return in body but never in spirit.[76] In rejecting the world for the monastic cell – he retired to the Cistercian community at Strata Florida where he later died – Cadell was acknowledging his mortality and, perhaps, his fear of death, which goes some way to explaining why such men, warriors all, felt compelled to lavish their wealth and attention on the church. They were as frail and as fearful as their less 'heroic' contemporaries and in patronising the church they hoped to atone for their sins. However, in some cases patronage was insufficent in itself to wipe the sin-slate clean, for though Cadell journeyed willingly to Rome, as had at least three native rulers previously in the ninth and tenth centuries, others were all but compelled to make penitential pilgrimages to the Holy City. The Book of Llandaff (*Liber Landavensis*) claims that in *c.* 1075 a certain Caradog ap Rhiwallon, who may possibly have been an otherwise unknown son of Rhiwallon ap Cynfyn of Powys (d. 1070), made a pilgrimage to Rome as penance for fratricide.

It is perhaps to be expected that, then as now, those on the point of death would almost inevitably turn to the church for succour and comfort even after a life of cruelty and debauchery. Increasingly, remorseracked princes were turning themselves in to the nearest or more regarded monastic community and donning the clerical habit of their favoured order among whom they spent their final days or hours. Yet there were others for whom the church had failed to persuade of the torments of purgatory, men like Owain Gwynedd and the Lord Rhys who stand out from their fellow princes in their preparedness to meet their maker while under penalty of excommunication. In effect, they were cast out of the church and the Christian community which in turn imperilled their souls for if they died without absolution then they were condemned to everlasting hell. In a society where belief in the reality of heaven and hell was near to being absolute, even the conventionally pious had much to fear from being excommunicated: indeed, it was the most terrible sentence the church could impose. Yet, in truth, it was rapidly becoming the rule rather than the exception, being imposed too often for frivolous reasons for it to be seriously regarded by any but the most pious. That said, neither was it to be lightly regarded since excommunication was the ecclesiastical equivalent of being declared an outlaw which was of more immediate concern and consequence for a ruling prince than for an unruly peasant. King John (d. 1216) found this out to his cost, for in his excommunication at the hands of Pope Innocent III (d. 1216) lay the means by which his vassals, both English and Welsh, might renounce their oaths of homage and fealty.

This underlines the fact that the church was more than just an institution intended to care for the spiritual welfare of its flock; it was a powerful organisation with as much temporal, especially political, as spiritual influence and authority. If the secular world often, and increasingly, intruded into the spiritual domain, so did the church involve itself in the world beyond the cloister. Innocent III had demonstrated how powerful and political, even international, the church could be, for in a career lasting eighteen years (1198–1216) he clashed with the rulers of England, France, Denmark, Bulgaria, Aragon and Sicily, all of whom had been subdued and forced to become vassals of the Holy See. By his power-broking he had come closer than any pope to subordinating the crowned heads of Europe to the papal ideal of 'theocratic government'.

The power of the papacy did not go unnoticed in Wales when, in 1244, Dafydd ap Llywelyn of Gwynedd attempted to protect his kingdom and assert his independence from Henry III by seeking to become a vassal of Pope Innocent IV. The price of princely submission and papal protection was calculated in the currency of the temporal rather than the spiritual world, being fixed, according to Mathew Paris, at the bargain rate of 500 marks (£333 6s. 8d.) per annum. In this instance, papal support was hardly worth having, at best it was half-hearted – the abbots of Aberconwy and Cymer were instructed to intervene in a dispute between Dafydd and Henry III which came to naught – and at worst counterproductive in that it fuelled Henry's enmity towards his nephew for involving outside agencies in what the Crown saw as an essentially internal dispute. Within nine months of taking up Dafydd's case against the Crown, the pope abandoned him to his fate having had a better offer – the hasty repayment of considerable sums outstanding – from Henry III.

It was an age of definition in which the nature and conflicting interests of church and state were brought more sharply into focus, often leading to bitter struggles for supremacy between prince and prelate. In their attempts to subordinate the church to the will of the Crown, and thereby channelling its considerable wealth and power to their own use, kings like Henry II and John fell foul of their own clergy quite apart from incurring the wrath of the papacy. There was no controversy like the one involving Henry II and Becket in Wales, nor was a Welsh prince ever excommunicated by a pope and his kingdom placed under interdict as happened to John, but there was tension and occasional confrontation between the chief representatives of church and state. While he may not have offended Pope Gregory X (d. 1276), Llywelyn ap Gruffudd's attempt to exercise his authority over the church in Gwynedd earned for him the undying enmity of its bishops Anian of Bangor (d.c. 1306) and Anian I (d. 1266) and II (d. 1293) of St Asaph. He sought their complete submission or, failing that, their acquiescence; they, on the other hand, aimed to retain their independence and enhance their freedom of action. They proved to be powerful enemies, contributing as near as much to Llywelyn's downfall as the armies deployed by Edward I for that purpose. Where possible, the native princes sought to enlist the goodwill and cooperation of their leading clerics on whom they relied for service as bureaucrats, diplomats and technocrats. They were men of considerable wealth and territorial influence, learned and often well connected; in short, probably the most important cogs in the machinery of princely government.

It was an age of change which witnessed the gradual transformation of the church in line with the broader principles being adopted by successive popes in the so-called papal reform movement of the eleventh and twelfth centuries. Among the more outstanding of the early reforming popes was, arguably, Gregory VII (d. 1085) who claimed for the papacy supreme legislative and judicial power within Latin Christendom, from which centralised and centralising position at the heart of western Europe, it was able to involve itself more fully in politics, finance and, of course, religious affairs. Secular concerns aside, the more devout put themselves at the forefront of the move for moral reform out of which, largely though not exclusively, came the monastic revival of the tenth and eleventh centuries. In Wales no less than in the rest of Europe the church was changing, evolving either naturally or by external force, and as it changed so did the princes' attitude to it and their patronage of it. Indeed, the princes had to deal with the church on two levels, as worshippers and as patrons, and it was in the latter connection that they truly revealed themselves for in exercising their patronage, particularly monastic, they sought to reconcile their faith and respect for the church with their desire to dominate and control it. Yet their relationship with the church in Wales was complicated as much by the interference of Canterbury as by the influence of change. The one stemmed from the desire on the part of successive archbishops of Canterbury, fully supported by the English Crown, to subjugate Wales, and the other from the evolutionary pressures associated with what may be termed the 'religious renaissance' of the eleventh and twelfth centuries. It was a challenge to which some of the more devout, or devious, princes met with considerable flair and imagination.

In a period which witnessed a near revolution in the organisation, administration and character of the church in Wales it is the distinction between monastic and secular, hoplessly blurred in the native church, which is important and goes to the very heart of this transformation. The pre-Norman church in Wales was very much monastic in origin and character, not that the Normans would have recognised it as such, and although it was fully part of Latin Chistendom it had remained outside mainstream European monastic developments. To those familiar with the traditions and practices of continental monasticism, based on the rigidly ordered and standardised Benedictine model, the Welsh monks appeared peculiar and a breed apart. True, they shared the same faith, doctrine and religious observances as their continental counterparts but their customs, among them clerical marriage, institutions, such as the *clas* or mother church, and organisation, as an independent community, differed markedly. The vast majority of Welsh monks or *claswyr* lived a secular life as members of a community attached to one of the many so-called *clas* or collegiate churches dotted throughout Wales. Headed by an abbot or, perhaps in no more than four instances as in the more important centres, a bishop, the ecclesiastical authority exercised by these *clasau* was in essence local. They dominated the religious life of their respective districts which, depending on their size and importance, might extend over a commote or a *cantref*. Even the influence of the richest and most powerful of them, the bishoprics of St David's, Bangor, Llandaff and Llandeilo Fawr, was felt further afield only in terms of the control they exercised over individual or satellite churches; it was in no way territorial.

It is probably fair to say that the Normans who first encountered the native church experienced something of a culture shock. Having resisted the influence of the so-called monastic revival, a movement which had left few corners of the Christian world untouched, Celtic monasticism struck no chord of experience or memory. Neither did it engender any sympathy in a people bent on the temporal as well as the spiritual conquest of Wales. Already in decline and in the throes of reform when the Normans arrived in Wales, the decentralised and fragmented native church was in no position to offer any resistance to those imbued with an almost missionary zeal to change it. The conquerors swept aside much of what they did not understand, destroyed that which they considered a threat but retained those features which might serve their purpose. In this way the church in Wales gradually evolved on new lines in which the distinction between the monastic and the secular was brought into sharper focus. Besides the customary, almost institutionalised, foundation of monasteries by individuals with an already impressive track record in such acts of conventional piety, the conquerors set about the bigger task of redrawing and reordering, and thereby subjugating, the church in Wales. Territorial boundaries, ranging from that of the diocese down to the humble parish, were fixed for the first time, cathedrals were founded, parish churches built and diocesian rule established. Both the secular and regular church in Wales was brought firmly under the ambit of Canterbury and the orbit of Rome.

This twelfth-century Anglo-Norman-inspired 'reformation' of the church in Wales did not go unresisted. With varying degrees of success, attempts were made to prevent the election of Anglo-Norman bishops to Welsh sees and to encourage the non-compliance of native bishops with the directives of Canterbury. Little could be done, however, to prevent the election of the Anglo-Normans Urban and Bernard as bishops of Llandaff (1107) and St David's (1115) respectively, or to the creation in 1143, of the new diocese of St Asaph and the consecration of its prelate Gilbert. On the other hand, Gruffudd ap Cynan succeeded in ousting the Breton Hervé from Bangor and, after a twenty-year struggle with the king of England, replacing him in 1120 with an Irishman, David the Scot. It was as much a matter of pride and patronage as a public demonstration of political power that caused Gruffudd's son Owain Gwynedd to reject Henry II's nominee for the vacant see of Bangor in 1163. So determined was he to ensure that the religious life of the kingdom and diocese be under the direction of his nominee, Arthur of Bardsey, that for seven years until his death in excommunication, he defied a triumvirate of king, archbishop and pope. Despite these 'successes', which probably did more harm than good to the cause of religion in Wales, the truth is, apart from Gwynedd, and there fitfully, the princes ultimately failed in their bid to resist the Anglo-Norman dominance of the secular church.

This failure to resist the reformation of the secular church was due in large measure to the fact that, in principle, the princes welcomed this religious renaissance. Their opposition stemmed not so much from religious differences as political ones, their overriding aim was control of this reformed church. If only we were able to unlock the meaning of the term 'church' as used by Gruffudd ap Cynan's anonymous biographer then we might better understand his motive in building them. If, for example, the writer meant church (*eglwys*) in the secular sense as opposed to monastery (*mynachlog*), as is suggested in the text, and if these churches (*eglwysi*) were not intended to be satellites of existing *clasau*, then it seems Gruffudd may be credited with contributing to the growth and development of the secular church in north Wales and in so doing, emulating his Anglo-Norman neighbours for whom the founding of parish churches was second only to establishing castles. Certainly, his concern to ensure the election of a Gwynedd-friendly prelate as bishop of Bangor suggests that a diocesian system was either in place or developing apace, neither of which could happen without the support of the ruling prince. The same was true in the native-held south where the progressive development of the parochial system and the gradual establishment of an administrative hierarchy was hardly resisted by a prince, the Lord Rhys, who may have been instrumental in securing for his son Maredudd (d. 1227), the archdeaconry of Cardigan.

The spirit of resistance was also evident in the princes' initial despoliation of the regular church. The first communities of monks who arrived from the continent, Benedictine, Tironian and Augustinian, were firmly, often brutally, suppressed, their buildings burnt and some of their number killed. Nor is this surprising, following as they did in the train of the conquerors and, more often than not, being endowed with the plundered property of the local *clas* church. It was soon recognised that the monastery, priory or church was usually accompanied by the building of a castle and borough, all visible symbols of conquest and settlement. As if to reinforce the insular nature and defensive mentality of these alien settlers, it was almost universally regarded as the primary duty of these imported French-speaking monks to care for the spritual welfare of their fellow countrymen. Their fellow Christians, the native Welsh, were to be ejected and excluded. Not without good reason did the abbot of Glouces-ter, Gilbert Foliot (d. 1148), advise the prior and monks of the Benedic-tine house at Ewenny to 'strengthen the locks on your doors and surround your house with a good ditch and an impregnable wall lest that people which as you say, gazes with shaggy brow and fierce eyes, break into it and destroy with one blow all your labour and sweat'.[77]

However, this general truth hides a more complex picture of differing attitudes and values which suggest that, with its own monastic tradition in decline, some princes early embraced the principles of continental mon-asticism. Among the first to do so was Gruffudd ap Cynan (d. 1137) who is said to have willed twenty pieces of silver apiece to the Bene-dictine houses at Chester and Shrewsbury. On the other hand, Mor-gan ab Owain (d. 1158), scion possibly of the royal family of Gwent or Morgannwg but reduced in status to lord of Caerleon, was among the first to acquire, in war, the patronage of the Benedictine priory of Goldcliff to which his subsequent beneficence is attested in charters issued during the 1150s. It was not long ere a Welsh prince took the next step of actually founding a house, and in 1170 Owain Cyfeiliog of Powys was the first to do so establishing a Cistercian community at Strata Marcella near Welshpool. In all, some fifteen Cistercian houses were established in Wales, more than any other order, and of these, eight owed their foundation to Welsh princes. Another two (Strata Florida, Whitland), possibly three (Basingwerk was, for long periods in the thirteenth century, under Welsh control), were beholden to the princes for their liberal patronage. Of the three, Whitland had most reason to be grateful, encouraged as it was, quite probably by the Lord Rhys, to establish three daughter houses in mid and north Wales in territories under native rule. Such was the strength of the numbers recruited at Whitland that in 1224 they ventured to Ireland and founded a daughter house at Tracton.

The triumph of Cistercian monasticism in Wales was due in large part to the strict nature of their spiritual devotion, their austerity and their rejection of luxury and wealth. This approximated closely to the eremit-ical life which, in pre-Norman Wales, was the closest thing the Welsh had to a truly monastic vocation and which they held in high regard. Among the more famous of these hermits was the Brycheiniog-born Saint Caradog (d. 1124) who had once served in the court of Rhys ap

Tewdwr of Deheubarth (d. 1093) but who ended his days in seclusion at St David's. Another reason for their success is the fact that their recruitment did not exclude Welshmen and within a relatively short time the heads of Cistercian houses in native-held territories were sporting names like Cynan (d. 1176) and Rhydderch (d. 1184), abbots of Whitland, Dafydd (d. 1185) and Cedifor (d. 1225), abbots of Strata Florida, Ithel (d. 1187) and Gruffudd (d. 1196), abbots of Strata Marcella. Clearly, these were men who were as Welsh as the land that bore them and as loyal as any native patron might hope to find. Consequently, within the territories of *pura Wallia* where the patronage of the princes was at its most potent, the careers of Welsh clerics prospered. In 1215, Cadwgan (d. 1236), successively abbot of Strata Florida and Whitland by dint of the patronage of a prince of Deheubarth, was promoted to the bishopric of Bangor, a post for which he was indebted to a prince of Gwynedd. There was a price to pay for such devotion: in 1212 King John ordered the destruction of Strata Florida 'which harbours our enemies'.[78] Similarly, in 1228 the monks of Cwmhir were punished by having part of their estate burned for siding with Llywelyn ab Iorwerth against King Henry III.

Besides their loyalty and service, the Cistercians responded to the princes' care and attention by contributing substantially to native literature and becoming, in effect, custodians of native cultural traditions. Between them, the various houses dotted across Wales – Basingwerk, Margam, Strata Florida and Whitland prominent among them – were responsible for compiling a lost Latin chronicle, copying at least one, possibly two, versions of the *Brut y Tywysogion*, translating into Welsh continental tracts like the Athanasian creed or the Charlemagne legends, preserving ancient manuscripts and building libraries which housed copies of the works of Geoffrey of Monmouth and William of Malmesbury (d.*c.* 1143). Spiritually and materially, they provided a refuge for those princes still living but weary of the secular world, and a place of rest for those wishing to secure not only their mortal remains but their immortal souls also. The noble and sometime warrior Einion ap Gwalchmai (d.*c.* 1223), court poet to Llywelyn ab Iorwerth, was certainly one for whom the secular world had lost its appeal, eschewing as he did 'crooked words, vain passion, lust for women, the planning of warfare, and other causes of woe'.[79] In fact, he hints at having donned the habit and adopted the lifestyle of a monk, for he sings 'Let us keep the midnight devotions, according to the practice. Let us not sleep, let us chant the canonical prayers'.[80]

Although the ruling elite developed a fondness for the Cistercians they were equally gracious, though perhaps less lavish in their patronage, of orders other than the white monks of Cîteaux. The Lord Rhys is probably to be counted among the most liberal and cosmopolitan benefactors of his day, patronising no less than four different orders of monks, Benedictine (Cardigan, Llandovery), Cistercian (Strata Florida, Whitland), Premonstratensian (Talley) and the Knights Hospitallers (Slebech), along with being the first prince to successfully found a nunnery (Llanllyr). At one stage in his forty-two-year career as prince of Deheubarth (1155–97), he could lay claim to the patronage of no less than eleven monastic communities within his domain. Unfortunately for the native *clas* churches, there was little in the way of either reward or patronage, and even once great churches like those at Llandeilo Fawr and Llanbadarn Fawr were eclipsed by the new monastic foundations. Within a decade of its foundation in 1164, Strata Florida, which, by his own admission, Rhys 'loved and cherished',[81] had succeeded Llanbadarn as the chief *scriptorium* in south Wales responsible for copying and keeping the native annals. In order to endow his foundation of the Premonstratensian order at Talley, the Lord Rhys imitated his Anglo-Norman neighbours by stripping the ancient *clas* church of Llandeilo Fawr of all its wealth in land and its authority over satellite churches and transferring them to the new house. According to Gerald of Wales, asset-stripping of religious institutions by secular 'patrons' was so common in Wales that 'Nobody has ever complained about their conduct' and in light of his experience of the practice even he had 'come to the conclusion that . . . it is better to say no more about this sorry state of affairs, for fear of infuriating this wicked people'.[82] It was in finding 'the church of Llanbadarn Fawr reduced to this sorry state' on visiting in 1188 that roused Gerald to anger, even to the point of naming the usurper of the church's rights and privileges 'an old man called Ednywain ap Gweithfoed, who had grown grey in iniquity, . . . usurping the office of abbot, while his sons officiated at the altar'.[83] With passion and conviction Gerald condemned these so-called 'patrons and defenders of the churches' who by 'their greed [and] in their impudence appropriating all church lands . . . leaving to the clergy nothing but their altars, with their tenths and oblations'.[84]

Despite this apparently 'wicked act of vandalism' perpetrated against Llandeilo and seeming lack of interest in either Llanbadarn or Llanddewi Brefi there is little to suggest that the Lord Rhys was inherently hostile to the *clasau* or that he intended their total suppression. Llanbadarn continued to function much as before as did Llanddewi Brefi, both of which were thought significant enough to be included in Gerald and Archbishop Baldwin's itinerary through Wales in 1188. It has been suggested that the dissolution of Llandeilo may have been a bold attempt on Rhys' part 'to revive the waning spirit of the *clas* through the medium of a new religious order peculiarly fitted for the purpose'.[85] The purpose which Rhys intended for his new foundation may, in part, have included the cure of souls in those churches and chapels, nine in all, transferred to its care. It was a task for which the Premonstratensians, unlike the Cistercians, were 'fitted for' and willing to undertake. It is noteworthy that when Talley was suppressed in 1536 it derived the more of its income from spiritualities (tithes and other receipts from dependant churches) than from its temporalities (rents and sales from their estates). In north Wales, where the pace of change appears to have been somewhat slower than in the south-west, ancient and modern coexisted for a while. Thus, for example, we witness Rhodri ab Owain Gwynedd (d. 1195), son-in-law to the Lord Rhys and the prince most likely responsible for founding the first Cistercian abbey in Gwynedd at Aberconwy in 1186, granting one-third of the vill of Neigwl to the *clas* at Clynnog Fawr. To the younger generation, his nephew Maredudd ap Cynan (d. 1212), there was no thought of *clas* when he granted another third of the same vill to his newly established Cistercian abbey at Cymer in 1198/9. The gradual shift away from the *clasau* towards the new monastic orders soon became a rush when, under Llywelyn the Great, at least four ancient foundations – Aberdaron, Bardsey, Beddgelert and Penmon – were transferred wholesale to the Augustinians.

These transfers, endowments and foundations created a land-rich monastic community which further enriched itself by its economic activities and trade. It has been estimated that within a quarter of a century of its foundation in 1186, the monastery of Aberconwy had accumulated an estate of near 40,000 acres. By the last quarter of the thirteenth century, Strata Florida too could boast an estate approaching 32,000 acres of which some 6,000 acres of arable land was actively farmed. The Cistercians it seems, were blessed with the instincts of the entrepreneur and they proved especially enterprising in exploiting the rural wealth of Wales. They were great pastoralists and although they turned later towards greater arable cultivation, much of their income derived from keeping sheep and sales of wool. Their continental connections enabled them to tap into an international market which drew merchants from as far afield as Flanders and Italy. In 1212, King John licensed the abbot and monks of Strata Florida 'to sell their wool and to send it without hindrance beyond the seas for three years'.[86] By 1252 the monks of Margam were selling their wool to merchants in London and Ghent. The export of wool and the import of stone for monastic building stimulated the Welsh economy as did the employment of masons, craftsmen and labourers for building and agricultural workers for farming. The princes no less than the kings of England were keen to encourage this economic development which contributed to the ever increasing circulation of wealth.

The influence of founders and benefactors was more explicitly manifest in the monasteries than in the secular church. It was in the monasteries that their rights were at their most intrusive since their ability to influence location, size, building, landed endowment and, possibly, personnel tended towards reinforcing a proprietorial sense. A hint of this may be glimpsed in the title the Lord Rhys ap Gruffudd assumed for himself in his charter, admittedly a later copy, to Strata Florida abbey in 1184, namely, *proprietarius princeps Sudwallie*.[87] Intended, no doubt, to apply in broader terms than simply the grant of property to the abbey, the assumption of this unique title, which may be translated as propri-etary or rightful prince of south Wales, might well reflect the bene-factor's search for legitimacy on two levels: firstly in political terms as ruler of a new, invigorated kingdom, though much reduced in size than that ruled by his grandfather Rhys ap Tewdwr (d. 1093), and secondly, in economic and legalistic terms by way of underlining his right to grant this territory to the monks at Strata Florida. In Welsh legal custom, as was the case elsewhere, propietary or *priodorion* rights were exercised over men, over land and over institutions, and although these monastic foundations were by way of gift or grant they nonetheless served to highlight the benefactors' sense of ownership.

This sense of ownership, be it manifest in the secular or in the regular church, was expressed in other ways also in so far as benefactors were keen to take advantage of local cults with which they purposely became closely identified. An example may be instanced in the case of the Lord Rhys who actively encouraged the cult of Saint David which became the dominant episcopal cult not just of west Wales but of Wales as a whole. The reasons for this are not difficult to find since the cathedral was more than just a church, it was a shrine, a centre of pilgrimage, a sacred store for holy relics, but more importantly, a mausoleum for the premier saint of Wales, Saint David. The cult of saints had powerful territorial associations which was a matter of great moment for a ruler like Rhys bent on re-establishing his dominion in a region of Wales not long ere it had been under Norman hegemony. The cult was vigorously propagated by both cleric and poet alike and perhaps not surprisingly, Rhys' own chief court poet or *pencerdd*, Gwynfardd Brycheiniog, was among those composing in the saint's honour. His poem, *A Song to Dewi*, was more than just a literary composition, it was also an effective piece of propaganda which bespeaks as much the exalted position of the Lord Rhys as of Saint David. Clearly, this was a site with which the premier ruler of native Wales would wish to be associated and although the cathedral lay well beyond the frontiers of late-twelfth-century Deheubarth, and consequently, outside the orbit of Rhys' power, this did not deter him from exerting his influence in the affairs of the church. This suggests itself most strongly in the incident recounted by Gerald of Wales in 1188, when the cathedral's chapter tried to persuade Lord Rhys to use his influence to prevent Archbishop Baldwin from celebrating Mass at the church's high altar. That he did not was probably more through choice than lacking the means to do so.

In being adopted and becoming the symbol of family pride, which had less to do with religion than politics and propaganda, greatly added to the prestige of a patron who took care to invest in and protect the saintly shrine, thereby making indivisible secular and spiritual lordship. This is evident in the policies adopted by the princes of Gwynedd who used their patronage of and close association with the church as an additional seat and tool of government. Llywelyn ap Gruffudd's itinerant court can frequently be found at Cistercian granges such as Cymer abbey's grange of Abereiddion at which the prince held an important council meeting in the summer of 1275. To help quell opposition and punish the recalcitrant, Llywelyn ab Iorwerth had the means to resort to excommunication and interdict made possible only with the acquiescence of compliant clerics. Thus were the lands of Madog ap Gruffudd Maelor laid under interdict sometime between 1215 and 1217 when he planned a marriage of which his overlord Llywelyn did not approve. Similarly, Llywelyn ap Gruffudd had his vassal Gruffudd ap Gwenwynwyn excommunicated in 1258 on account of his breaking an oath of fealty. On the other hand, such cynical use of the church and its authority tended to rebound on those most active and opportunistic in its exploitation. Both Llywelyn ab Iorwerth and his grandson were themselves victims of the weapon of excommunication pronounced by English bishops at the behest of a king of England.

Aside from the considerable economic and political benefits (and pitfalls), we need not doubt the sincerity of the princes' motives in founding religious houses, some of which became closely identified with particular ruling families by acting as mausoleums. The burial patterns of the princes reveals much about them as patrons and devotees of the church and the esteem in which some religious houses, churches and cathedrals were held. In wishing to be buried in the cathedral church of St David's, rather than in one of his own monastic foundations, Rhys was hardly setting a precedent. Quite the contrary, it is in keeping with the burial traditions followed by his compatriots from the north, the princes of Gwynedd, Gruffudd ap Cynan (d. 1137) and his son Owain Gwynedd (d. 1170), both of whom were buried in the cathedral church at Bangor. Lacking a cathedral they could call their own, the princes of Powys, such as Madog ap Maredudd (d. 1160), had to content themselves with being buried at the ancient *clas* church of Meifod. Not that this was any less exalted than St David's (though probably more so than Bangor) for they were following an ancient burial ritual which was linked to the cult of St Tysilio, the patron saint of Meifod. Similarly, it is likely that Rhys too was conforming to tradition by following his kingly ancestors to seek the shelter of St David's, which, according to Professor J.E. Lloyd, 'was for him, as for his fathers, the holiest place in Wales'.[88] That there is no written or sepulchral evidence to suggest that the pre-twelfth-century princes of Deheubarth, and before them the rulers of the sub-kingdom of Dyfed, were ever buried at St David's need not preclude its having happened. Given its religious and cultural significance, it is inconceivable to imagine these rulers not wishing to be buried in the 'holiest place in Wales'.

It is not until the mid to late twelfth century that we witness a significant change in the burial patterns of the princes as their increasing patronage of the continental monastic orders draw them away from the English-controlled cathedrals (with the exception of Welsh-held Bangor) and native *clas* churches. As a result, from the 1170s, dynastic mausoleums were established at Strata Florida, Strata Marcella, Valle Crucis, Cwmhir and Aberconwy by the rulers of Deheubarth, Powys Wenwynwyn, Powys Fadog, Rhwng Gwy a Hafren and Gwynedd respectively. That other monasteries too were thought fit for the burial of princes, such as Cymer, Talley and Whitland, can be substantiated from the written record, but their complement of royal corpses pales in comparison with the aforementioned houses. Not that inspection of these sites would yield anything of significance, since time and fate have not been kind to the princes and little now remains of what may have once been fine tombs. Nor have any distinctive burial chapels, which might label a section of the fabric with a familial identity, survived; but that they existed is amply testified in contemporary poetry and suggested by archaeological remains. Nevertheless, we have no way of knowing how these princely families chose to represent themselves or what sculptural decoration they wished to adorn their sepulchral monument. Perhaps the anonymous mason who worked on refashioning the tomb of the Lord Rhys sometime in the middle of the fourteenth century got it right by representing the princely incumbent as a warrior dressed in the garb of a knight in full armour.

Patronage was as much a servant of politics as it was of the arts and religion, and the princes were keenly aware of the power of patronage in augmenting their political authority. Indeed, the more astute among them did not attempt to rule without exercising it. They were in a privileged position to be able to shape the fortunes of their respective principalities and they did so by giving favours, encouragement and support to those individuals and institutions able to do them good. Patronage for priests and poets contributed as much to maintaining the social order through peace, law and justice as the other agencies at the disposal of the ruler. Indeed, if adroit patronage was indispensable to successful rulership so, in equal measure, were piety and propaganda specifically tailored to the needs of the prince.

Notes

1. G. Williams, *Welsh Poetry, Sixth Century to 1600* (London, 1973), 32.
2. C.W. Lewis, 'The Historical Background of Early Welsh Verse', in *Guide to Welsh Lit.*, I, 16.
3. *Journey & Description*, 240, 246.
4. Lloyd, *Hist. Wales*, II, 532.
5. Ibid. The translations appended here are selections from Gwalchmai's poem *Exultation* (Welsh *Gorhoffedd*). For a full rendition of the poem in translation, see G. Williams, *Welsh Poetry*, 32–5.
6. *Autobiog.*, 82–3; *Gwaith Cynddelw Brydydd Mawr*, ed. N.A. Jones and A.P. Owen (2 vols, Cardiff, 1991–5), II, 185–90.
7. G. Williams, *Welsh Poetry*, 38.
8. Ibid.
9. Ibid., 36.
10. Ibid., 37.
11. *The Law of Hywel Dda*, 39.
12. Ibid., 20.
13. D.M. Lloyd, 'The Poets of the Princes', in *Guide to Welsh Lit.*, I, 163.
14. *The Law of Hywel Dda*, 20.
15. Ibid.
16. Ibid.
17. *Guide Welsh Lit.*, I, 158.
18. Ibid.
19. Ibid., 157.
20. C.W. Lewis, op. cit., I, 129.
21. J.E.C. Williams, 'Meilyr Brydydd and Gruffudd ap Cynan', in *Gruffudd ap Cynan*, ed. K.L. Maund, 173, 184, 186.
22. *Guide Welsh Lit.*, I, 129, 134.
23. Lloyd, *Hist. Wales*, II, 529.
24. *Guide to Welsh Lit.*, I, 141–2. There is some dispute regarding the bardic credentials of the story-tellers.
25. *Mediaeval Prince*, 73. On the other hand, J.E. Caerwyn Williams has translated the original Welsh phrase *telynyaur penkerd* as either 'harpist of a master craftsman' or 'master craftsman harpist'. Idem, *The Poets of the Welsh Princes*, 9; BT. Pen., 71; BT. RBH, 167; B. Saes., 183. The B. Saes. alone names him the son of Eilon.

26. *Journey & Description*, 223.
27. Ibid., 239.
28. Ibid., 236.
29. *Autobiog.*, 102.
30. Ibid., 82–3.
31. *Journey & Description*, 203.
32. F. Heer, *The Medieval Mind* (London, 1963), 101.
33. *Autobiog.*, 162–3.
34. A. Breeze, *Medieval Welsh Literature* (Dublin, 1997).
35. *Journey & Description*, 223.
36. See G.H. Doble, *Lives of the Welsh Saints*, ed. D.S. Evans (Cardiff, 1971).
37. T. Jones, 'The Early Evolution of the Legend of Arthur', *Nottingham Medieval Studies*, VIII (1964), 15–6; B.F. Roberts, 'Tales and Romances', in *Guide to Welsh Lit.*, I, 222.
38. J. Lindsay, *The Troubadours and their World of the Twelfth and Thirteenth Centuries* (London, 1976), 23.
39. Ibid.
40. *Journey & Description*, 252.
41. J.E.C. Williams, 'Aberteifi, 1176', *Taliesin*, 32 (1976), 30–5.
42. Idem., *The Poets of the Welsh Princes*, 9.
43. Idem., 'Meilyr Brydydd and Gruffudd ap Cynan', op. cit., 170.
44. See *The Treatise of the Laws and Customs of England commonly called Glanvill*, ed. G.D.G. Hall (London, 1965).
45. *Mediaeval Prince*, 81.
46. Ibid., 82.
47. J.B. Hilling, *The Historic Architecture of Wales* (Cardiff, 1976), 33.
48. Dylan Iorwerth, 'The Mystery at Morgraig', *Cadw: Heritage in Wales*, 7 (1997), 17–19.
49. C. Kightly, *Chieftains and Princes* (Cadw: Cardiff, 1994), 20.
50. Ibid.
51. R. Avent, 'Castles of the Welsh Princes', *Chateau Gaillard*, XV (1992), 7–18.
52. D.M. Lloyd, 'The Poets of the Princes', in *Wales Through the Ages*, ed. A.J. Roderick (2 vols, Llandybie, 1959), I, 102.
53. R.A. Griffiths, 'The Making of Medieval Cardigan', *Ceredigion*, XI (1990), 106–7.
54. Ibid., 127.
55. See D.J.C. King, *Castellorum Anglicanum* (2 vols, London, 1983).
56. J. Bradbury, *Philip Augustus* (London, 1998), 21.
57. Ibid., 22.
58. Ibid., 23.
59. *BT. Pen.*, 17, 52, 104.
60. Ibid., 79.
61. *Journey & Description*, 253–4.
62. Ibid., 253.
63. Ibid., 171.
64. *Autobiog.*, 250.
65. *Journey & Description*, 202.

66. Ibid., 114.
67. Ibid., 76.
68. *BT. Pen.*, 50.
69. D.G. Walker, *The Normans*, 28.
70. Ibid., 28. Although Orderic Vitalis was speaking of one man in particular, Robert of Rhuddlan, his comments are equally applicable to his subject's warrior contemporaries.
71. J.H. Huizinga, *The Waning of the Middle Ages* (London, 1950), 163.
72. *Journey & Description*, 180–1.
73. D.M. Lloyd, op. cit., I, 180–1.
74. *BT. Pen.*, 56, 176–7.
75. Ibid., 58.
76. Ibid.
77. *Letters and Charters of Gilbert Foliot*, ed. A. Morey and C.N.L. Brooke (Cambridge, 1967), 47, no. 10.
78. S. Williams, *The Cistercian Abbey of Strata Florida* (London, 1889), appendix, xx.
79. D.M. Lloyd, op. cit., 181–2.
80. *Dictionary of Welsh Biography* (London, 1959), 202.
81. British Library, Add. Ms 24839.
82. *Journey & Description*, 181.
83. Ibid., 180.
84. Ibid.
85. T. Jones Pierce, 'Strata Florida Abbey', *Ceredigion*, I (1950), 21–2.
86. C.66/9, m.9; quoted in D.M. Robinson and C. Platt, *Strata Florida Abbey/ Talley Abbey* (Cadw: Cardiff, 1992), 14.
87. *Monasticon Anglicanum*, v, 632.
88. Lloyd, *Hist. Wales*, II, 529.

chapter seven

CONCLUSION: THE PRINCES AFTER CONQUEST

Do not you believe in God, foolish men?
See you not that the world is ending?
Ah, God, that the sea would cover the land!
What is left to us that we should linger?
No place to escape from terror's prison,
No place to live: wretched is living!
No counsel, no clasp, not a single path
Open to be saved from fear's strife.
Head cut off, no hate so dreadful,
Head cut off, thing better not done,
Head of a soldier, head of praise.
Head of a warlord, dragon's head,
Head of fair Llywelyn: harsh fear strikes the world,
An iron spike through it.
Head of my prince – harsh pain for me – Head of my soul
rendered speechless.
Head that owned honour in nine hundred lands,
Nine hundred feasts were his.
Head of a king, his hand hurled iron,
Head of a king's hawk, forcing a gap.
Head of a kingly wolf out-thrusting,
Head of heaven's kings, be his haven.[1]

If, as has often been argued, the poet's muse is the public expression of a people's private thoughts, then the death of Llywelyn was evidently greeted with an hitherto unparalleled outpouring of grief. Although elegies had been written for other equally consequential and revered rulers there is something in the quality of this poem which marks it out as an outstanding work of astounding insight. Written, probably, early in 1283, this extract of Gruffudd ab yr Ynad Coch's poignant and celebrated elegy on Llywelyn ap Gruffudd serves as a fitting conclusion not only for the death of one prince but for the end of an age of princes.

Arguably, there was but one Welsh prince and one princely or royal dynasty in Wales when native independence was extinguished in 1282–3. In a dynamic career spanning nearly forty years, Llywelyn ap Gruffudd had seen to it that he, and his family of Gwynedd dynasts, alone would be recognised as the premier rulers of native Wales. Twice, in 1258 and, more importantly, in 1267, he had succeeded in underlining his hegemony by formally and publicly binding the other native dynasts or princelings to his rule. Where there had once been many princes and equality in status there was now but one prince and an aristocracy bound to him by ties of homage and fealty. By the same token, where once in the eleventh century the native dynasts of Deheubarth and Powys were kings, they were now, in the second half of the thirteenth, no longer even princes and nor did they rule kingdoms or principalities. They were reduced to the status of lords or barons holding their ancestral lands as tenants-in-chief of the Gwynedd-based prince of Wales who, in his turn, would do homage and fealty to the king of England on their behalf. There was no room in Llywelyn's pre-conquest polity for princes other than himself and in no sense would he have subscribed to Sir Maurice Powicke's view that 'the prince of Gwynedd was to be the keystone in an arch of kings'.[2] The Normans may have done for Welsh kingship by the killing in 1093 of Rhys ap Tewdwr, but it was not strictly the English who did for the Welsh princes with the killing in 1282 of Llywelyn ap Gruffudd, but, and in more senses than one, the Gwynedd dynast himself.

This is not to suggest that Edward I would have acted any differently: there was no room in his post-conquest polity even for one native prince let alone many. Indeed, as early as the 1240s the English Crown had come to regard and treat the native rulers of Wales as barons rather than princes.[3] Even the unique status of the princes of Gwynedd was not entirely safe, for if the political circumstances had been more favourable during the middle decades of the thirteenth century it is clear that the Crown would have denied them the use of the princely title. This was evidently the aim purposed by Edward I when in 1282 he determined on the complete destruction not only of a native principate but also of their use and style of prince. Following the killing of Llywelyn in December 1282, his brother Dafydd assumed the mantle of leadership, but with his capture, trial and execution for treason in October 1283 the war came to an end. The ancestral lands of the Gwynedd dynasty were annexed by the Crown, its heirs, the children of Llywelyn and Dafydd both male and female, were either imprisoned for life or deposited in a nunnery. The title and dignity of the Welsh principate was set aside until Edward revived it in favour of his eldest son and heir in 1301. One member of the Gwynedd dynasty alone survived, Rhodri (d. 1315), but, marginalised during the lifetime of his elder brother Llywelyn, he proved as pliant a vassal of the Crown as he had a 'baron' of the prince. His support for and service in the king's forces during the wars of independence, 1276–7 and 1282–3, earned for him an estate in Cheshire, an English wife and an annuity of 40 marks for life.[4] More importantly for the Crown, he exchanged his claim to the title and dignity of a Welsh prince for that of an English knight, thus it is as Sir Roderick de Tatsfield that he became known rather than as Prince Rhodri ap Gruffudd, the grandson of Llywelyn the Great and last of the direct line of the dynasty of Gwynedd. Not that Rhodri had ever adopted the style of prince let alone entertained any such claim to the principate either during the lifetime of his brother Llywelyn or after the latter's death, an event which left him the sole representative of the royal dynasty. Indeed, when his distant cousin Madog ap Llywelyn (d. 1295), a cadet of the dynasty of Gwynedd, raised the standard of rebellion and claimed the title prince of Wales in 1294, Rhodri did not stir either in support or opposition to what turned out to be a shortlived and ill-fated revolt.[5] Clearly, the Crown had succeeded in destroying utterly the reality if not the notion of a Welsh principate.

If the fate of the princely dynasty of Gwynedd had been sealed by the Edwardian conquest, what of the other princely dynasties of the fragmented and devolved former kingdoms of Deheubarth and Powys? They did not entirely disappear either at the hands of Llywelyn ap Gruffudd or his and their conqueror King Edward I. They continued, albeit under a different guise. Publicly and politically, before and after 1282–3, the dynasties had no choice but to accept a dimunition in their status and enforced change in the nomenclature of their power and authority. Privately, however, and in some cases not so privately, it is likely that they persisted in thinking of themselves as royal in blood and status. Certainly, Gruffudd ap Gwenwynwyn of southern Powys railed constantly against Llywelyn's persistent attempts to impose his authority over him. To Gruffudd it was not merely a simple case of *him* kneeling at the feet of Llywelyn either in swearing fealty or in seeking pardon, an act of submission entirely in keeping with the accepted feudal practice of the day, but in the humiliation of *him* as a descendant of King Bleddyn ap Cynfyn and Prince Madog ap Maredudd of Powys kneeling before a ruler of Gwynedd. It may be that he and his ilk were not allowed to forget their royal roots, least of all by the bardic poets who continued to extol their 'princely' virtues. Although most applauded the *machtpolitik* of the Gwynedd dynasty, some poets like Y Prydydd Bychan (d.*c.* 1270) and Llygad Gwr (d.*c.* 1288) were reluctant to abandon the princely form of address in their poems to such as Rhys Gryg (d. 1233) and Maredudd ab Owain (d. 1265) of Deheubarth, and to Gruffudd ap Madog ap Gruffudd Maelor (d. 1269) of Powys, respectively. This 'pressure' from a powerful group of propagandists might have done much to shape their thinking if not contribute to their actions. In the case of Gruffudd ap Gwenwynwyn it seems that hard political reality rather than deference to the opinions of his bardic contemporaries lay at the root of his decision to seek an alternative to the overlordship of Llywelyn.

Although Gruffudd would not stand in the same relationship to the king of England as he might have done had he accepted Llywelyn's overlordship, at whose court he would have been among the prince's 'leading men', and nor would he ever compare but insignificantly with an English magnate, nevertheless his rendering of fealty and homage to an English king was evidently preferable to that of a Welsh prince. Not unsurprisingly, he alone of the Welsh princelings survived in the brave new world of post-conquest Wales. His unswerving support of the Crown during the whole of Llywelyn's principate (1258–82) ensured for him a place in the new order, and it was more as a Marcher lord than as a Welsh baron that Gruffudd ruled the former kingdom of Powys Wenwynwyn or southern Powys. Upon his death in 1286, his heir Owain, adopting the distinctly un-Welsh name of de la Pole, succeeded and it was through him and his descendants, including his daughter and heiress Hawise and her husband John Charlton, that the dynasty of Powys Wenwynwyn continued. The princely family of Powys were not alone in abandoning the native patronymic and adopting the names of their conquerors. Morgan Fychan, lord of Afan and the only descendant of the last king of Glamorgan to retain a degree of authority in the former kingdom, assumed the name de Avene and his family continued in the male line until 1350.

However, not all of the Crown's princely supporters prospered in the new order. The killing of the prince of Wales in 1282 may have freed those of his 'barons' who had sided with the Crown from their obligation to him but they had merely exchanged one overbearing overlord for another. For example, Rhys ap Maredudd (d. 1292), lord of Dryslwyn, scion of the dynasty of Deheubarth and the most powerful princeling in south-west Wales, found to his cost that Edward was no more benevolent an overlord than Llywelyn had been.[6] Having resisted Llywelyn's attempts to make him his vassal, Rhys had sided with the king during the Welsh wars of independence, 1276–7 and 1282–3, and expected to be rewarded for his loyalty. His expectations were soon dashed however, for although he was rewarded by a grateful king with substantial tracts of land in Cantref Mawr, his chief desires to rule an independent lordship under a nominal royal suzerainty and to add the castle of Dinefwr, the ancient royal seat of Deheubarth, to his possessions, were denied him. Disgruntled and with the added pressure of a pressing royal administration based in nearby Carmarthen, Rhys rebelled in 1287. Outside his household and tenanted landholdings the rebellion was largely unsupported, it was quickly crushed and within five years the fugitive Rhys had been captured and executed (1292) thus bringing to an ignominious end that particular branch of the near-defunct dynasty of Deheubarth.

If this is what the Crown's princely supporters could expect, what of its enemies? The majority were either killed, imprisoned or simply dispossessed of their ancestral lands. Those few that managed to retain or, after pardon obtain, portions of their territories survived as minor landholders of high lineage. After the execution of Rhys ap Maredudd, his cousin Llywelyn ab Owain, fifth in descent from the Lord Rhys, remained the sole representative in direct line of the dynasty of Deheubarth to freely hold territory within the bounds of the former kingdom. His minority in 1282–3 probably saved him from the fate that befell his other living relatives like Rhys Wyndod and his brothers who died in prison (1302) or Rhys Fychan (d. 1302) who died after a period of military service abroad. Llywelyn ab Owain's inconsiderable share of the family patrimony amounted to but a commote and a half in southern Ceredigion near Cardigan. The dynasty of Powys Fadog or northern Powys continued in the main line via Gruffudd Fychan who clung precariously to Glyndyfrdwy in the commote of Ederinion. Although his son Madog added to the patrimony with half the commote of Cynllaith even this only amounted to a fraction of their former territorial wealth the bulk of which had been given as reward to English Marcher lords and out of which the lordships of Bromfield and Yale and Chirk were created. Ironically, it was from this line that was sprung Owain ap Gruffudd Fychan, better known to history as Owain Glyndwr, who led the last native rebellion against the English Crown in 1400. Lauded by the poets for his princely lineage and supported by them in his claim to be the true prince of Wales, his rebellion generated a great deal of enthusiasm in the country, and although it caused the Crown serious concern its ultimate failure was perhaps inevitable.

The Edwardian conquest had been as much a disaster for the dynasts of Deheubarth and Powys as it had been for the dynasty of Gwynedd. The defeat and death of Rhys ap Maredudd (1292) and Madog ap Llywelyn (1295), the second of which accounted for the representatives of a number of royal offshoots such as the descendants of the dynasty of Gwent, demonstrated quite clearly that the restoration of princely title and authority had ceased to be a practical possibility after 1283. Even the poets, those conservators of myth and tradition with a vested interest in keeping alive hopes of a princely restoration, are silent in the century after the conquest. Until the last quarter of the thirteenth century their celebration in song of princely achievements or their praise heaped on individual princes and princelings may often have been exaggerated but it was, nonetheless, rooted in reality. The fourteenth century, on the other hand, witnessed a discernible shift in their attitude resulting in an almost complete divorce between poetry and politics. They continued to praise their patrons and exalt the virtues of their lineage but it was very much in terms of recalling a glorious past or in prophesying a hoped-for glorious future that they did so. Only in respect of Owain Glyndwr at the beginning of the fifteenth century did the poets dare speak of Welsh princes and revive their belief in the restoration of a native principate.

The importance of the princes in the history of Wales cannot be overstated. Any study of the history of Wales between, roughly, the middle of the ninth to the end of the thirteenth century cannot but make mention of its rulers be they called kings, princes or lords. Their capacity to shape and influence the political, social, religious and economic developments in their respective polities is suggestive of an impact that simply cannot be ignored by historians working in one or other of those particular fields. The extent to which they have earned the attention of historians is made manifest in the titular currency afforded by such as 'The Age of the Princes' which have appeared in the contents pages of serious works of history.[7] Elsewhere the 'Wales of the Princes' has been described as an 'epoch' which came to an end with the fall of Llywelyn ap Gruffudd.[8] That they have lent themselves to describing an 'age' and 'epoch' in the history of Wales points unmistakably to their importance and their worth as a subject of study.

Historically important they may be, but assessing their achievements is an altogether different matter since, with the passage of time, it is more likely to be subjective than objective. Nationalists especially have tended to view this period as a golden age of Welsh independence and, accordingly, they have sometimes oversimplified its history or, by assessing the Welsh princes in a purely modern context, have exaggerated their achievements. Although the Welsh did not lack the concept of themselves as a people, the Welsh princes were not self-consciously Welsh, they did not think in nationalistic terms and nor did they act in the interests of Welsh nationhood. Nevertheless, as the late Professor Gwyn Williams observed: 'Many historians, aware that the feudal principalities of princes elsewhere made nations, have largely accepted the verdict of nineteenth-century Welsh nationalism and identified the house of Aberffraw as the lost and legitimate dynasty of Wales'.[9] Consequently, in a conflation of folklore and history, Llywelyn ap Gruffudd became Llywelyn the Last. In the uniquely controversial view of Professor Williams, 'Wales of the Princes had to die before a Welsh nation could be born'.[10] In other words, had the Welsh princes continued and had the native principality survived, the progress of the Welsh people towards nationhood would have been impeded rather than assisted. Conquest and colonisation, in his view, shaped Wales and made her a nation, not the golden 'age of the Princes'.

In purely historical terms, the achievements of the Welsh princes as individuals must be made in a contemporary context which will inevitably vary according to the time in which they lived and limited by the opportunities that were available to them. The truly 'great' princes are those who to some degree succeeded in transcending their times and, with an eye for profit, ruthlessly took advantage of their opportunities. They are also those princes most likely to be celebrated in song by bards, referenced in official records by clerks and referred to in chronicles by monastic scribes. Consequently, in the period between 1063 and 1283 it is, arguably, only possible to highlight the achievements of no more than half a dozen princes most of whom hail from Gwynedd, among them Gruffudd ap Cynan (d. 1137), Owain (Gwynedd) ap Gruffudd (d. 1170), Llywelyn ab Iorwerth (d. 1240) and Llywelyn ap Gruffudd (d. 1282), Madog ap Maredudd (d. 1160) of Powys and Rhys ap Gruffudd (d. 1197) of Deheubarth. Beyond their undoubted achievements as warriors and politicians in their own small spheres they, like Rhys ap Gruffudd, can at least lay claim to some success in the legal and cultural field which went beyond petty boundaries and benefited the whole nation. Nevertheless, their petty rivalries were apt more to assist in the destruction of Wales than save it, so it is in their collective achievement that they should perhaps be assessed. It was by means of their tenacity, courage and selfish desire to rule that enabled Wales to postpone the fate of Anglo-Saxon England in 1066, and though they failed until the thirteenth century to unite politically, without doubt the greatest achievement both of Llywelyn ab Iorwerth for setting the precedent and Llywelyn ap Gruffudd for realising it, this resistance meant that the nation could enjoy not only a separate existence and history to that of England but the space to develop as a people united socially, culturally and linguistically. Even the close proximity of Anglo-Norman society served mainly to benefit the Welsh whose own culture, by virtue of their princes' cosmopolitan willingness to imitate and adopt, was enriched as a result. Indeed, the princes provided the link between two cultures and though they were the guardians of one they did not hesitate to take from the other, but in doing so modified its effects on their own.

Notes

1. Extracted in part from T. Conran, ed. and trans., *Welsh Verse* (Bridgend, 1992), 163–4 and *The Oxford Book of Welsh Verse in English*, ed. G. Jones (Oxford, 1977), 32–3.
2. F.M. Powicke, *The Thirteenth Century* (London, 1953), 386.
3. For this and fuller details of the fate of the princes after conquest, see A.D. Carr, 'An Aristocracy in Decline: The Native Welsh Lords after the Edwardian Conquest', *WHR*, 5 (1970), 103–29.
4. A.D. Carr, *Owen of Wales: The End of the House of Gwynedd* (Cardiff, 1991), 5–7.
5. J. Griffiths, 'The Revolt of Madog ap Llywelyn', *TCHS*, 16 (1955), 12–24; G. Roberts, 'Biographical Notes: Madog ap Llywelyn', *BBCS*, xvii (1956), 43–4.
6. J.B. Smith, 'The Origins of the Revolt of Rhys ap Maredudd', *BBCS*, xxi (1965), 157–62; R.A. Griffiths, 'The Revolt of Rhys ap Maredudd, 1287–88', *WHR*, 2 (1966), 121–43.
7. For example, J.E. Lloyd, ed., *History of Carmarthenshire* (2 vols, Cardiff, 1935–9), D.M. Lloyd, ed., *The Historical Basis of Welsh Nationalism* (Cardiff, 1954) and, more recently, A.D. Carr, *Medieval Wales*.
8. G.A. Williams, *When Was Wales?*, 85.
9. Ibid.
10. Ibid., 86.

GENERAL BIBLIOGRAPHY

This book is based, as far as possible, on original sources most of them translated from Latin and Welsh. This is a highly selective and brief guide to works of use on the general topics covered by each of the chapters. All books were published in London unless otherwise stated.

Barbier, P., *The Age of Owain Gwynedd* (1908).

Benson, R.L. and Constable, G., eds, *Renaissance and Renewal in the Twelfth Century* (Oxford, 1982).

Binchy, D.A., *Celtic and Anglo-Saxon Kingship* (Oxford, 1970).

Binns, A., *Dedications to Monastic Houses in England and Wales* (Woodbridge, 1989).

Carr, A.D., *Llywelyn ap Gruffudd* (Cardiff, 1982).

Carr, A.D., *Medieval Wales* (1995).

Cowley, F.G., *The Monastic Order in South Wales, 1066–1349* (Cardiff, 1977).

Crouch, D., *The Image of Aristocracy in Britain 1000–1300* (1992).

Davies, R.R., ed., *The British Isles, 1150–1500: Comparisons, Contrasts and Connections* (Edinburgh, 1988).

Davies, R.R., *Conquest, Coexistence and Change Wales 1063–1415* (Oxford, 1987). [Paperback edition entitled *Age of Conquest: Wales, 1063–1415* (Oxford, 1990).]

Davies, R.R., *Domination and Conquest: The Experience of Ireland, Scotland and Wales* (Cambridge, 1990).

Davies, W.E., *Wales in the Early Middle Ages* (Leicester, 1982).

Charles-Edwards, T.M., 'The Heir-Apparent in Irish and Welsh Law', *Celtica*, IX (1971), 180–90.

Charles-Edwards, T.M., Owen, M.E. and Russel, P., eds, *The Welsh King and his Court* (Cardiff, 2000).

Edwards, J.G., 'The Royal Household in the Welsh Lawbooks', *TRHS*, XIII (1963), 163–76.

Griffiths, W.L., *The Welsh* (Harmondsworth, 1950).

Hallam, E., 'Royal Burial and Cult of Kingship in Medieval England, 1060–1330', *Journal of Medieval History*, 8 (1982), 359–80.

Howell, M., 'Regalian Rights in Wales and the March: The Relation of Theory to Practice', *WHR*, VII (1975), 269–88.

Jack, R.I., *Medieval Wales* (1972).

Jarman, A.O.H and Hughes, G.R., eds, *A Guide to Welsh Literature* (2 vols, Swansea, 1976; repr., 1979).

Jenkins, D., 'Cynghellor and Chancellor', *BBCS*, XXVII (1976), 115–18.

Jenkins, D., 'Kings, Lords and Princes: The Nomenclature of Authority in Thirteenth-century Wales', *BBCS*, XXVI (1976), 451–62.

Jolliffe, J.E.A., *Angevin Kingship* (1963).

Jones, G.R.J., 'The Defences of Gwynedd in the Thirteenth Century', *Transactions of the Honourable Society of Cymmrodorion* (1969), 29–43.

Jones, N.A. and Pryce, H., *Yr Arglwydd Rhys* (Cerdydd, 1996).

Jones, T., 'The Early Evolution of the Legend of Arthur', *Nottingham Medieval Studies*, VIII (1964), 15–16.

King, D.J.C., *Castellarium Anglicanum: An Index and Bibliography of Castles in England* (London, 1983).

Knowles, D. and Hadcock, R.N., *Medieval Religious Houses. England and Wales* (2nd. edn, 1971).

Koch, J.T., 'When was Welsh Literature first written down?', *Studia Celtica*, XX/XXI (1985–6), 43–66.

Lewis, C.W., 'The Treaty of Woodstock, 1247: Its Backgound and Significance', *WHR*, II (1964), 37–65.

Lindsay, J., *The Troubadours and their World of the Twelfth and Thirteenth Centuries* (1976).

Lloyd, J.E., *A History of Wales from Earliest Times to the Edwardian Conquest* (2 vols, 1911; repr. 1939).

Maud, R., 'David, the Last Prince of Wales', *Transactions of the Honourable Society of Cymmrodorion* (1968), 43–62.

Maund, K.L., ed., *Gruffudd ap Cynan: A Collaborative Biography* (Woodbridge, 1996).

Maund, K.L., *The Welsh Kings* (Stroud, 2000).

Pierce, T.J., *Medieval Welsh Society*, ed. J.B. Smith (Cardiff, 1972).

Pryce, H., 'Owain Gwynedd and Louis VII: The Franco-Welsh Diplomacy of the First Prince of Wales', *WHR*, XIX (1998), 1–28.

Richter, M., 'David ap Llywelyn, the First Prince of Wales', *The Welsh History Review*, 5 (1970–1), 205–19.

Richter, M., 'The Political and Institutional Background to National Consciousness in Medieval Wales', in *Nationality and the Pursuit of National Independence*, ed. T. Moody (Belfast, 1978), 37–55.

Roderick, A.J., 'The Feudal Relations between the English Crown and the Welsh Princes', *History*, XXXVII (1952), 210–12.

Roderick, A.J., 'Marriage and Politics in Wales, 1066–1282', *WHR*, IV (1968–9), 1–20,

Smith, J.B., 'Offra Principis Wallie Domino Regi', *BBCS*, XXIV (1966), 362–7.

Smith, J.B., 'Owain Gwynedd', *Transactions of the Honourable Society of Cymmrodorion*, 32 (1971), 8–17.

Smith, J.B., 'The Treaty of Lambeth, 1217', *English History Review*, 94 (1979), 562–79.

Smith, J.B., 'Magna Carta and the Charters of the Welsh Princes', *English History Review*, 99 (1984), 344–62.

Smith, J.B., *Llywelyn ap Gruffudd Prince of Wales* (Cardiff, 1998).

Stephenson, D., *The Governance of Native Wales* (Cardiff, 1984).

Treharne, R.F., 'The Franco-Welsh Treaty of Alliance in 1212', *BBCS*, XVIII (1958), 60–75.

Turvey, R.K., 'King, Prince or Lord? Rhys ap Gruffydd and the Nomenclature of Authority in Twelfth-century Wales', *Transactions of the Carmarthenshire Antiquarian Society*, XXX (1994), 5–18.

Turvey, R.K., *The Lord Rhys Prince of Deheubarth* (Llandysul, 1997).

Turvey, R.K., 'The Defences of Twelfth-Century Deheubarth and the Castle Strategy of the Lord Rhys', *Archaeologia Cambrensis*, clxiv (1998), 103–32.

Walker, D.G., *The Norman Conquerors* (Swansea, 1977).

Walker, D.G., ed., *A History of the Church in Wales* (Penarth, 1976; repr., 1991).

Walker, D.G., *Medieval Wales* (Cambridge, 1990; repr., 1994).

Williams, G., *Welsh Poetry, Sixth Century to 1600* (1973).

Williams, G.A., 'The Succession to Gwynedd, 1238–1247', *BBCS*, XX (1962–4), 393–413.

Williams, G.A., *The Welsh in their History* (1982).

Williams, G.A., *When Was Wales?* (1985).

INDEX